Committees and Commissions in India
1977

Concepts in Communication
Informatics & Librarianship-51

General Editor : **S.P. Agrawal**

Committees and Commissions in India 1977

Volume 15

PART B

A Concept's Project

Compiled by a team of professionals
under the auspice of
VIRENDRA KUMAR

CONCEPT PUBLISHING COMPANY, NEW DELHI 110059

ISBN 81-7022-485-3 (Vol. 15, Part B)

First Published 1993

Published and Printed by
Ashok Kumar Mittal
Concept Publishing Company
A/15-16, Commercial Block, Mohan Garden
NEW DELHI 110059 (India)

Lasertypeset by
Printing Express
H-13, Bali Nagar
NEW DELHI 110015

CONTENTS

PART B

PART C

PART D

PART B

16

COMMITTEE ON CONSUMER PRICE INDEX NUMBERS, 1977– REPORT[1]

Chairman Shri Nilakantha Rath, Professor, Gokhale Institute of Politics and Economics, Poona

Members Smt. Maniben Kara; Smt. Parvathi Krishnan; Smt. Renuka Devi; Shri Prasanabhai Mehta; Shri B.N. Sathaye; Dr. M.K. Pandhe; Shri Kanti Mehta; Shri V.I. Chacko; Shri R.L.N. Vijayanagar; Shri V.R. Rao; Shri M.A.M. Rao; Shri M.T. Shukla

M. Secy. Shri R.S. Deshpande

Appointment

The Consumer Price Index (CPI) Numbers for the working class, compiled by the Labour Bureau of the Government of India, are important indicators of the changing economic situation in the country. Apart from serving as a guide for policy formulations, these index numbers are utilised for regulating the dearness allowance paid to thousands of manual workers and other employees. Naturally therefore, the entire organised working class is vitally interested in the correctness of the index. The CPI numbers compiled by Labour Bureau as well as by several State Governments, had been criticised in the past, and several Committees had been set up by the Central and the concerned State Governments to look into one technical aspects or the other of the certain specific centres' indices. The current series of CPI numbers compiled and published by the Bureau, have also come under severe criticism. Despite the Bureau's attempt from time to time to reply to such criticism and explain the indices, the general impression that the index number do not properly reflect the actual

---

1. New Delhi, Ministry of Labour, 1978, 204 p.

price situation, has persisted, consequently, there was a growing feeling that these index numbers should be examined in all aspects, and the deficiencies therein, if any, should be corrected. At a Tripartite Labour Conference held in the first week of May 1977, several trade union representatives suggested that a Committee should be appointed to go into the various aspects of CPI Numbers and make recommendations. So the present series of the Consumer Price Index Numbers for industrial workers are compiled by the Labour Bureau on base 1960=100 and are based on the Family Budget Enquiries conducted in 1958-59. In order to ascertain the shifts in the consumption pattern of the working class since 1958-59, the Labour Bureau had undertaken fresh family budget surveys in 1971 in respect of 60 centres. However, there has been demand from various quarters that before the new series are released the Index Numbers should be reviewed in all their aspects and the deficiencies in the series, if any, be rectified before the new series are introduced. So the Government of India, Ministry of Labour Constitute a Committee on Consumer Price Index Numbers vide its Resolution No. U/24025/4/77-LB dated May 31, 1977.

Terms of Reference

(i) To review the various aspects of the Consumer Price Index Numbers for industrial workers including the criteria and the methodology for deriving the weighting diagram, the linking factor, methods of compilation of the index and the price collection system;

(ii) To study and report on:

(a) the existing price collection procedures and machinery;
(b) the desirability and mode of associating the representatives of the trade unions and employers with the processes of price collection work; and

(iii) To make recommendations on the above matters.

Contents

Introduction; Consumer Price Index; Background; Scope and Coverage of the Index Series; Review of 1960 and 1971 Series; Introduction of the 1971-based C.P.I. Numbers and the Linking Factor;

Price Collection Procedure and Machinery; Association of User Interests; Summary of Main Recommendations; Acknowledgements; Minutes of Dissent; Appendices.

Recommendations

Selection of Centres

8.1 The present basis of the selection of Centres and the present pattern of the selection from three distinct groups, namely, Factory, Mines and Plantations may continue. (Para 3.3).

Coverage of Workers

8.2 Once a centre has been selected on the basis of its relative strength among factory, mine of plantation centres, as at present the subsequent family living surveys should cover all manual workers in the three sectors in the Centre and not be confined to only factory, mine or plantation workers (Para 3.4). The scope of the surveys should be enlarged so as to include manual workers in other establishments. As a step towards this, the next family living survey should cover manual workers in ports and docks, electricity and generating and distributing establishments, public transport undertakings and railways (Para 3.11). Having decided the categories of manual workers to be covered in the family living surveys, all manual workers in these categories should be covered irrespective of their income, as at present (Para 3.12). Contract labour engaged in factory, mine of plantation centres should be covered in the family living surveys, if necessary, by adopting tenement sampling methods (Para 3.15).

Some Old Series of CPI

8.3 There are three centre indices for Beawar, Cuttack and Berhampur, which do not form part of the all-India index, but are currently in use. The users of these indices should be persuaded to discontinue using these and to adopt suitable alternative ones, failing which the Bureau should arrange to update the weighting diagram through fresh family living surveys (Para 3.5).

Combination of Centre Indices

8.4 In the 1971 series, indices for Bombay-Thana and Calcutta-Calcutta (I.R.) should be combined and a single index published in each case (Para 3.6).

Parallel Series

8.5 It is desirable that the parallel series of the same centre are discontinued. However, if some State Governments are compiling their series on the basis of accepted procedures and methodology, and want to continue them for their specific requirements, the Labour Bureau may discontinue publishing its series but continue compiling them for the all-India index. (Para 3.8).

8.6 The Labour Bureau and the State Government should pool up their resources and apportion them between themselves to avoid waste of efforts (Para 3.9).

State/Regional Index

8.7 The question of compiling the State level indices and regional indices may be examined in consultation with the TAC and the Standing Consultative Committee recommended by us (Paras 3.21 and 3.23).

Price of Rationed Commodity

8.8 Where rationing is introduced ration price should be utilised for index compilation with proper splicing for quality changes (Paras 4.4 and 4.5).

Weight for Ration Price

8.9 In compiling the price index for an item sold in the ration shop in modified rationing areas, the weight attached to the ration price should be based on the actual off-take and not on the admissible quantity (Para 4.5).

Black Market Prices

8.10 It will not be advisable to insist on the collection of black market prices for purposes of index compilation (Para 4.13)

The current practice of the Labour Bureau of distributing the weight of the non-ration quantum of a commodity under statutory rationing in all other items of the food group is the best alternative available and should continue to be followed in such situations. (Para 4.18).

Rent Index

8.12 The present method of compiling house rent index needs improvement. The house rent index in the mining centres should not be kept frozen at 100 as at present. Henceforth, the house rent index for the self-owned tenements in the mining centre should be based on the repair, maintenance, etc., cost index to be compiled by taking the raw material cost and wages of skilled and unskilled workers at the mining centres (Paras 4.20 and 4.22).

Till such centre specific indices become available for correcting the current indices in the 1960 and 1971 series a common repair, maintenance, etc., cost index for all mining centres may be prepared by taking a simple average of the price indices for bricks and tiles from the wholesale price index of India and the simple average of the indices of wage rates of skilled and unskilled construction workers for the Delhi centre (Para 4.23). This rent index should also be used for compiling the rent index for free houses provided to the mining workers as well as the rented houses in the mining centres (Para 4.25).

8.13 For the rent index for the factory centres, the pattern of the rent survey currently carried out by the Labour Bureau does not take into account new houses from time to time and therefore, should be changed. Henceforth, the rent survey should be based on a new and a larger sample taken every year from an up to date list of workers (Para 4.29).

8.14 For correcting the current indices, the weight given to the house rent index should be apportioned between old and new houses. For the new houses, the weight should be determined on the basis of the rate of growth of households in the centre as revealed by the population census date for 1961 and 1971. The remaining weight should be assigned to old houses. The rent index for the new houses should be the overall consumer price index, excluding the rent index, for the centre. For the old houses, the rent index calculated on the basis of the present six monthly surveys should be used (Paras 4.31 and 4.32).

8.15 House rent index for plantation centres should not be kept frozen at 100 as at present. The weighted average house rent index for all the non-plantation centres may be taken as the house rent index for each plantation centre for the current period as well as in future (Para 4.24).

Other Free Items

8.16 For firewood, coal and medicine provided free of cost by employers in some centres, the price index should not be kept at 100 or reduced to zero. The price index of these commodities in nearby centres should be imputed in such cases (Para 4.34).

When State abolished school fees or provides text-books free to the students, the weights of these item in the index should be distributed on all other items of the index *pro rata.* Where text-books are not provided free, the average price of all the prescribed text-books for all the classes up to the secondary stage should be taken for indexing (Para 4.35).

Tobacco and Intoxicants

8.18 Whenever expenditure on tobacco and liquor and other intoxicants is reported in the household expenditure surveys, the items should be included in the index subject to the following:

(a) If expenditure on liquor and intoxicants is reported in the survey even if there was prohibition, no open market price quotations would be available and therefore, the weight of this item should be distributed *pro rata* on the other items of the sub-group.
(b) If in the above situation, prohibition is subsequently lifted, the open market price of the item should be collected and the index used after proper splicing.
(c) If there was no prohibition in the base year but is introduced later, the weight of the item should be distributed *pro rata* on the other items in sub-group (Para 4.38).

Clothing Items

8.19 The specification should be given in greater detail. There should be a greater check and supervision of price data relating to clothing by the regional offices of the Bureau. The State level CPI Committees may arrange for verification of data in all doubtful cases an in such cases splicing may be resorted to. In case the currently specified variety is considered to be not commonly used by the working class, the specification should be changed in consultation with the State Committee and its price adopted after splicing. Instead of collecting prices for ready-made garments, their weights should be attributed to the relevant cloth and tailoring in proper proportion. Tailoring charges may be included in clothing group rather in 'Miscellaneous'. For including controlled cloth in index scheme, no special procedure is necessary (Para 4.43).

Medicines

8.20 When ESI Scheme is introduced after the base year of the index, the division of the workers' expenditure on medical services between the ESI contribution, and private doctor's fee and medicines should be ascertained for assigning proper weights to the two categories of medical expenses for arriving at the index (Para 4.50).

Doctor's Fee

8.21 A larger sample of doctors that at present from each market may be chosen wherever possible to arrive at the average of the doctor's fee (Para 4.53).

Tram Fare at Calcutta

8.22 For 1960 index the average of the first and the second class tram fare may be taken in the current period. For 1971 series both the base price as well as the current price may be taken as the average of the first and the second class fares. (Para 4.54).

Cinema Tickets

8.23 Henceforth the cinema ticket charge for the lowest but one class should be used in the index after splicing (Para 4.55).

Quantitative and Qualitative Charges

8.24 (i) Item of prepared food/drinks such as cup of tea/coffee, saltish snack like *idli, dosa,* etc., should not be priced separately. Instead their weights should be imputed to their constituent items including fuel (Para 4.56).

(ii) The practice of pricing prepared sweets per unit of specified weight should be followed in all the centres (Para 4.56).

Durable Consumer Goods

8.25 Durable consumer goods should not be priced separately in the index when less than one per cent of households report expenditure in the family living surveys but its weight should be imputed to other relevant item/items (Para 4.58).

Imputation

8.26 The imputation details should be thoroughly checked for the 1971 series in respect of every one of the 60 centres and necessary corrections carried out before the series is introduced. Specifically (i) items on which significant expenditure has been reported should be separately priced and not imputed, (ii) items having higher weight should not be imputed to items having lower weight and inappropriate imputations should be corrected (Para 4.59).

Unit of Measure

8.27 The units specified for collection of price data of all items of groceries and spices should be those in which the working class households make their purchases. Henceforth whenever necessary changes in units should be incorporated and their price indices be appropriately spliced. (Para 4.63).

Introduction of the 1971-based CPI Series

8.28 The new CPI Numbers on base 1971 should be introduced at the earliest, simultaneously discontinuing the compilation and publication of 1960-based series of the index numbers (Para 5.5).

Conduct of the Fresh Family Living Surveys

8.29 A new family living survey should be conducted at the earliest, i.e., by 1980-81. The survey results should also be made available at the earliest and in any case in about 18 months from the date of completion of the field investigations (Para 5.6).

Interval Between Two Surveys

8.30 The interval between two surveys should be preferably be five years (Para 5.7).

Linking Factor

8.31 The linking factor between the 1960 and the 1971 series should be calculated with the help of the ratio method and should be based on the monthly index numbers beginning with January 1971 to the latest month before the introduction of this series.

Additions to Markets

8.32 Where new working class areas and markets develop or where other conditions justify a change of or addition to existing markets, the Labour Bureau should effect such a change/addition in consultation with the State Level Committees (Para 6.5).

Change of Shops

8.33 Though the change of shops too frequently may not be desirable, the need for a change should be examined periodically and shops may be changed whenever considered necessary and justified (Para 6.6).

Price Collection Machinery

8.34 Where the number of markets in a centre is only one or two the present system of part-time price collection may continue; and the Labour Bureau may arrange with the concerned State Governments for allowing them more time for this work. In centres in which the number of markets covered is more than three, full-time Price Collectors should be appointed (Para 6.9).

Training Courses

8.35 Training courses for price collectors and price supervisors should be arranged regularly by the Labour Bureau (Para 6.10).

8.36 It is preferable that the Labour Bureau entrusts the work of price collection to the State Bureau of Economics and Statistics. The price supervisors should preferably be of middle level. A Supervisor should not be burdened with more than four markets to supervise (Para 6.11).

Regional Offices of the Labour Bureau

8.37 Regional Offices should be strengthened and put under the charge of Deputy Directors and sub-regional offices opened in States where the number of Centres does not justify a full-fledged regional office (Para 6.13).

Association of User Interests

8.38 There may not be any objection if a representative of the trade union or organisations of employers' in a centre accompanies a price collector as an observer [Para 7.10(i)]

8.39 Price quotation should be displayed regularly on the notice board or desk of the price collecting agency at the centre [Para 7.10(ii)].

State Level Committee

8.40 At the State level, a Standing Committee consisting of representatives of trade unions and organisations of employers and officials of the State Government and the Labour Bureau should be constituted to meet once a month to scrutinize the price data and also examine other related questions [Para 7.10(iii)].

All India Committee

8.41 At the all-India level a Standing Advisory Committee consisting of representatives of trade unions and organisations of employers, the Chairman of the TAC and the Director, Labour Bureau should be constituted in the Ministry of Labour to advise the Government on broad issues and provide a continuing forum for consultation on matters relating to the index (Para 7.10).

Regular Seminars on CPI

8.42 The Labour Bureau should organise once a year at least in each State one day seminar of trade union workers where the various aspects of the index can be explained, their doubts clarified and their suggestions entertained (Para 7.12).

17

P. JAGANMOHAN REDDY COMMISSION OF INQUIRY (REGARDING NAGARWALA CASE), 1977 – REPORT[1]

Chairman P. Jaganmohan Reddy
Secretary Shri S. Vohra, ICR (Retd.) upto March 23, 1978
Alterations Shri J.K. Ahluwalia, thereafter.

Appointment

The Central Government by its notification No. S.O. 389(E) [No. VI/11034/8/77-S&P (D.I.)] dated 9th June 1977, appointed this Commission to inquire into matters specified in the Annexure to that notification. By this notification, it required this Commission to enquire into and ascertain whether there was, on the part of any public servant or person in authority any deviation from any rule or established procedure, or any suppression of, or omission to verify, any relevant fact or circumstance in relation to, or connected with, the chain of events commencing with the taking out of a sum of rupees sixty lakhs from the State Bank of India, Parliament Street, New Delhi, on May 24, 1971 by Shri Ved Prakash Malhotra, the then Chief Cashier of the said branch of the State Bank of India, including the subsequent criminal proceedings against Shri R.S. Nagarwala, son of late Shri S. Nagarwala and his death.

Terms of Reference

(a) to examine and evaluate the evidence which has already been obtained, or may be obtained by the Commission or may be produced before it with regard to matters mentioned in the Annexure to the notification;

----

1. Controller of Publications, Government of India, New Delhi, 227 p.

(b) to make such further inquiry as the Commission may consider desirable in order to obtain, to the extent possible, a full picture of all the facts and circumstances relating to the matters referred to in the Annexure; and

(c) to inquire into any other matter arises from, or is connected with or incidental to any act, omission or transaction referred to in the annexure aforesaid. Seven matters were listed in the Annexure, viz.:

Annexure

(1) The taking out of the sum of Rs. 60 lakhs from the State Bank of India, Parliament Street, New Delhi, on May 24, 1971, by Shri Ved Prakash Malhotra, the then Chief Cashier of the said Branch of the State Bank of India, the manner and the circumstances of taking out of the said sum, the source and ownership of the said sum, the accounts, if any, from which the said sum was taken out, the manner in which the said sum was accounted for in the books of the said Branch of the State Bank of India prior to its taking out and also subsequent to its return to the said Branch of the State Bank of India.

(2) The transfer of the aforesaid sum by the said Shri Ved Prakash Malhotra to another person alleged to be one Shri R.S. Nagarwala son of late Shri S. Nagarwala.

(3) The filing of a complaint with the Parliament Street Police Station, New Delhi by the officers of the said Branch of the State Bank of India relating to the taking out of the said sum and the investigation of the case by the Police authorities.

(4) The arrest of the said Shri Nagarwala, the recovery of the whole or part of the said sum from him and the subsequent criminal proceedings against him.

(5) The involvement, if any, of other persons with the said Shri Malhotra or Shri Nagarwala in any of the aforesaid transactions.

(6) The death of Shri Nagarwala during the pendency of the criminal proceedings against him.

(7) The death of the investigation officer, Shri D.K. Kashyap.

Contents

Preliminary; Who was Nagarwala?; Who is Malhotra?; Nagarwala

Story – The popular belief; The taking out of the sum of Rs. 60 lakhs from the State Bank of India, Parliament Street, New Delhi, on May 24, 1971, by Shri Ved Prakash Malhotra, the then Chief Cashier of the said Branch of the State Bank of India, the manner and the circumstances of taking out of the said sum, the source and ownership of the said sum, the accounts, if any, from which the said sum was taken out, the manner in which the said sum was accounted for in the books of the said Branch of the State Bank of India prior to its taking out and also subsequent to its return to the said Branch of the State Bank of India; The transfer of the aforesaid sum by the said Shri Ved Prakash Malhotra to another person alleged to be one Shri R.S. Nagarwala son of late Shri S. Nagarwala; The involvement, if any, of other persons with the said Shri Malhotra or Shri Nagarwala in any of the aforesaid transactions; The filing of a complaint with the Parliament Street Police Station, New Delhi, by the Officers of the said Branch of the State Bank of India relating to the taking out of the said sum and the investigation of the case by the Police authorities; The arrest of the said Shri Nagarwala, the recovery of the whole or part of the said sum from him and the subsequent criminal proceedings against him; The death of Shri Nagarwala during the pendency of the criminal proceedings against him; The death of the investigating officer, Shri D.K. Kashyap; Conclusions; Appendices I to IX.

Conclusions

The difficulty in this case is that a story has mostly been built on assumptions which are mistakenly taken as equivalent to facts for the consumption of the public and the same story is often repeated. It is when one proceeds on *a priori* assumption, without their being supported by proved facts, that doubts keep on being repeated and, by sheer repetition, bring back to the mind unresolved those very doubts by almost carrying conviction to the mind which had stated with those assumptions.

Notwithstanding the difficulties adverted to above, namely, the thoroughly defective Police investigation, and their attempted concoction, the unwillingness of persons who are said to have furnished information to those who published those views to come forward to permit their names being disclosed to this Commission and several other restrains under which the Commission had to work, the evidence highlights certain conclusions:

In setting out these conclusions I am conscious of the fact that I am relying on certain statements made by police officers gathered during the investigation in respect of some of these conclusions. No doubt, under Section 162 of the Cr. P.C., a statement whether oral or reduced to writing, made to a police officer during investigation under Chapter XII of the Code is inadmissible in evidence, the statement could be used, in terms of the proviso to the Section, for limited purposes only when a witness is called for the prosecution. The person using it must be the accused or, with the permission of the court, the prosecution. The use of such statement could only be for purposes of contradicting such witnesses under Section 145 of the Evidence Act and the written statement must be proved. It would, therefore, appear that the statement of the person made to the police, whether the person is neither called for the prosecution nor for the defence, cannot be made use of in any manner unless the statement comes under Section 32(1) of the Evidence Act. There are, however, certain decisions which seems to have laid down that this Section does not control Section 8 of the Evidence Act and a statement made to a police officer in the course of investigation which accompanies or explains conduct is relevant under Section 8, may be admitted in evidence. In some decisions, it was held that the prohibition contained in this Section extends even to statements which are admissible in evidence of conduct. It is, however, clear that a statement made during investigation can be used in a subsequent civil proceeding. Under regulation No. 19 made by virtue of the powers conferred on the Commission under Section 8 of the Commissions of Inquiry Act to regulate its own procedure, it is provided that technical rules of the Evidence Act, as such, do not govern the recording and admissibility of evidence before the Commission, subject, however, to the fundamental principles of natural justice and the basic principles underlying the primary provisions of the Evidence Act being followed as a guide. In so far as this Commission is concerned, this is neither a criminal trial nor a civil trial. As it is a fact finding Commission, I will be justified in relying on such material as is placed before it as long as it is not abhorrent to the principles of natural justice or it does not do any violence or transgress any fundamental rules of evidence, such as hearsay, etc.

The following can be said to be established on the evidence:

(1) Malhotra received a telephone call at about 11.30 a.m., as a consequence of which Malhotra took out Rs. 60 lakhs and handed it over to Nagarwala.

(2) Malhotra believed that the persons who telephoned to him were Haksar and Smt. Indira Gandhi, Prime Minister of India, that Rs. 60 lakhs be handed over to a person who would give a particular code word to be answered by another code word.

(3) Haksar and Smt. Indira Gandhi did not phone Malhotra.

(4) There is no evidence to show that Smt. Indira Gandhi had a personal account anywhere near the amount withdrawn by Malhotra. There were certain accounts of funds which were operated by her and someone else jointly. I have referred to these accounts earlier but even in these accounts, it is not shown that there were any amounts which would cover the withdrawal of such a heavy amount for the disbursal of which he was expecting to receive a cheque/voucher/receipt. Her own personal account had only Rs. 150 to her credit.

(5) Malhotra was not personally known to Smt. Indira Gandhi to such an extent that she could trust him with any secret work or entrust him with such a large sum of unaccounted money. Nagarwala had once met her for help which she gave to get his compensation due after discharge from the Army and again in 1967 regarding Vietnam War. Neither Smt. Gandhi nor Haksar admit that they remember meeting Nagarwala but there can be no doubt that Nagarwala had met them and discussed Vietnam War. Smt. Gandhi denies that Nagarwala was related to her husband. There is, however, sufficient evidence to show that Nagarwala had great regard for Smt. Gandhi and even after conviction, his letter to her showed a familiarity with which no stranger would write. It may be that Nagarwala was giving out that he was a friend of Smt. Indira Gandhi.

(6) Malhotra and Nagarwala were known to each other as Nagarwala was frequently visiting State Bank of India to get his drafts encashed, and also to get change, for which he had met Malhotra. Haksar, in his first statement, said that Malhotra, when he saw him on the day of the incident, mentioned Nagarwala by name as the person who had defrauded him. Later, in his deposition he explained that the person whose name was

not then known and later came to be identified as Nagarwala, was referred to as Nagarwala when narrating what Malhotra told him on the date of the incident.

(7) Nagarwala confessed that he played a hoax by mimicking the voice of Haksar and Smt. Indira Gandhi and it was he alone who was responsible for the hoax but this confession was not voluntary.

(8) Nagarwala could not mimic or at any rate could not mimic the voice of a female much less of Smt. Indira Gandhi.

(9) Police hurried the case with ugly haste and managed to extract a confession from Nagarwala and by adopting a device had the case transferred to another Magistrate who acted on inadmissible evidence and convicted Nagarwala on a questionable plea of guilty.

(10) The Magistrate circumvented trial by a Sessions Court by giving a consecutive sentence.

(11) The Bank's Safe Vault contained unaccounted boxes.

(12) Books of Vault room not produced – Vault Register seized on 24th May 1971 not produced – nor extract of that book though shown to have been filed in the retrial not produced. The Jotting Register and the Stock Register were only seized on 1st June 1971 but no entries were made in these two books after 24th May 1971 till the date of seizure. New books, i.e., Vault Register, Chief Cashier's Jotting Register and Stock Register were opened in which entries of 24th May 1971 were said to have been copied and subsequent transactions continued to be enterred therein. Neither the Jotting Register nor the Stock Register maintained up to 24th May 1971 have been produced and although extracts of these books of 24th May 1971 are said to have been filed in the retrial proceedings, even these have not been produced. In view of the suppression it could be inferred that if these were produced they would not have shown the 60 lakh entry.

(13) If the money (Rs. 60 lakhs) is Bank's money, it has been taken out contrary to all Rules and Regulations and without proper entries, nor can (a) the money of the Bank be taken out or paid on the instructions of any one who has not got the amount to his/her credit in an account with them, (b) no money can be taken out and paid out on telephonic instructions, (c) no money of the Bank can be drawn out of the cur-

rency chest without the joint custodian being told of the purpose of drawing the amount, (d) no money of the Bank can be drawn, without a cheque, (e) no money of the Bank can be taken out without its being entered in the Insurance Register, (f) no money larger than Rs. 25 lakhs can be taken out of the Bank's premises at any one time, (h) no money can be taken out without the Armed guard, and (i) no money can be taken out except in the Bank's van. Everyone of these instructions and requirements have been deliberately transgressed by Malhotra.

(14) Khanna, Batra, Rawal Singh, U.D. Sharma, Satpal, Manbahadur, Santosh Kumar (driver) and Sinha (Security Officer) all knew that money was taken out by Malhotra contrary to rules but none reported to the higher officers till the police came and informed them that Malhotra had been defrauded.

(15) Malhotra admitted and repeatedly insisted that he used to take moneys to VIPs though not such large amounts – and obtain cheques from them.

(16) Malhotra on all accounts was not excited or upset till he came to know from Haksar that he (Haksar) had not phoned and the whole thing was a hoax played on him and that he should go and inform the police at once. He is then stated to have said "Mein Margaya, Mein lut gaya, etc., . . ".

(17) That all the investigating officers knew Malhotra well even before the incident, i.e., Kashyap, Bose and Markandy Singh. Apart from these, Suraj Balram, Mehra and Chadha, the last three Security Officers of Smt. Indira Gandhi, also knew him well even before the incident.

(18) Not necessary for Malhotra to give taxi number to get at the taxi driver who drove away Nagarwala and the story of Malhotra giving taxi number cannot be believed. This is supported by case diary in which Nagarwala is made to give the same taxi number after it was discovered.

(19) Tandon and Gautam Kaul, the former Joint Secretary in the Prime Minister's Secretariat and the latter cousin of Smt. Indira Gandhi, were very much active in the Police Station during investigation of Malhotra and Nagarwala. Tandon conveyed Smt. Gandhi's message that the culprit should be traced and the money recovered quickly particularly as her name was involved. Gautam Kaul was hovering around and impeding the

investigation though Kaul denies it and his presence during investigation where he had no business probabilises Rajpal's complaint.

(20) A high ranking official of the State Bank of India was in the Parliament Street Police Station along with Tandon. Letters, Exs. C-200 and C-201, say it was Chairman, Talwar, the then Chairman in his subsequent affidavit says he was not in Delhi but was in Bombay at that time.

(21) Enquiry confined only to the question whether there was "a conspiracy to tarnish the image of the Prime Minister". No other enquiry was considered necessary. In fact, it was taken as prohibiting an inquiry into the question of whose money was given by Malhotra and whether Smt. Indira Gandhi had kept any money in the Bank and whether it was her money that was paid to Nagarwala.

(22) Nagarwala when arrested had a scooter tyre and tube in which there were three bundles amounting to Rs. 30,000 which he claimed was his share. At that time he is also stated to have said that there were others involved and if he disclosed their names, he would be killed.

(23) Nagarwala at first insisted on being taken to Smt. Indira Gandhi or some other authority but after reward was settled by the police party in Mufti went to Captain's house and got the suit cases with money recovered.

(24) Nagarwala got his hair dyed and got himself clean shaved after he relieved Malhotra of Rs. 60 lakhs and ordered an Air-conditioned taxi for the next day to come to Parsi Dharamshala to go to Ranikhet.

(25) Nagarwala, according to newspaper reports, bargained for a reward of 10 per cent (Rs. 6 lakhs) and ultimately settled for Rs. 2 lakhs, besides the Rs. 30,000 found in the scooter tyre, though, according to Rosha, deposing before the Commission, he (posing as a Bank official) promised to consider him for a reward if he got the money discovered. The newspapers, it may be pointed out, were given the above information reported by them, by the police officers among whom was Rosha who is now reticent to disclose to the Commission which he freely disclosed to the Press.

(26) Nagarwala refused to disclose the name of the woman who phoned him at 7 p.m. on 24th May, 1971 to Parsi Dharamshala

and wanted to talk to him. The woman refused to give her name. Police gave out that they knew the woman who phoned as Smt. Indira Gandhi and it will be disclosed when Nagarwala makes his confession.

(27) The Bank tried to trace the three bundles of new notes being part of the recovered money from the special register which would have indicated, if these were found therein, that they were part of the recovered money and, by this process, to show that the recovered money was taken out of the currency chest. As no list of the numbers of new notes was made either at the time of the seizure or at the time when the court had given these notes in *superdari* or at the time when the police handed them over to the Bank in compliance with the *superdari* order, I had held that it would not be possible to rely on this fact to establish conclusively that these new notes formed part of the recovered money. Nonetheless, we have the evidence of Bose, that, at the time of the seizure, the numbers of the notes were recorded in 14 or 15 pages. When I asked Bose whether these 60,000 numbers were noted, he said 'yes'. I cannot rely on his statement also because nothing was said in the seizure report about a list having been made, nor was this list filed in the court, nor is it possible to count 60,000 pieces in the time available, nor could 14 or 15 pages be considered sufficient to note down the numbers of 60,000 notes. Assuming that each page has 5 columns and 20 lines on each sheet of 2 pages, 200 numbers can be written; at this rate, one would require 300 pages to write out 60,000 numbers. Even making allowance for deduction in respect of 12 new bundles where only the first and last number of each bundle is required to be noted and assuming that the pages could have more lines and more columns to take in more numbers, the minimum number of pages required would be 200 to 250. Even if these numbers were noted, the only purpose could be to link the withdrawal of the 60 lakhs currency notes from the currency chest with those that had been recovered. I have already shown that insofar as the old notes are concerned, they are of no assistance in this regard since the numbers of used notes are not recorded in the special register. In the recovered notes, it is indisputable that, except for 11 or 12 bundles, all of them were old notes. The list of such 11 or 12 bundles of new

notes could be contained in one sheet and if that was done these would have been a means of checking if these tallied with the numbers in the said register. I cannot, however, give any importance to the statement of Bose that such a detailed list giving the number of each and every hundred rupee note was noted. While making a seizure of any article or thing, the police are enjoined in give details and description of that article or thing as later could be identified in court. If so, even where a list is made of the currency notes, all that could reasonably be assumed is that each bundle in the 60 lakhs was the same bundle which was part of the Rs. 59,94,300 recovered. In such an event, the statement of Bose that there were 14 or 15 pages would be correct. Even if the list so made is not produced, there is nothing to infer that the notes recovered were not the notes handed over by Malhotra to Nagarwala. Thus this finding is a neutral finding in the sense that while it may not positively prove that these notes were drawn from the currency chest, it does not necessarily follow that they were not withdrawn from the currency chest.

(28) Nagarwala's allegation that he was induced by the police to make a confession gets support from the evidence and circumstances in which the confession, if it be a confession at all, is made.

(29) Nagarwala attempted to get Malhotra included as a co-accused but failed.

(30) Nagarwala made statements to show that he will unmask all those who were concerned – that some people would like to see that he does not get out of the hospital alive, that he will tell Pudumjee the whole story when he gets out.

The above facts which have been highlighted show that there are certain aspects of Nagarwala story which if properly investigated at the time of the incident would have given some answers but without that we are unable to find the answers.

The Home Secretary directed the Inspector General of Police, Delhi vide Ex. C-146 dated 29th May 1971 to investigate if there was a conspiracy to "tarnish the image of the Prime Minister". In his evidence before the Commission, the then Home Secretary, Govind Narain stated that the Prime Minister was kept informed of the progress of the case. There was a specific issue of the certificate of

Commendation issued to V.P. Malhotra and also the question about Nagarwala's antecedents about which the Prime Minister was informed. He has also stated that the Prime Minister enquired once or twice from him regarding the progress of the case. It is curious, therefore, to note that the then Prime Minister in her evidence before the Commission stated otherwise, viz., that she took no interest in the case and that she made no enquiry about it as it was a matter of little importance compared to the international issue of Bangladesh which engaged her full attention. The Prime Minister or any member of the Government did not consider it proper to institute any inquiry to settle the dust of doubt and controversy which was being raised all the time and which came to thicken all the more as time passed. The two agencies, the Intelligence Bureau and the Research and Analysis Wing of which Kao was the head, both under the Home Ministry and the Prime Minister's Secretariat were hardly likely to enquire into this with the kind of directions they had received or envisaged by their own closeness to the then Prime Minister to be helpful in any inquiry about the possible involvement of the then Prime Minister. The result is that facts have become more difficult to ascertain and in view of the absence of any evidence which has not been forthcoming, there still remain unanswered questions.

The investigation of the case was incomplete not only in respect of the question of the involvement of the name of Prime Minister but, in fact, even the ordinary aspect of the investigation of Malhotra regarding the breach of trust in parting with Rs. 60 lakhs of Bank's money was not investigated. As investigation if undertaken would also have thrown light on the question whether the money belonged to the Bank or whether it was kept in Bank's custody by someone, the possibility of keeping such money not being ruled out. The failure to investigate this aspect has affected the chance of finding out the truth on this important aspect.

Apart from the police, the trial Magistrate also made no attempt to go behind the confession of Nagarwala. He did not examine either Malhotra or other witnesses to find out if the version given by Nagarwala was corroborated. He seems to have ignored all norms of caution by merely concentrating on the conviction and sentence with ugly haste which is an anathema to judicial notions. This not only resulted in miscarriage of justice as pointed out by the Appellate Court in respect of Nagarwala but in my view also resulted in failure to bring out facts which would have thrown light on the allegation of the involvement of others besides Nagarwala and Malhotra.

Then again, questions relating to Nagarwala also remained unanswered. What was the motive of Nagarwala in getting the money? Surely, as Pudumjee said, he was not a squealer, nor, as he said, when he had asked Nagarwala since when he had become a philanthropist in wanting to help Bangladesh, because from what he knew of him, the only recipient of philanthropy would be Nagarwala himself to which Nagarwala said it was a long story and he was no fool. This seems to be Pudumjee's estimate of a very dear friend of his which he did not hesitate to say, with due apologies to a deceased friend by placing his views about him before the Commission. Nagarwala did have that morning some plan to try on the Bank to see if he could get something from Malhotra. As I said, he told Bagli when Bagli offered him a lift at 10.30 a.m. to Connaught Place that he (Nagarwala) had to make one or two telephone call. Was Nagarwala meeting anybody to make the calls or was he making calls to others besides making calls to Malhotra?

It has been seen that Malhotra according to Rajpal had admitted and persisted in admitting during investigation that he had earlier taken monies from the State Bank for VIPs and got cheques from them. Though the amount was not so big but small, Malhotra would not disclose the name of the VIP. When the police had this information they did not pursue it to find out who it is or did they know and are not telling the Commission for fear of throwing the earlier investigation in doubt. Once the case diaries had been prepared and a version of the purposes of the police objective built up it will be difficult for those who took part in the investigation to go against that story even if the truth is otherwise. That was the difficulty with Hari Dev, when he was reluctant to tell the truth.

From what Kanhaya Lal Gauba said it would appear that Nagarwala was probably giving out that he know Smt. Gandhi and was certainly taking probably gubly and in eurogistic terms as one of her great admirers. That this was so was believed by some of Nagarwala's Parsi friends. Gauba says that sometime in March 1971, a month or two before the incident, when he was staying in the India International Centre Shri and Smt. Daruwala, friends of his, invited him to dinner to meet an interesting person, Nagarwala, who they said knew Smt. Gandhi well. At the dinner, Smt. Daruwala introduced Nagarwala to him as the boy-friend of Smt. Gandhi. When asked what interesting conversation they had with Nagarwala, Gauba said he was more interested in chicken than the conversation. In fact, Nagarwala did not talk much. Another fact to be noticed is that when Nagarwala was arrested, he said that Rs. 30,000 which he had in his possession in the scooter tyre and tube was his share and if he disclosed the names of the persons who were with him in the episode, he would be killed. Then he wanted a reward and then wanted to disclose where the money was, to Smt. Gandhi and wanted the police to take him to her. Ultimately, according to the newspaper after settling for Rs. 2 lakhs and being allowed to keep 30,000 he showed the place where he hid the money. Somehow Nagarwala always felt confident that he could write to Smt. Gandhi and felt that he could approach her. In a matter like the Vietnam War he though he could invoke Smt. Gandhi's mediation between the U.S.A. and Vietnam. Had even gone to see the U.S. Ambassador in India but ultimately could not see him as he was not there but saw Shri Miller and gave him a similar memorandum as he had sent to Smt. Gandhi on the lines. Nagarwala said that he had spoken to her when he saw her on the 15th December 1967. It is also evident that she had asked him to see Haksar whom he saw on the 18th December 1967. The copies of contemporaneous letters written by him in January 1968 confirm his statement that he had seen both Smt. Indira Gandhi and Haksar though they do not recall his visits. All this would confirm the estimate of Pudumjee and his other Parsi friends that Nagarwala was a clever operator and was a man who was living by his wits. This however by itself does not involve Smt. Gandhi or Haksar or Miller.

I have also held that it is a reasonable inference that Nagarwala know Malhotra to the extent of making requests to him for his assistance to cash cheques or drafts and get change for higher currency notes to lower denomination, etc., all of which may have given Nagarwala an opportunity to get an idea of the type of man Malhotra was, the manner in which he transacted business and his readiness to oblige. There is, however, no evidence to show that there was anything more intimate than this between Malhotra and Nagarwala though the Intelligence Agency initially seems to have thought that Malhotra and Nagarwala were known to each other, used to meet each other in the Parsi Dharamshala and played cards together. It was suggested that the person who may be visiting Parsi Dharamshala may be Captain O.P. Malhotra but Captain O.P. Malhotra said that he neither plays cards nor he drinks. There is also no evidence to show that V.P. Malhotra, Chief Cashier, plays cards or was visiting the Parsi Dharamshala. If these facts had been ascertained, perhaps some light might have been thrown.

A am not prepared to accept that on the 24th of May 1971, Nagarwala got a sudden idea of a plan when sitting under a fan in the State Bank of India on a hot summer day and at the spur of the moment he telephoned Malhotra. Perhaps, for some time, Nagarwala might be toying with the idea of trying on Malhotra something like what he did. As pointed out earlier, that morning, as the evidence of Bagli would show, at about 10.30 a.m., Nagarwala was contemplating making a couple of telephone calls. Were these the telephone calls which he ultimately made and was it from somewhere else with the assistance of some other person, whether male of female has to be inferred because if he could not mimic either the story of mimicking Indira Gandhi is wrong and that Smt. Gandhi herself spoke, or he had someone else with him who mimicked her voice. Since Malhotra also joins Nagarwala and says that he heard Smt. Gandhi's voice, I must take it, on a reasonable appreciation of the evidence in view of the denial of Indira Gandhi, that she herself did not speak on the phone but that her voice was mimicked over the phone which is what Malhotra heard.

The D.I.G. Police, Rosha, said the Nagarwala had not planned what he did because from the way he was running from pillar to post with the money showed that he could not have any plan. This may, to some extent, be true. But he did have a plan to try to see whether he could get Malhotra deliver the goods and, if successful, he may have wanted to hand it over to someone who was expected to meet him and if he was not there, he would have to run from pillar to post. He then had to plan his get away and in this attempt, he changed taxis, threw away his felt what, had his hair dyed, got himself clean shaved showing that he must have had a moustache or a beard or both, arranged for a car next morning to take him away, kept Rs. 30,000 in a scooter type and tube, etc. Of course, what he is alleged to have said subsequently may support what I said because of what he said to Pudumjee which, I believe and which would indicate a bitterness at someone who has let him down and who might even be happy to see that he does not get out of the hospital alive. Why should anyone feel that way, why should Nagarwala express about such an involvement of someone else, if he was the only one concerned, and that too in respect of this matter; what was it all about; again these must remain unanswered questions. Alternatively, if his estimate of Malhotra is right and on mere telephone call from the Prime Minister, he might deliver the amount, he would execute his plan whatever that be; if he did not respond, nothing was lost.

When he says in his interrogation that he left clues to lead the police to him so that they could discover the money, was he expecting anyone to believe that story or was he only trying to create a defence for himself? If, in fact, he was successful in dealing with Malhotra and getting such a large sum of money and had no intention of defrauding but only to draw the attention of the government to the Bangladesh problem, he should have immediately returned it after giving it sufficient publicity. If he wanted to attract the attention of public to Bangladesh problem and its recognition, his taking away the money from the Bank and going away to Ranikhet would not have highlighted that problem, except to say that somebody by a stratagem had defrauded the Bank which would have made him an ordinary criminal without any redeeming qualities such as Nagarwala wanted for himself, much less to make him a patriot serving the interests of the country. Then again why did he pick up the figure of sixty lakhs? Is that figure hit upon as it forms the span of life according to Hindu belief? This has been highlighted by some to say that 60 lakhs had been obtained from some source and this was kept in the Bank and that was the amount that has been delivered to Nagarwala as a courier. Again, if Nagarwala had said that he was going to catch an I.A.F. plane at 1 p.m., why was no investigation done to find out whether any plane was actually due to leave, or had it actually left at 1 p.m.? The Commission tried to get the records of the airport but unfortunately these records are said to have been destroyed, according to the normal instructions, after 12 months. If the police had investigated this case at that time instead of attempting to gain supersonic speed in getting a conviction, many of these questions may have been answered.

The questions which I have been indicating throughout this Report were the questions which eminently needed a thorough investigation by the police and other authorities. At any rate, it has been demonstrated sufficiently that the theory of hoax set up by Nagarwala cannot be believed, and if believed, will itself be considered to be a hoax, in view of the several facts unearthed. Though these may not be sufficient to enable me to give a positive finding as to what actually took place, yet they raise several doubts. But, alas! these questions were left untouched as if the respective authorities were afraid of finding out what had happened. Once a case had been crystallised and records built up on certain lines, it may not be possible altogether to demolish the edifice built up by the authorities, nor is it possible in view of the reluctance of all those who know about it not to disclose to the Commission hat they know and also in view of the untruths and reluctance of all those who have taken part in it, particularly Malhotra, the surviving participant in the drama, to tell the truth, the whole truth and nothing but the truth. In the circumstances, it has approximating to what in reality actually took place, particularly when we are confronted with unanswered questions after so long a lapse of time.

Nevertheless, there are certain incontrovertible facts which demolish the story that was put out by the authorities as can be seen from the following:

(1) Suppression of original accounts written on 24th May 1971 and the writing of fresh accounts beginning as on the day, leading to the inference that if the original books were produced they would not have shown the entry of Rs. 60 lakhs in those books. The admission of Khanna and Rawel Singh that even those original books were not closed even though the cash transactions were closed at 2.30 p.m. that day because the money was not recovered or that Malhotra had not given a voucher for the taking away of the money and the amount of Rs. 60 lakhs drawn was not shown therein, would establish that fact.

(2) The non-action, including the failure to report to the higher officer, on the part of those concerned with the taking out of the money from the currency chest and taking that money out of the Bank, on their own admission, leads to an inference that such transactions may not be unusual.

(3) The keeping of unaccounted boxes in the Vault Room contrary to the Rules of the Bank that noting is the Vault Room should remain unentered in the books kept in the Vault Room itself. That there is at least one instance which came to the notice of the Commission when the Bank first produced a small box and later two big boxes said to be those in which Taparia, Secretary and Treasurer had kept his belongings and deposited them in the Vault Room in the safe deposit. Taparia

took out one of the boxes on 15-4-1974 'took delivery of some articles' from the box 'and then locked it and left it in safe custody' and made an entry in his own handwriting against the original entry No. 16/293 in the Register 'seal broken and now locked without seal'. Attempt was made by the Bank by writing the numbers in the safe deposit register pertaining to Taparia on each box on a small piece of torn label in a fresh ball-point pen just before their production before the Commission, leading to the inference that these may not be the boxes. There are also indications that there were labels showing that these boxes contained stationery articles, etc. This would show a gross irregularity and transgression of the rule that no safe deposit article is allowed to be opened while in custody by the depositor and that if he wants to take out something from it, he has to surrender and discharge the deposit receipt and take the article out of the Vault. It is only then that he can open it, take out or it, as heretofore, and redeposit as if it is a fresh deposit by obtaining a fresh deposit receipt, which would then have a different receipt number corresponding to the fresh entry made in the Safe Deposit Articles Register that day. That Taparia could transgress all these rules, rebuts the regularity of the Bank's strict adherence to the procedures for the custody of safe deposit articles. This would give room for allegations that unaccounted money could be kept in such boxes by high ranking Bank officials and taken out in this manner whenever required. I do not, however, say that in the above instance o Taparia in respect of what took place in April 1975, any such inference can be drawn. Even so, the fact that such things can take place is not completely ruled out. No wonder the Bank in its submissions condemned in no uncertain terms this practice though in another breath sought to be little the contribution of Justice Rangarajan to the discovery of such a serious lapse and the inherent possibilities of misuse or abuse by Bank officials of the facilities provided to them by the Bank.

(4) The fact that the Prime Minister did not have either in her personal account or any other account, which she was jointly operating with others, any amount which would remotely approximate to the money which Malhotra withdrew from the Bank and handed over to Nagarwala, makes the statement of

Malhotra that he expected a cheque/receipt/voucher from Smt. Gandhi for this amount incredible. For a hardened Cashier to say that the prime Minister of a country could issue a cheque on Government account without knowing on what account that would be given is to merely hazard a defence of a position which he could not defend. While rejecting his plea that he did all this under a spell, one can only say that he is not telling the truth.

Though these findings may also raise some presumptions that inasmuch as the money that was taken out was not entered in the registers as required to be done if the money was drawn from the currency chest; that it was possible to keep other peoples money in unaccounted boxes or that monies may be paid out without any protest or report to the higher officers, by the manner in which the three who were directly connected with the drawing of cash and paying out, viz., Khanna, Batra and Rawail Singh, had kept quiet when such a large amount as sixty lakhs was taken out, in my view, may not be sufficient to hold without further evidence aliunde that the story as generally believed that the money belonged to the former Prime Minister and that the same was paid at her instance or believed by Malhotra to be at her instance is established.

There are several lacunae before the generally believed version, mentioned above can be said to be not constitute a complete chain of events, leading to the only conclusion that that version is established. These lacunae are:

(a) whether the money was first drawn by the Bank from the currency chest and paid out without it being entered in any books of the Bank with the hope of getting a voucher authorising the drawing of money from the unaccounted source and replenishing the same. In respect of this, there is no evidence to show what correlation there is between a voucher/cheque/receipt and the unaccounted money. This will determine the mechanism by which the operation can be determined and the persons involved in the operation identified.

(b) whether the unaccounted money has been paid from unaccounted source initially and when it was discovered that it was paid to the wrong person, money is drawn from the currency chest and replaced subsequently and made over to the person to whom it may belong. This theory also has serious defects inasmuch as it will involve not only a series of operation but would show that the money either has been drawn out of the currency chest after 2 or 2.30 p.m. when Malhotra discovered the fraud or alternatively after the money was recovered late in the night when no money from the currency chest need be drawn out. The money so recovered could be paid direct to the person whose unaccounted money it lost.

To supply an answer to these would force me to leave the safe haven of facts which required to be established by evidence and enter the realm of conjectures and speculation. Unless these crucial facts are established, the other facts adverted to are merely inferences which may be explained away due to the concerned persons acting in a reckless and irregular manner tending to raise an inference that they were willing to oblige people they know or overawed by the belief that the Prime Minister of the country had the power to direct a Nationalised Bank to pay out or bring money without any regard to rules and regulations. If such was the case, why should the Prime Minister ring up a Chief Cashier as Smt. Gandhi said that itself is a big assumption. The manner in which the police had investigated and some of the unacceptable statements in their investigations as adverted to instead of clearing the mystery has greatly contributed to it and, to quote a phrase of a great leader of the Second World War used in a different context, has further deepened the enigma wrapped up in the heart of a mystery. With this remark, I must take leave of this episode.

18

HIGH-POWERED EXPERT COMMITTEE ON COMPANIES AND MRTP ACTS, 1977 – REPORT[1]

Chairman Justice Shri Rajindar Sachar, Judge of the High Court of Delhi

Members Shri S. Ranganathan; Shri R.D. Gattani; Shri Bedabrata Barua; Shri F.S. Nariman; Shri Shantanu N. Desai; Shri M. Srinivasa Rao; Shri D.C. Mothari; Shri Keshub Mahindra; Shri K.P. Tripathi; Shri K.K. Ray

Secretary Shri M.K. Kukreja

Alterations Shri K.K. Ray ceased to be the Secretary of the Department of Company Affairs from the 1st January, 1978 but continued as Member-Secretary of the Committee up to 28th February, 1978 when he retired from the Indian Administrative Service. Therefore, Shri Ray continued only as Member

Appointment

This Committee was constituted by Government in terms of the Ministry of Law, Justice and Company Affairs (Department of Company Affairs) Resolution No. 7/6/77-CL.V dated the 23rd June, 1977.

Terms of Reference

The Committee was "to consider and report on what changes are necessary in the Companies Act, 1956, and the Monopolies and Restrictive Trade Practices Act, 1969, with particular reference to the modifications which are required to be made in the form and structure of the Companies Act, 1956, and the Monopolies and Restrictive Trade Practices Act, 1969, so as to simplify them and to make them

---

1. Ministry of Law, Justice and Company Affairs, Department of Company Affairs, Government of India, New Delhi, 1978, xx + 368 p.

more effective, wherever necessary".

The Committee was called upon to consider the provisions of the two Acts and report, *inter alia*, on:

(i) classification and formation of companies and the constitution of Board of directors with special reference to protection of the interests of shareholders who are in a minority;

(ii) exercise of managerial powers, and protection of shareholders' and creditors' interests and their relations, *inter se*;

(iii) measures by which workers' participation in the share capital and management of companies could be brought about;

(iv) provisions which are required to be made to prevent mismanagement with special reference to safeguarding of company's own interests and the public interest;

(v) measures necessary to promote professionalisation of management and regulation of managerial and executive remuneration commensurate with their responsibilities;

(vi) measures by which re-orientation of managerial outlook in the corporate sector could be brought about so as to ensure the discharge of social responsibilities by companies;

(vii) what changes are required to be made in the Companies Act, 1956, to streamline the winding-up procedures so as to expedite the realisation and distribution of assets to the creditors and contributors;

(viii) whether it is desirable to enact special provisions applicable to the Government companies as a class so as to exclude the provisions of the Companies Act, 1956, generally in their applicability to such companies;

(ix) what adaptations and modifications are necessary in the provisions of the Companies Act, 1956, in their application to entrepreneurs in medium and small scale sectors carrying on business as joint stock companies;

(x) what further changes are required to be made in the Com panies Act, 1956, regarding the establishment of places of business and operation of foreign companies in India;

(xi) what improvements, if any, are required to be made in the present administrative structure and procedures regarding the enforcement of the provisions of the Companies Act, 1956, and the Monopolies and Restrictive Trade Practices Act,

1969;

(xii) what changes are required to be made in the Monopolies and Restrictive Trade Practices Act, 1969, in the light of the experience gained in the administration and operation of said Act; and

(xiii) any other matter incidental or ancillary to the administration of the Companies Act, 1956, and the Monopolies and Restrictive Trade Practices Act, 1969, having regard to the growth and development of trade, commerce and industry.

Contents

Introduction; Nature and Scope of the Terms of Reference and the Approach of the Committee; Concepts and Definitions; Classification of Companies; Management Structure and Professionalisation of Management; Managerial and Executive Remuneration; Shareholders' Protection and Prevention of Mismanagement; Accounts and Audit; Inter-corporate Investments and Loans; Public Deposits; Workers' Participation in Management of Companies; Social Responsibilities of Companies; Political Donations – Section 293A – Prohibition regarding making of Political Contribution; Government Companies; Winding-up of Companies; Administrative Machinery; Simplification and Over-all Review of the Companies Act not covered in other parts of the Report; Summary of Recommendations (Part A); Concepts and Definitions under the M.R.T.P. Act; Concentration of Economic Power; Monopolistic, Restrictive and Unfair Trade Practices; Administrative Machinery under the MRTP Act; Summary of Recommendations (Part B); Appendices I to XVII.

Recommendations

Part 'A' – Companies Act, 1956

Concepts and Definitions (Chapter III)

18.1 Having regard to the relevance of existing concepts and definitions to the changes being suggested in the present law, the need for a more rational arrangement of the provisions of the Act and also in view of certain departures from the existing scheme as suggested by the Committee, appropriate recommendations are being made relating to the concepts and definitions by way of consolidation and re-arrangement, modifications, additions and deletions. (Para 3.1)

18.2 The existing definitions of 'alter' and 'alteration' and 'modify' and 'modification' may be combined in one section. (Para 3.2)

18.3 The existing definition of 'member' in clause (27) of Section 2 may be replaced by the definition of 'member' in Section 41. The latter section may be deleted. (Para 3.2)

18.4 Section 2(41) relating to definition of 'relatives' may be redrafted on the lines of the provisions of Section 6 along with an Explanation that if one is related to the other within the meaning of this clause, the latter shall also be deemed to be related to the former. Schedule I-A may be amended to include brothers and sisters of mother and father. Section 6 may be deleted. (Para 3.3)

18.5 'Articles' and 'memorandum' may be redefined as suggested. (Para 3.3)

18.6 The existing definition of 'Board' may be modified as suggested. (Para 3.3)

18.7 The definition of book and/or paper may be modified to include book of account. (Para 3.3)

18.8 The definition of 'company' may be simplified to indicate company registered under the existing Act or any other Acts, ordinances, etc., before the commencement of the existing Act. (Para 3.3)

18.9 The definition of 'Company Law Board' may be simplified as suggested. (Para 3.3)

18.10 The definition of 'Court' may be amplified to include the Registrar and the Company Law Board as it has been elsewhere suggested that they may be clothed with powers to impose penalties for contravention of certain provisions. (Para 3.3)

18.11 The definition of 'debentures' should be modified to exclude issue of unsecured debentures. (Para 3.3)

18.12 The definition of 'investment company' as in section 372(10) and Note (1) to Schedule VI may be modified to exclude a private company and to include only those public companies who are carrying on business of only underwriting or dealing in shares, debentures or other securities. The revised definition should be incorporated in the definition section and section 372(10) and Note (1) to

Schedule VI may be deleted. This will prevent investment companies from functioning as catalyst of corporate control. (Para 3.3)

18.13 The existing definition of 'officer' may be modified to exclude reference to managing agents and secretaries and treasurers and to include 'an accountant' as defined. (Para 3.3)

18.14 The definition of 'officer in default' in Section 5 should be split up to spell out what constitutes default in the matter of imposition of penalty and in the matter of imprisonment or fine or both. (Para 3.3)

18.15 The definition of 'prescribed' in clause (33) of Section 2 may be amplified to include rules made by the Company Law Board. (Para 3.3)

18.16 In the existing definition of 'shares' in Section 2(46), reference to 'stock' may be omitted. (Para 3.3)

18.17 In the existing definition of 'turnover' in Clause (b) of Explanation to Section 43A may be shifted to definition section itself. (Para 3.3)

18.18 New definitions have been suggested to be added as follows: (Para 3.4)

(i) Accountant
(ii) Auditor
(iii) Free reserves
(iv) Managing/whole-time director
(v) Professional Manager
(vi) Recognised shareholders' association
(vii) Worker/Worker-director.

18.19 Clauses (3), (4), (16), (18A), (24), (25), (34) and (44) of Section 2 may be deleted, either because they have become redundant or are otherwise no longer necessary to be retained here. (Para 3.5)

18.20 For those expressions and definitions not defined in the 'Definition' section itself, attention should be drawn in this section by way of cross-reference. (Para 3.5)

18.21 References to words and expressions which have become redundant may be suitably changed or omitted. (Para 3.5)

Classification of Companies (Chapter IV)

18.22 While the basic classification of companies into public and private limited may be retained, a few structural changes within this broad classification are called for. (Para 4.1)

18.23 The class of unlimited companies should be abolished and clause (c) of sub-section (2) of Section 12 and Section 32 should be deleted. The existing unlimited companies should be compulsorily required to convert themselves into limited companies. (Para 4.2)

18.24 Guarantee companies must, in future, be required to be formed only as public limited companies and for the purposes enumerated in Section 25 of the Act. The Central Government should be empowered to issue directive to the existing guarantee companies for either getting themselves registered under the provisions corresponding to the present Section 25 of the Act of converting themselves into companies limited be shares. (Para 4.3)

18.25 The definition of a 'private company' will remain as at present in Section 3(1)(iii) of the Act. Such a company will, however, be prohibited from accepting deposits or borrowing money from the public, except from its own directors, shareholders and their relatives. It shall also be prohibited from borrowing long-term loans of more than three years from public financial institutions in excess of rupees ten lakhs. Whenever the turnover of a private company exceeds rupees one crore in any financial year or whenever, in any financial year, twenty-five per cent or more of the paid-up share capital of the private company is held by one or more public limited companies, or whenever, in any financial year, twenty-five per cent or more of the paid-up share capital of a public limited company is held by the private company, certain provisions of the Act as are applicable to public companies shall also apply to such private companies. (Para 4.5)

18.26 The proviso to sub-section (1) of Section 31 should be deleted. It should not be permissible for a public company to convert itself into a private company. (Para 4.6)

18.27 In order to encourage the growth of small scale sector, private companies may, henceforth, be classified into two groups – (1) small companies and (2) others. Small companies would be those private companies which have a paid-up capital of not exceeding rupees five lakhs. Such small companies would be eligible for further exemptions and privileges in respect of certain specified matters when they satisfy two conditions. Firstly, the small company must not have a body corporate, other than a Government company or statutory body, or a public financial institution or a bank, as its shareholder. Secondly, the small company must not invest in the shares of another body corporate. Powers of purely executive nature in respect of such companies should be exercisable at the local level by the Registrar or the Regional Director. Powers of the Court under the Act should be exercised by the District Judge. (Para 4.9)

18.28 The law relating to foreign companies shall be rationalised. Where a body corporate incorporated outside India is engaged in agricultural (including plantation), production, processing, mining, manufacturing, distribution of goods, generation of power or construction activities in India, the body corporate must register itself as a company under the Act. Where not less than fifty per cent of the paid-up share capital of a body corporate incorporated outside India is held by one or more bodies corporate incorporated in India or by one or more citizens of India, it must register itself as a company under the Act before establishing or operating a place of business in India. Sub-section (2) of Section 591 should be deleted. Sections 603 to 608 relating to prospectus issued by foreign companies may be deleted and suitable provisions including the prospectus provisions, contained in Part III of the Act, should be made. Provisions of clauses (c), (e) and (f) of Section 433 should be made applicable to foreign companies. All the provisions relating to winding up of companies (following the applicability of these clauses of Section 433) shall apply to foreign companies. Some other modifications will have to be made. (Para 4.12)

18.29 The Government may like to consider such matters as require urgent attention for suitable incorporation in the law as regards the additional disclosures or compliances to be made by multinationals in public interest, pending the recommendations of the U.N. Commission of Transnational Corporations. (Para 4.13)

Management Structure and Professionalisation of Management (Chapter V)

18.30 Some of the provisions of the Act have proved to be ineffective to meet present day need of corporate management and administration. It would be a valid generalisation to say that managerial powers should be exercised not merely for the interest of the shareholders but also in the interest of the creditors, consumers, overall growth of the economy and also keeping in view the considerations of public good. Professionalisation of management is, therefore, not a mere concept but is, in fact, an inevitable necessity for the well-being of the company itself. In our country, the development of a distinct managerial class cannot be said to have taken place in any systematic manner. It is the abolition of managing agency system which had a salutory effect in helping companies to re-orientate themselves to the changed situation which called for management by the techno-structure. There is growing evidence that more and more professional people are taking up positions in companies previously held by owner-managers. This process of professionalisation of management needs to be carried forward. (Paras 5.1 to 5.5)

18.31 It is difficult to legislate on professionalisation of management without defining professional management. There are certain areas which are beyond doubt within the competence of professionally qualified people. On the other hand, instances are not rare where professional approach has been developed and applied by people without professional qualifications but having considerable experience. The term 'professional manager' has thus been defined to take into account the element of specialised knowledge as well as specialised experience, more intensive or extensive experience being insisted upon for a professional manager not possessing the specified qualifications. (Para 5.6)

18.32 While the conceptual and practical aspects of the problem of workers' participation in management are dealt with in Chapter XI, compulsory adoption of the two-tier board is not recommended. (Para 5.7)

18.33 The question of 'minority of shareholders' finding representation on the Board of Directors is beset with practical difficulties of definition and implementation. The Committee has, however, recommended a number of safeguards to protect shareholders' rights and interest. (Para 5.8)

18.34 Public limited companies having a paid-up capital of rupees fifty lakh or more must have at least one managing or whole-time director. Large size companies cannot be successfully managed without somebody being specifically charged with substantial powers of management. (Para 5.9)

18.35 The form of management by 'manager' is very rare. Definition of 'manager' in clause (24) of Section 2 should, therefore, be deleted. Reference to 'directors who are managers' occurring in Section 318 should also be dropped. The provisions of sections 384 to 388A relating to managers need also to be deleted. Section 197A is to be suitably redrafted to incorporate that when a company has only one managing or whole-time director, he shall be deemed to have the management of the whole or substantially the whole of the affairs of the company. Where there are more than one managing or whole-time director, they shall be deemed to have been entrusted with substantial powers of management. (Para 5.10)

18.36 It should be provided that provisions of Section 265 will be subject to any proportion which a company is required to maintain as regards worker-directors. Suitable references are also to be made in sections 266 and 270 to provide that there shall be no stipulation in the articles as regards qualification shares to be obtained by a worker-director. (Para 5.11)

18.37 Consistent with the Committee's general approach requiring Governmental approval only in exceptional cases, provisions of Section 269 regarding appointment of managing and whole-time directors in public companies need to be replaced by new provisions as suggested. These include:

(i) Appointment of a whole-time or managing director by a public limited company by a special resolution, if he has completed age of 30 years and is not above 65 years, and is not a relative of any director or is not a shareholder or a relative of a shareholder holding, in either case, more than two per cent of the paid-up equity capital of the company, and further that certain prescribed formalities have been complied with;

(ii) On a complaint from a specified number of shareholders or on own information, the Central Government may refer to the Company Law Board to decide whether any person appointed as managing director, who has been convicted of an offence specified in certain statutes, is or is not fit and proper person to hold that office. This reference is subject to certain safeguards, and decision of the Company Law Board will be subject to an appeal to the High Court. The said managing director can thereafter be removed by the High Court or the Company Law Board, as the case may be;

(iii) Appointment of a whole-time or managing director, who does not fulfil the prescribed conditions, can be made only with the previous approval of the Company Law Board. The said Board may also approve the appointment, notwithstanding any of the aforesaid provisions.

(iv) Section 268 may accordingly be deleted. (Para 5.12)

18.38 No person will be allowed to hold office of managing director in more than one public company unless certain specified procedure has been followed and, in addition, approval of the Company Law Board will be necessary, except in the case of holding-subsidiary companies. (Para 5.13)

18.39 Statutory prescription of a general statement of duties of directors is neither helpful nor desirable. The existing law, however, needs to be a strengthened to ensure greater degree of effective participation by directors. (Paras 5.14 and 5.15)

18.40 Director will retire at the age of 70, unless his continuance is approved by a general meeting of the company for which special notice has been given. (Para 5.16)

18.41 The total number of twenty directorships that can be held by directors as per present law may continue but in computing this number, alternate directorships and directorships in private companies should also henceforward be included. This ceiling of twenty, in case of a managing or whole-time director will, however, be reduced to ten.

18.42 In order to ensure more effective compliance of the various provisions requiring a company or its officers to file certain statutory returns and documents with the Registrar, provisions of Section 283 should be extended to provide for vacation of office by directors in case of persistent default in filing certain specified documents and returns. (Para 5.21)

18.43 Section 283 should be amplified to provide for additional grounds on which a whole-time director or a worker-director will become disqualified to continue in office. (Para 5.22)

18.44 To ensure more effective participation in management by the Board as a whole, Board meetings should be held at least once in every two months (as against once in three months at present). (Para 5.23)

18.45 With the same end in view, certain specified matters, e.g., investments, borrowings, statutory liabilities, should be required to be placed before the meetings of the Board of Directors. (Paras 5.23 and 5.24)

18.46 A director who has not placed his dissent on record shall be presumed to have assented to the action of the Board, subject to certain safeguards. (Para 5.25)

18.47 Certain specified powers given in Section 293 to the Board shall be exercised only by a special resolution in general meeting. (Para 5.26)

18.48 Notice of the meetings of the Board of Directors should be given ordinarily at least seven days prior to the date of the meeting. (Para 5.27)

18.49 Section 203 should be amended so as to empower the Court to direct that a person shall not without leave of the Court be a director of the company even when winding-up proceedings are not pending before it. (Para 5.28)

18.50 The Court should be empowered to disqualify a person (under Section 203) who has been convicted of any offence involving fraud or dishonesty. (Para 5.29)

18.51 Power should be conferred on the Court to disqualify a person, who is found to be not competent to act as a director, from acting as a receiver, manager or liquidator. (Para 5.30)

18.52 A worker-director should not be deemed to hold any office of profit. (Para 5.31)

18.53 Section 317 should be deleted and provisions thereof, if necessary, may be taken care of along with provisions of Section 269. (Para 5.31)

18.54 Sections 322 and 323 need to be deleted as they are virtually a dead letter. (Para 5.32)

18.55 Workers' participation at the Board level would require consequential changes in certain sections which have been specified. (Para 5.33)

Managerial and Executive Remuneration (Chapter VI)

18.56 Despite differing views expressed in the Committee, it would have made an attempt to come to some definite conclusions regarding the regulation of managerial and executive remuneration. However, in view of the recommendations of the Bhoothalingam Committee on Wages, Incomes and Prices Policy (including top managerial salaries) which have since been submitted to the Government and on which an integrated policy is to be determined by the Government in consultation with all interests, this Committee is not making any specific recommendation, except that, in view of the professionalisation of management recommended elsewhere, managerial remuneration should be left to be regulated by the company itself by special resolution in general meeting after adequate safeguards are taken. Regulation of managerial remuneration may be subject to the guidelines of 11th November, 1969, now being followed by the Government till such time as the Government announces the decision in the light of its recommendations in the Bhoothalingam Committee Report. (Para 6.7)

18.57 The statutory guidelines should provide for classification of companies into four categories according to size based on effective capital, viz., A, B, C and D and the maximum and the minimum salary payable to managerial personnel of each category may be fixed accordingly. Minimum remuneration in excess of the limits of the period laid down in the guidelines would require the prior approval of the Central Government. (Para 6.8)

18.58 The wide powers now given to the Government in the matter of approval of every appointment and re-appointment of working directors may be modified to provide for such approval only in special circumstances, such as, in case of relatives of directors or where the proposed appointee is himself a shareholder or a relative of a shareholder holding in either case more than two per cent of the paid-up equity capital of the company or in case of appointment of expatriate directors. (Paras 6.11 and 6.13)

18.59 Powers of appointment/re-appointment within the statutory guidelines should be exercised by the companies only at a general meeting through special resolution and as an item of special business. Explanatory statement on such resolutions should contain all the particulars and justification in terms of the existing requirements in sections 269(3), 309 and 637AA of the Companies Act. The statement should indicate if the proposed managing/whole-time director was at any time involved in any prosecutions under the various specified economic offences. The Board's annual report to the shareholders should state that the statutory guidelines have been complied with. Breach of the guidelines would be cognizable by the Company Law Board on the basis of a complaint made to it. (Para 6.12)

Shareholders' Protection and Prevention of Mismanagement (Chapter VII)

18.60 Proper balance between shareholders' rights and the right of management should be maintained. Shareholders' individual membership rights and corporate membership rights should be strengthened with a view to make their participation effective and meaningful. There should be better management at Board level and remedies against oppression by majority over minority shareholders and against acts of mismanagement should be improved and quickened. Powers of Courts to deal with such matters should be enlarged. Recognition of shareholders' associations needs to be encouraged. Vigilence over corporate activities and corrective measures over erring companies needs to be strengthened. (Paras 7.1 to 7.4)

18.61 Proxy holder should have a right to speak as well as right to vote on show of hands. To facilitate this, the two-way proxy form with suitable modification should be a mandatory requirement for all public companies. (Para 7.5)

18.62 A legal right of intervention should be provided to shareholders in exercising control over and issuing directions to the Board without disturbance to their day-to-day managerial autonomy by amending Section 291. (Para 7.7)

18.63 The twin proof requirements in Section 397, namely, a continuous course of oppressive conduct and circumstances justifying winding-up of companies in onerous. Single act of oppression should be sufficient. Provision for necessity of circumstances justifying winding-up of the company be deleted. (Para 7.12)

18.64 Additional avenue of relief to individual shareholder – substitution of new Section 397. (Para 7.12)

18.65 The same circumstances as in Section 397 (as redrafted) should also be sufficient grounds for the Central Government to exercise its power under Section 408(1). Orders under this Section should be passed after giving an opportunity to the management to be heard. (Para 7.12)

18.66 Directors appointed by the Central Government under Section 408 should report every three months on matters which the Government ought to know. (Para 7.12)

18.67 The power under Section 409 presently exercised by the Central Government should be exercised by the Company Law Board (as re-constituted) in future. Prescribed percentage of shareholders also to have the right to complain. (Para 7.12)

18.68 Interim orders under Section 409 should be operative for a period of two months only unless extended further. Final orders should be passed by Company Law Board within six months. (Para 7.12)

18.69 Any party aggrieved by the order of Company Law Board would have a right of appeal to the High Court. The appeal should be decided by the High Court within six months. Meanwhile the order of thc Company Law Board should remain undisturbed. (Para 7.12)

18.70 Shareholders' association should be recognised on the same lines as of recognizing Stock Exchanges. They should be entitled to avail the rights to apply to the Court/Central Government/Company Law Board in cases of oppression or mismanagement. (Para 7.13)

18.71 Single shareholder or the shareholders' association (in the case of public companies) should be entitled to apply to the Court under sections 397 and 398 and not the Central Government to move a petition regardless of the prescribed percentage of members under Section 399(1)(a) and (1) (b). (Para 7.13)

18.72 None of the office-bearers of shareholders' association should be concerned with the management of the company. (Para 7.13)

18.73 In order to ascertain how companies funds are utilised, Inspecting Officer should be empowered to inspect the accounts of partnership firms and joint ventures in which the company has an interest. (Para 7.15)

18.74 Inspection of companies under Section 209A should be carried out only after giving prior notice, unless for reasons to be recorded by the Regional Director it is considered unnecessary. (Para 7.16)

18.75 Company Law Board like Court under Section 237(a) should also have power to order investigation into the affairs of the companies. (Para 7.17)

18.76 Persistent default by the companies in complying with the statutory requirements should be an additional ground for *suo moto* investigation by the Central Government under Section 237(b). (Para 7.18)

18.77 Investigation into the affairs of related companies should be carried out only after giving an opportunity to the concerned party to be heard. (Para 7.19)

18.78 Provisions relating to Special Audit in Section 233A have not been made use of frequently and are redundant, and should be deleted. (Para 7.20)

18.79 Right of companies to refuse to register transfer or transmission of shares should be exercised within two months of the date of lodging of the transfer deed or request for transmission and for reasons to be recorded in writing. Default should be punishable. Such order to be appealable to the Company Law Board. (Para 7.21)

18.80 An appeal should lie to the High Court on the grounds mentioned in Section 100 of C.P.C. against the orders of Company Law Board. (Para 7.21)

18.81 In order that members may move any resolution, the additional requirement with regard to the value of their shares being not less than one lakh rupees as provided in Section 188(2) should be removed. (Para 7.21)

18.82 Special notice required under sections 225, 261, 284 could be given by a single members. Section 190 should be amended. (Para 7.21)

18.83 In case the minimum subscription is not received by a company within 120 days, all monies received from the applicants should be refunded forthwith with increased rate of interest at 12 per cent. (Para 7.21)

18.84 The copies of the minutes of the general meeting of companies should be supplied by companies on request to the shareholders and to recognised shareholders' association free of cost. (Para 7.21)

18.85 Section 108(1A) to (1D) for getting transfer of shares endorsed be deleted as they have served no useful purpose and have delayed the free transferability of shares. (Para 7.21)

18.86 On a complaint that shares have been dealt with for a period for six months or more in any recognised stock exchange without the same being lodged for registration with the company, the Company Law Board may make proper inquiries and may freeze the voting rights attached to those shares. (Para 7.21)

18.87 As a substitute for the present requirement of the prescribed authority dating the transfer-form, the transferor while signing should put the date. (Para 7.21)

18.88 A public company other than Section 25 companies, should be expressly prohibited by Statute from having any power to expel any of its member notwithstanding its articles or resolution of the Board. (Para 7.21)

Accounts and Audit (Chapter VIII)

18.89 The Committee has felt the need for simple, adequate and meaningful disclosure by the companies, for the benefit of the shareholders, the management, the workers and the community at large and also keeping in view the objective of professionalisation of management for improving the working of the companies. To achieve the objectives, the following recommendations are made. (Paras 8.1 to 8.5)

18.90 Maintenance of accounts by companies on mercantile system only should be made obligatory as maintaining accounts on 'cash' basis may not reflect a true picture of the state of affairs of the company. Section 200 may be suitably amended. (Para 8.6)

18.91 Presently the Registrar of Companies as also the Income-tax Officer can extend the 'Financial Year'. To simplify and to reduce the paper work in the Registrar's office, it should be provided that the 'Financial Year' should consist of eighteen months, if so permitted by the Income-tax Officer (Section 210). (Para 8.7)

18.92 As preparation of balance sheet in vertical form, which is not prescribed in Schedule VI, has become a fairly common practice now, Section 211 should be amended whereby companies can adopt vertical form of balance sheet at their option as per model given at the end of the chapter. (Para 8.8)

18.93 Companies should be allowed to round off the figu.es in the balance sheet to the nearest thousand or hundred or ten rupees to facilitate publication of accounts in a more intelligible form. (Para 8.9)

18.94 Companies should be required to attach with their, balance sheets, the balance sheet and the profit and loss accounts of firms, joint ventures in the same manner as it is incumbent on a holding company to attach to its own balance sheet a copy of the accounts, etc,. of the subsidiary companies so as to enable shareholders to know how the funds of the company are utilised. (Para 8.10)

18.95 With a view to achieve the objectives of professionalisation, all companies with a paid-up capital of twenty-five lakh rupees or more should be required to employ:

(a) A Chief Accountant or a Financial Controller;
(b) A Cost Accountant and an Internal Auditor, if such companies are engaged in any manufacturing or other specified activities.

Accountant and the Cost Accountant must be members of the Institute of Chartered Accountants of India and the Institute of Cost and Works Accountants of India respectively. Persons holding such offices at the coming into force of these provisions, though not members of the said Institutes, may, however, continue to function as such. (Paras 8.11 to 8.13)

18.96 In the case of companies with a paid-up capital of twenty-five lakh rupees or more, engaged mainly in the construction of ships or in the manufacture or processing of goods or in mining or in generation and distribution of electricity and if the cost audit for that industry has been ordered, the Cost Auditor is also to certify in the balance sheet, the figures of stock-in-trade, stores, spares, raw materials, tools and work-in-progress. (Para 8.14)

18.97 The Committee feels that many malpractices in the published accounts flow from the fact that those who are responsible to maintain the accounts are not held responsible for the figures shown in the published accounts. It is, therefore, suggested that the statements of accounts of the company with a paid-up capital of twenty-five lakh rupees or more should be authenticated, prior to their submission for audit, by the Accountant of Financial Controller of the company and additionally for stock-in-trade, stores, spares, raw materials, tools and work-in-progress by a Cost Accountant if such a company is engaged mainly in manufacture or other specified activities. (Para 8.15 to 8.16)

18.98 The report of Directors under Section 217 should contain additional information, brief particulars of which are given below:

(i) Deposits received, total repayment made and outstandings;
(ii) Certain types of prosecutions launched against the company and their results;
(iii) Unclaimed and unpaid dividends;
(iv) Investments in other bodies corporate, firms or joint ventures, exceeding five per cent of the company's paid-up capital and free reserves, as have not yielded any returns during the year and reasons therefor;
(v) Any material liability incurred by the company from the date of closing of the accounts to the date of adoption by the Directors of such accounts; or matters likely to adversely affect profits and lost, or asset and liability position of the company during the current year;
(vi) Commitments and liabilities for which no provisions have

been made;

(vii) Steps taken for discharging social responsibilities towards different segments of society, quantifying wherever possible in monetary terms;

(viii) Losses incurred by the company in those activities which account for not less than ten per cent of company's total turnover;

(ix) Certain accounting ratios;

(x) Key factors preventing fall utilisation of installed capacity of plant and machinery;

(xi) Number of shares held by each Director, carrying two per cent or more of the total voting power;

(xii) Contracts with the company and its subsidiaries in which a Director, his spouse or dependent children have interest to the extent of one per cent or more of total purchase, sale, payment or receipt; and

(xiii) Compliance with statutory norms and guidelines relating to managerial appointment, remuneration and inter-company investments and loans. (Para 8.17)

18.99 Disclosure of the information under Section 217(2A) be amended to provide that:

(i) Information relating to employees drawing remuneration of three thousand rupees or more per month has not served any practical purpose. This may be filed with the Registrar along with Annual Return and shall be open for inspection by members or public;

(ii) The company shall be bound to furnish on demand by any shareholder, information regarding all executives receiving remuneration in excess of that drawn by managing or whole-time director;

(iii) Information required to be furnished along with the balance sheet shall be limited to:

(a) particulars of Directors and their relatives drawing remuneration of not less than three thousand rupees per month or thirty six thousand rupees per annum;

(b) particulars of executive in receipt of remuneration in excess of that drawn by managing or whole-time directors, if such executive by himself or along with his spouse and dependent children holds not less than two per cent of equity shares of the company; and

(c) Category-wise statement showing number of employees drawing remuneration of less than five hundred rupees, between five hundred and one thousand rupees and between one thousand and two thousand rupees, etc. (Para 8.18)

18.100 All payments including remuneration, salaries and perquisites to managing director/whole-time director, directors and employees drawing three thousand rupees or more per month should be quantified in monetary terms and shown separately in profit and loss account. (Para 8.19)

18.101 The Committee was informed that Chartered Accountants who are in whole-time employment elsewhere are sometimes admitted as partners in firms so that the firm could take credit for the specified number of audits. To counter this, it is suggested by way of addition of Explanation III in Section 224(1C) that:

> For calculating the specified number of audits, a person practising as Chartered Accountant singly and a partner of a firm of Chartered Accountants, in full-time employment elsewhere, shall not be reckoned. (Para 8.20)

18.102 Maintenance of Cost Accounting Records in certain types of industries and their continuous audit is a step not only in the direction of consumer protection but also an advantage to the company itself. Cost audit, therefore, ordered in respect of any particular industry should be continued every year unless the Central Government decides to discontinue such audit in that industry. (Para 8.21)

18.103 Cost Auditor is appointed by the Board of Directors with the previous approval of the Central Government. The Committee sees no reason for distinction in the procedure for appointment of a Financial Auditor and a Cost Auditor and, therefore, recommends that the provisions relating to appointment, resignation, etc., of a statutory auditor should also apply to a Cost Auditor. (Para 8.22)

18.104 Unfair profits can, sometimes, be made by dealing in shares by the use of confidential information generally available to 'insiders' like a company's Director, Statutory Auditor, Cost Auditor, etc. To deal with this aspect, the main suggestions of the Committee are listed below:

(i) Any Director, Statutory Auditor, Cost Auditor, Financial Accountant or Financial Controller, Cost Accountant, Tax and Management Consultant or Adviser and whole-time Legal Adviser or Solicitor of the Company and any private company, partnership firm or trust in which the above category of persons have pecuniary interest should notify the Board their intention to buy or sell the shares of the company. They are prohibited from purchasing or selling shares, prior to or after two months of the close of the accounting year unless permitted by the Board;

(ii) Details of the number of shares and price at which they are bought or sold by the above category of persons should be annexed to the published accounts;

(iii) The above requirements should also apply to the spouses and dependent children of the above persons;

(iv) All public companies should be required to maintain a register disclosing dealings in shares of the company by the above persons, including dealings of their spouses and dependent children and also of those persons who are in full-time employment of the company and drawing a salary of three thousand rupees or more per month. This information should also form part of the published accounts;

(v) Persons establishing to have suffered an identifiable loss by reason of misuse of information by any of the above categories of persons should have civil remedy before the Company Law Board;

(vi) Notices of certain specified transactions within the given time will have to be furnished to the company. (Paras 8.23 to 8.29)

18.105 For the benefit of investing public, creditors and others connected with the affairs of the company, it has been recommended that all public companies listed in any Stock Exchange should publish an abstract in a summarized form, of half-yearly unaudited accounts of the company within sixty days of the close of the half-year highlighting the important developments in company during the period under report. (Para 8.30)

18.106 In the accounts of companies, a specific provision relating to gratuity to employees, payable under any law or agreement, must be made. (Para 8.31)

18.107 There are references to 'free reserves' in the Act. As the term has not been defined yet, the same has been provided with a definition.

Due to continuous increase in prices, providing depreciation on 'historical cost' will not be adequate to replace an old or obsolete asset. It has been recommended that companies should set aside ten per cent of their profits after tax as a Replacement Reserve which should be treated on par with depreciation. (Paras 8.32 to 8.33)

18.108 To protect the independence of the statutory auditors, certain provisions relating to their resignation, etc., have been suggested. (Paras 8.34 to 8.35)

18.109 Many companies at the initial stage of operation or when incurring losses do not provide for depreciation but indicate only a note on accounts. As depreciation is a charge, it is recommended that profit and loss account should be made up only after providing for depreciation and there should be no provision to indicate *unabsorbed* depreciation. (Para 8.36)

18.110 It has been felt that general instructions for preparation of balance sheet and profit and loss account have grown in bulk over the years through successive amendments. In this process, while certain duplications have crept in, certain necessary requirements have been missing. With a view, therefore, to see that the accounts reflect a true state of affairs of the company, certain changes in Schedule VI have been suggested. (Para 8.37)

Inter-corporate Investments/Loans (Chapter IX)

18.111 Omission of the expressions 'same group' and 'same management' from the Companies Act consequent on the proposed transfer of Sections 108A to 108H to the MRTP Act is recommended. These expressions basically have a bearing on the objectives underlying the MRTP Act. (Para 9.3)

18.112 With a view to preventing the present practice of using investment companies as a vehicle for corporate control, a revised definition of investment company has been suggested in Chapter III as meaning a public company limited by shares and carrying on business of only underwriting in or dealing in shares, debentures, or other securities.

18.113 Investment in preference shares and debentures (the latter in case of companies under the same management), which are at present included within the purview of Section 372, should be excluded. The debentures and deposits should, however, be included for purposes of inter-company loans. Investments should also include contributions by way of capital formation to firms, joint ventures or other associations of persons as such investments tend to deplete the funds available for deployment outside the investing company's own business. (Para 9.5)

18.114 Existing exemption in favour of private companies in the matter of inter-corporate investments should continue. (Para 9.6)

18.115 Capacity of the investing company to invest in shares or by way of loans should be related only to its 'free reserves' (including that part of the paid-up capital which is represented by capitalisation of profits made after the commencement of the Amendment Act incorporating these suggested changes) and not to subscribed capital or net worth as at present. Subscribed or paid-up capital should normally be invested in company's own fixed capital assets. While providing for a more rational basis for determining genuine surplus for investment in shares or loans, an absolute ceiling should be prescribed beyond which no company should make investments or give loans. This ceiling is proposed at sixty per cent in the aggregate, of which investments should in no event exceed thirty per cent. To ensure that inter-company investments do not operate as instrument of insidious corporate control, investments should be permitted in the interest of the growth of the economy only in certain specified categories of cases (promoting a new company; taking over a sick unit and taking over an existing company – the last one after making the same offer to all shareholders and with the approval of the Company Law Board). In view of absolute ceiling, and investments being permitted for certain specified purposes only, Government approval should be dispensed with except where, in public interest, the Government may permit investment notwithstanding any of the proposed provisions. The provisions for intercompany investments and loans can also be usefully combined into one section. Combined redraft of Sections 370 and 372 is accordingly suggested. (Para 9.7)

18.116 The Committee is anxious that its recommendations in this chapter are put into effect immediately. (Para 9.8)

Public Deposits Protection to Depositors (Chapter X)

18.117 Depositors as a class are like any other creditors of the company having dealings with the companies in different manner. Legislative protection to this class can be by compelling companies which accept deposits to disclose more about their affairs so that depositors can form their own opinion about the soundness of the companies. Rules framed in this behalf are quite exhaustive. Law cannot afford protection beyond a certain limit to any single or special class of creditors of companies. Nevertheless as the class of depositors include many trusting and unwary citizens some further tightening of law is recommended. (Paras 10.1 to 10.8)

18.118 In the application form for deposits and in 'the Directors' report the details regarding outstanding deposits should be disclosed. It should also be stated that deposits rank *pari passu* with other unsecured creditors of the company. (Para 10.7)

18.119 Suggestions for extending insurance coverage to public deposits with companies is not feasible since there are practical difficulties. (Para 10.9)

18.120 Private companies, in order that they retain their private character, should not be allowed to invite or accept deposits from public in future. Private companies which have already accepted deposits earlier should be allowed sufficient time to pay of the deposits in a phased manner. (Para 10.10)

18.121 As an additional measure of protection and to tackle cases of more serious default Section 58A should be amended to provide that where 10 per cent of the matured deposits remain unpaid for over a period of six months in spite of claims from depositors having been made, the company and its directors should be deemed to be in default unless the company applies to the Court who would be empowered to pass all appropriate orders which the Court may, in the circumstances consider necessary. The company should bear all expenses in giving effect to the order of the Court. On failure of the company to apply, it will be deemed to be in default and would be penalised. (Para 10.11)

18.122 Sub-section (8) of Section 58A does not and should not permit the Central Government to grant exemption or relaxation to any companies from payment of deposits which have matured for repayment. (Para 10.11)

18.123 A depositor who has not been paid either the interest or the principal or both should have a right to move the Court without any authorisation as presently required under Section 621 of the Act. (Para 10.11)

18.124 A company which has defaulted in paying either the interest or the principal, should be prohibited from inviting or accepting further deposits. No company should be allowed to invite or accept deposits with a view to pay off earlier deposits. (Para 10.11)

18.125 Percentage for acceptance of deposits in relation to paid up capital and free reserves as at present should be changed to only with reference to 'free reserves' (as re-defined). (Para 10.11)

18.126 With a view to controlling the undesirable activities of brokers in canvassing for deposits, it would be necessary for stock exchanges to shoulder the responsibility of regulating such activities of brokers. The Government should also look into this matter and take remedial measures immediately. (Para 10.12)

Workers' Participation in Management of Companies (Chapter XI)

18.127 Workers' participation at the Board level is recommended. To start with, such participation may be limited to companies employing 1,000 or more workmen as defined in the Industrial Disputes Act, 1947 (excluding casual or badli-workers). This would apply both to Government and non-Government companies. Companies employing a lesser number of workmen would, however, have the discretion to have such participation at their Board level. (Paras 11.3, 11.10 and 11.11)

18.128 Every company proposed to be covered under the scheme of workers' participation recommended by the Committee should arrange to hold, under the supervision of the Labour Department of the State Government concerned and at its expense and premises, a secret ballot in which all workmen who have been in service of the company for six months would participate to decide whether or not to have workers' participation. If 51 per cent of the eligible workmen of the company vote in favour, the company would be legally bound to provide for workers' participation at the Board level and implement the scheme without any avoidable delay. (Paras 11.12, 11.13 and 11.18)

18.129 Decision regarding the proportion of worker-directors on the Board requires detailed consultation with companies, trade unions and workers' representatives. Government should, therefore, initiate talks in this regard immediately for implementing the scheme. (Para 11.14)

18.130 The method of nomination for elections to be made by

workers directly. No worker will be eligible to stand for election unless his candidature is proposed by least ten workmen of the same company. (Para 11.17)

18.131 Arrangements should be made for the casting of votes by all the workmen conveniently at each establishment at their places of work. (Para 11.19)

18.132 The choice of the worker-director will be only from amongst the workmen belonging to the company. (Para 11.20)

18.133 The tenure of a worker-director would be for a period of three years. (Para 11.21)

18.134 Vacancies in the office of the worker-director will be treated as casual vacancies and will be filled with the approval of the other sitting worker-directors. Where there is no other worker-director on the Board, election of a worker-director will be held within three months. (Para 11.22)

18.135 No distinction will be made between a holding and a subsidiary company, each having 1,000 workmen or more, in regard to the election of worker-directors. Each of them will be entitled to have separate worker-director on the respective Boards. Foreign companies will also be covered by the scheme of workers' participation. (Paras 11.23 & 11.24)

18.136 Two-tier Board system obtaining in some European countries is not considered suitable for this country. (Paras 11.25 and 11.26)

18.137 In order to ensure effective participation by workers' representatives at the Board level Section 292 should be amended to provide that certain decisions are necessarily taken only at the Board level and no delegation to Committees of the Board or to other functionaries is made. (Para 11.27)

18.138 Worker-director should not, because of Section 299/300 of the Companies Act, be barred from participating in Board meetings while dealing with issues concerning workers, e.g., wages, bonus, etc. In the case of workers, wages/salary and other benefits will not be treated as an office of profit for the purposes of Section 314. (Para 11.29)

18.139 For proper performance of their duties, the worker-directors should be imparted training and be made familiar with subjects like Commercial Law, Elements of Accountancy, by the Government. Government must fund the expenses. (Para 11.30)

18.140 No reason to expect that worker-director will in any manner so act which is either detrimental to the interests of the company or in breach of the confidentiality of the information vouchsafed to them as members of the Board. (Para 11.31)

18.141 The Committee is hopeful that the participation of workmen at the top management level in a company will lead to greater industrial harmony and mutual trust and genuine endeavour by both, to work in the larger interests of the economy and welfare of the country. (Para 11.32)

18.142 The question is equity participation by workers is a vexed one and not easy of solution. While business interests do not approve of conversion of part of bonus payable to workers into shares due to difficulties in servicing capital, labour itself is vehemently opposed to such a suggestion. In the absence of mutually acceptable formula, the Committee is unable to suggest any mandatory participation of any workers in the equity capital of a company. (Paras 11.36 and 11.37)

18.143 Ten to fifteen per cent of all new shares issued in future should, however, be reserved exclusively as workers' shares and should be offered to the employees of the company and failing that only to the existing shareholders or to the public. For this purpose, Section 81 should be suitably amended. (Para 11.38)

Social Responsibilities of Companies (Chapter XII)

18.144 In the development of corporate ethics, a stage has been reached where the question of social responsibility of business to the community can no longer be scoffed at. The plea of the companies that they are performing a social purpose in the development of the country can only be judged by the test of social responsiveness shown by them to the needs of the community. (Paras 12.1 and 12.4)

18.145 Acceptance of the concept of social responsibility must be reflected in the information and disclosure that the company makes available for benefit of various constituents like the shareholders, creditors, workers and the community. Openness in corporate affairs is the first principle in securing responsible behaviour. (Para 12.5)

18.146 The Committee is happy to note that some of the enlightened business houses in our country are showing a recognition of the social responsibility owed by the corporate sector. No enlightened management can really remain aloof to the national problems such as unemployment, over-population, rural development, environmental protection including conservation of resources, control of pollution and provision for clean drinking water. (Para 12.6)

18.147 Accountability of the public sector to the people through Parliament must find its parallel in the private sector in the form of social accountability which is, in our view, a mere extension of the principle of public disclosure to which a corporation must be subject. Every company, apart from being able to justify itself on the test of economic viability, will have to pass the test of a socially responsible entity. (Paras 12.7 and 12.8)

18.148 In order to ensure implementation of the concept of social responsibility and dissemination of adequate information in this regard, a provision should be made in the Act that every company, along with directors' report shall also give a Social Report, which will indicate and quantify in as precise and clear terms as possible the various activities relating to the social responsibility aspects which have been carried out by the company in the previous year. (Para 12.12)

Political Donations – Section 293A – Prohibition Regarding Making of Political Contribution (Chapter XIII)

18.149 Prior to the coming into force of the Companies Act, 1956, by and large companies had not provided in their memoranda of association for any enabling power to make contributions to political parties. (Para 13.2)

18.150 The pressure for making such contributions had increased by the time of General Elections in 1957 and in the two cases involving alterations of memoranda considered by the Bombay and Calcutta High Courts, the danger inherent in permitting such contributions was pointed out by the Courts. (Paras 13.3 and 13.4)

18.151 Parliament took note of this danger and put a ceiling on such contributions through Section 293A inserted by the Companies (Amendment) Act, 1960. The Santhanam Committee, however, found this amendment ineffective and called for a total ban on all such contributions. (Para 13.5)

18.152 A total ban on such contributions was laid down in 1969 by the insertion of a new Section 293A in the Act. During the period the permissive provisions were in force, the main, if not almost the sole, beneficiary of such contributions was the then ruling party. (Para 13.6)

18.153 An attempt was made to revoke the ban and permit the giving of political donations by companies by the Amendment Bill 80 of 1976, which, however, did not become law and lapsed. (Para 13.7)

18.154 Removal of existing ban on political contributions by companies would benefit only the larger companies because irrespective of whether the limit is in terms of percentage of profit or otherwise, the bigness of a company will determine the bigness of the contribution and this will necessarily lead to more unhealthy influence. (Para 13.10)

18.155 Danger of permitting money to play any important role in election has been recognised by the Election Law also. (Para 13.11)

18.156 Many democratic countries have placed limits on what a candidate or a political party can spend on elections. Even in countries like the USA, the unrestricted flow of money for elections is not permitted. The modern trend and practice is to make it unlawful for companies to make any contribution to political parties or for a political purpose. (Para 13.12 and 13.13)

18.157 There are equally weighty reasons against removing the ban on political contributions. There is a sharp divergence of views as to who should have the right (the Board, the shareholders or the workers of the company) to determine which political party should be the recipient. In such a situation the right course is to treat the company's fund as a trust fund in which various parties have a stake and, therefore, to continue the existing prohibition on such contributions. (Para 13.14 and 13.15)

18.158 An Explanation should be inserted in Section 293A of the Companies Act on the lines of Section 19(3) of the UK Companies Act, 1967 to clarify what is meant by political purpose and to cover any donation or subscription or payment to a political party or to a person carrying on or proposing to carry on any activity for public support for a political party. Any expenditure incurred by the company including on advertisement, souvenirs, brochures, tract, pamphlet or the like publication of a political party directly or indirectly should be deemed to be a contribution for a political purpose. (Para 13.16)

18.159 Any member of office-bearer of a political party or any other person who receives from the company directly or indirectly an amount by way of contribution for a political purpose in contravention of Section 293A should be punishable with imprisonment up to three years and with fine. (Para 13.17)

18.160 Section 293A should be redrafted on the lines suggested in the previous paragraphs. (Para 13.18)

Government Companies (Chapter XIV)

18.161 Keeping in view the recommendations for simplification of the Company Law there will be no case for Government companies claiming exemption from the provisions of the law. (Para 14.8)

18.162 There is need to provide safeguards for preserving the autonomy of Government companies so as not to defeat the legislative intent to separate the commercial activity of the Government from bureaucratic intervention. Accordingly, a model set of Articles framed as at Annexure II to the Chapter should be statutorily prescribed by way of compulsory regulations for all Government companies. Under these regulations, the Board of Directors of Government companies will be entitled, among others, to create posts, to make appointments to posts carrying a monthly salary of below Rs. 2,500 per month, to authorise variations up to ten per cent in the approved estimates of any work of capital nature already covered by a detailed Project Report – approved by the Central Government, and to authorise the undertaking of works of a capital nature in advance of the preparation of Project Report, where the cost of individual works involved is less than Rs. 100 lakhs. The Central Government would, on the other hand, be entitled to appoint the Chairman, Managing Director and other executive and functional directors, fix their salaries and allowances and also create and make appointments to posts carrying a salary of Rs. 2,500 per month or more. (Para 14.11)

18.163 Definition of 'Government company' should make it explicit that a Government company is a public limited company of a separate type by itself. [Paras 14.12 and 14.13(1)]

18.164 Section 617 dealing with the definition of a Government company should be enlarged to make it clear that a company in which not less than 51 per cent of the paid-up share capital is held jointly or severally by the Central Government, by one or more State Governments, by one or more Government companies or by one or more bodies corporate owned or controlled by the Central or State Government shall be deemed to be a Government company. [Para 14.13(1)]

18.165 In the case of shares held on behalf of the President or the

Governor in a Government company, provision should be made for facilitating automatic transfer of shares to be recorded in the register of members notwithstanding any other provisions in the Act to the contrary. [Para 14.13(3)]

18.166 The statutory provisions relating to meetings and proceedings shall apply only subject to the articles of association of the Government company. [Para 14.13(4)]

18.167 Provisions relating to investigation shall also apply to a Government company. [Para 14.13(5)]

18.168 Government companies should be exempted from the provisions relating to managerial appointments and remuneration. No compensation for loss of office should also be payable to the directors of a Government company. Provisions relating to appointment of relatives should, however, continue to apply to Government companies as well. [Para 14.13(6)]

18.169 A panel of chartered accountants be maintained by the Comptroller and Auditor-General of India from which Government companies should be free to appoint auditors subject, however, to such guidelines as may be laid down by the Comptroller and Auditor-General. The existing statutory restrictions on the number of audits which a firm of chartered accountants can take at a time and also the principle of rotation of auditors after a specified period as per guidelines of C&AG should continue to be applicable. While retaining the existing scheme in sub-sections (4) and (5) of Section 619, the C&AG should be requested to make available his report or comments within a given time-frame to enable Government companies to conform to the time-limit of six months permitted under the law for the holding of annual general meeting. [Para 14.13(7)]

18.170 While the provisions applicable to non-Government companies in regard to penalties and prosecutions should be applicable to Government companies also, no Court should take cognizance of any offence under the Act alleged to have been committed by any Government company or any officers thereof except on the complaint in writing of a person authorised by the Central Government. [Para 14.13(8)]

18.171 No distinction need be drawn between wholly-owned Government companies and Government companies in which private participation exists in the matter of extending the exemptions and modifications, as the extent of private holding was found to be only one per cent of the total paid-up capital of all Government companies. (Para 14.14)

Winding-up of Companies (Chapter XV)

18.172 Provisions dealing with winding-up procedures have long remained a neglected area in the Act. Delay in termination of winding-up proceedings and blocking of corporate assets is injurious both to the shareholders and to the economy in general. Problems in obtaining the statement of affairs filed by the Directors and the difficulties faced by the Official Liquidators in the realisation of assets necessarily delay early termination of winding-up proceedings. These need attention and the Committee's recommendations are directed towards this goal. (Paras 15.1 to 15.9)

18.173 Section 454 should be amended to ensure the filing of a statement of affairs and provide information about the custody of books before the winding-up order is passed. (Para 15.14)

18.174 The following additional provisions should be made in Section 454:

(a) Where the petition for winding-up is filed by the company itself, the petition should be accompanied by a duly prepared statement of affairs as required by Section 454. The petition should specify as to who has the custody of the books of account and papers and name the officers and/or directors who would produce the books, papers, etc., after the order of winding-up. The statement regarding custody and production of books must have been approved by the Board of Directors, and the petition must include this averment;

(b) In other cases, the Court should be empowered at the time of giving directions under Rules 96/99 of the Companies (Court) Rules, 1959, to direct the company to file, within such time as may be allowed by the Court, a declaration, which should be approved and/or verified by the Board of Directors of the company and accompanied by the consent in writing of person/persons charged with the responsibility of production of books of account and for filing statement of affairs, containing the required particulars; and

(c) In the event of default in filing the statement of affairs and/or production of the books of account within the prescribed period, all the directors on the date of filing of the winding-up petition should be deemed to be in default. There should be a minimum fine of rupees one thousand. (Para 15.19)

18.175 (a) Power to extend time for filing the statement of affairs should be left only with the Official Liquidator – Section 454(3) should be amended.

(b) Expenses in connection with preparation of the statement of affairs should be borne by the directors and not paid out of assets of the company – Section 454(4) should be amended;

(c) The onus of proving reasonable excuse for default should be on the person who alleges it – Section 454(5) should be amended. (Para 15.20)

18.176 The liquidator should only pay a fixed court fee in any suit, proceeding or claim brought by him on behalf of the company. (Paras 15.22 and 15.27)

18.177 Section 456 should be amended to empower the Liquidator, on the lines of Section 132 of the Income-tax Act, 1961, to carry out search and seizure, after obtaining the leave of the Court. He should also be entitled to seek the help of police. (Paras 15.23 and 15.27)

18.178 A provision similar to sub-sections (1) and (2) of Section 45-F of the Banking Regulation Act, 1949, be inserted in the Companies Act dispensing with the necessity of producing original books. (Paras 15.24 and 15.27)

18.179 Section 458A should be amended to provide for exclusion of a period of three years from the date of winding-up order for purposes of limitation. In the case of directors, there should be no period of limitation for enforcement by the company of any claim based on a contract. In other claims against directors, the period of limitation should be six years. (Paras 15.25 and 15.27)

18.180 There should be quicker and summary procedure for recovery of any amount due to the company. Provision on the lines of Section 45-T(3) of the Banking Regulation Act 1949, should be provided. (Para 15.27)

18.181 (a) Section 530 should be amended to provide that notwithstanding Section 178 of the Income-tax Act, 1961, arrears of taxes which have become due and payable within twelve months next before the 'relevant date' alone should have priority;

(b) Costs and expenses of winding-up shall be determined by the Court and not by the Commissioner of Income Tax. Section

178(3) of the Income Tax Act should be suitably amended;

(c) A provision should be made in tax laws for the assessment of companies in liquidation to be placed under the charge of one Income Tax Officer;

(d) Salaries, wages up to Rs. 12,000 will have priority over taxes; and

(e) In Section 530(1), existing clause (b) the period of four months should be increased to twelve months; and in sub-section (2) rupees one thousand should be increased to rupees twelve thousand with a view to enable the workers and other employees of companies in liquidation to recover a major share of their dues. (Para 15.36)

18.182 Section 467 should be amended to empower the Official Liquidator to settle the list of contributories. Only the list of persons who dispute should be referred to the Court. (Para 15.38)

18.183 Section 542 should be amended:

(i) to make it clear that actual dishonesty is not a necessary ingredient of a charge under the section;

(ii) to make directors and others personally responsible if they carry on the business in a reckless manner. It should cover civil liability only;

(iii) empowering the Court while hearing applications under sections 542 and 543 to pass interim orders including freezing and prohibiting any dealings by the directors of their private properties so as not to render ineffective all final orders as may be passed by the Court; and

(iv) to clarify that Section 542 should apply in the case of working companies also and not only to companies in liquidation. (Para 15.40)

18.184 Section 543 should be amended to provide that misfeasance proceedings will lie against a director if he has acted with gross negligence. (Para 15.40)

18.185 The present procedure in Section 545 is time consuming. Instead the voluntary liquidator should be empowered to straight away initiate action against offenders without any reference to the Registrar and the Central Government. (Para 15.40)

18.186 There should be additional grounds for winding-up, namely:

(i) when a company obtains additional deposits to pay off old deposits;
(ii) If the security of the creditor entitled to the benefit of a floating charge is in jeopardy. [Para 15.41(1)]

18.187 The Registrar of Companies should be empowered to move a petition for winding-up on the grounds of 'public interest'. [Para 15.41(2)]

18.188 A provision should be made to provide for the vesting of property of the company in the liquidator in compulsory winding-up. [Para 15.41(3)]

18.189 A provision enabling the Court to recall or rescind the winding-up order should be made in the Act. [Para 15.41(4)]

18.190 A provision enabling the liquidator to appoint a 'special manager' of the estate and business of the company should be provided. [Para 15.41(5)]

18.191 (a) Section 536 should be amended to empower the Court to validate any disposition of property of the company, on such terms as it may think fit. During this period, the Court should be empowered to sanction carrying on the business of the company and acts incidental thereto;

(b) It should be clarified that orders under Section 536(2) could be passed by the Court even though no order for winding-up is actually passed. [Para 15.41(6)]

18.192 Power to arrest directors and officers who are about to abscond should be provided in Section 477 on the same lines as power to arrest absconding contributories in Section 479. Expenses incurred for appearance before Court should be borne by the person summoned. [Para 15.41(7)]

18.193 Section 494 should be amended to give right to any member who desires his interest to be purchased by the Official Liquidator. [Para 15.41(8)]

18.194 If a branch of foreign company doing business in India is unable to pay its debts, the said branch should be deemed to be a company within the meaning of the Act and liable to be wound-up. [Para 15.41(9)]

18.195 Sections (464, 465, 503 and 504) relating to Committee of Inspection should be deleted since they have not served any useful purpose. [Para 15.41(10)]

18.196 The Official Liquidator should keep records for a period of ten years prior to the 'relevant data' and have a power to destroy all other records which are not required by him. [Para 15.41(11)]

18.197 The Central Government should take up with the State Governments the question of exempting debts due to companies in liquidation from the purview of Debt Relief Acts. [Para 15.41(12)]

18.198 The Court should be empowered to order enquiry against the conduct of the Official Liquidator. [Para 15.41(13)]

18.199 The expenses incurred by the liquidators in connection with taking possession and subsequent sale of assets of the company in liquidation should be treated as liquidation expenses for tax benefits. [Para 15.41(14)]

18.200 With a view to preserving the industrial activity, the Official Liquidator should make efforts to dispose of the undertaking of the company as a going concern notwithstanding the winding-up proceedings. (Para 15.42)

18.201 Tenancy rights of the company in liquidation which are at present not saleable under the Rent Acts, should be allowed to be sold by the Official Liquidator, as this will increase the assets of the company. (Para 15.42)

18.202 The practice of employing company-paid staff should be minimised and the offices of the Official Liquidator should normally be manned by regular Government employees only. (Para 15.43)

18.203 (a) Section 435 should be amended to vest power in the High Court to delegate some of its powers to the Company Law Board as recommended to be reconstituted.

(b) All matters relating to winding-up of small companies should be with District Courts. (Para 15.45)

18.204 (a) The two separate sets of sections 489 to 497 (dealing with members voluntary winding-up) and 500 to 509 (dealing with creditors voluntary winding-up) should be combined to provide for only one type of voluntary winding-up.

(b) Sections 495, 498, 502, 503 and 504 should be deleted as a consequence of only one type of voluntary winding-up being suggested. (Para 15.46)

(c) Winding-up subject to supervision of Court should be abolished and sections 522 to 527 be deleted. (Para 15.47)

18.205 Under Section 488, the declaration of solvency should also contain a statement regarding the address where books and other records of the company are kept, and also name, address, designation of person/persons who is/are charged with the responsibility of producing the books, records, etc., and also the statement of affairs if required by the voluntary liquidator. (Para 15.48)

18.206 Scrutiny by the Official Liquidator under Sections 497(6) and 509(6) should be discontinued. Consequential changes in sub-sections (3), (6A) and (6B) of Section 497 and in Section 509 should be made. (Para 15.53)

18.207 It is not necessary to have a report of the Official Liquidator before ordering dissolution. However, the dissolution will be effective only six months after holding of the final meeting. (Para 15.54)

18.208 As an additional safeguard on the dispensing of the report of the Official Liquidator under Section 559, the Registrar of Companies also should be empowered to move the Court for declaring the dissolution as void and the period of two years be increased to five years. (Para 15.55)

18.209 The Official Liquidator need file only one, instead of two, set of accounts under Section 462 for the period made up to the 31st March each year. A copy of the same account should be simultaneously filed with the Registrar of Companies. (Para 15.56)

18.210 In case of voluntary liquidation the present six monthly report by voluntary Liquidator should be retained. There should be a single form of accounts for purposes of submitting reports to the Court as well as to the Registrar. (Para 15.57)

18.211 Number of sections in Part VII should be reduced by re-arrangement as indicated in the Annexure to this Chapter. [Para 15.41(15)]

Administrative Machinery (Chapter XVI)

18.212 The Company Law Board should be statutorily constituted as an independent quasi-judicial body on the pattern of the Income-tax Appellate Tribunal with permanent Benches in the different regions, including Delhi region. (Para 16.9)

18.213 The Companies Act, 1956, incorporates concepts of social philosophy and protection of public interest as adumbrated in the Constitution. To achieve these objectives, the administration in discharge of its duties and functions must act in a quasi-judicial manner. While matters of purely administrative nature should continue to be exercised by the Central Government, other matters which require exercise of quasi-judicial powers should be entrusted to the Company

Law Board as reconstituted. The Board should function independently of the Central Government ensuring speed and efficiency in discharge of these functions. There should be power to impose penalties for default in compliance of statutory obligations in place of the existing routine prosecutions. (Paras 16.1 to 16.8)

18.214 Procedure for recruitment of Members to the Company Law Board as reconstituted should be on the lines of recruitment of Chairman and Members of the Income-tax Tribunal appointed by a Selection Board constituted under Rules framed for the purpose under Article 309 of the Constitution. (Para 16.9)

18.215 Professional qualification and experience in law or accountancy should be prescribed as the eligibility qualification for Members of the Company Law Board. (Para 16.10)

18.216 Modifications should be made to the existing provisions relating to the constitution and functions of the Company Law Board. Power to constitute the Company Law Board should remain with the Central Government and power to constitute the Regional Benches should be with the Company Law Board; the Company Law Board alone should have powers to frame rules and procedure for the conduct of its business and that of its Regional Benches; the Company Law Board including its Regional Benches should have powers of the Court under the Code of Civil Procedure; the Chairman of the Company Law Board should be a person who is qualified to be appointed as a judicial Member. He should hold office until he attains the age of 65 years or has served for a period of five years as a Chairman, whichever is earlier; the other Members of the Board must be persons having legal and/or accountancy qualification, in addition to the experience of working and administration of the Companies Act and allied statutes and of corporate sector; the Company Law Board or any of its Regional Benches should not be subject to the control of the Central Government. (Para 16.11)

18.217 Broadly while the existing pattern of exercise of various powers by the Central Government, the Company Law Board and the Court should continue, the said powers should be re-allocated to these authorities as per Annexures IA (Company Law Board), IB (Central Government) and IC (Court) respectively. (Para 16.12)

18.218 The penal provisions which are scattered throughout the Act should be consolidated at one place and grouped according to the nature of the offence and punishment. (Paras 16.13 and 16.14)

18.219 In place of the existing practice of imposing fine only by the Courts, there should be power with the Registrar/the Company Law Board to impose penalty. The Registrar's power to impose penalty should be limited to Rs. 500 in the first instance; Imposition of penalty beyond Rs. 500 in the first instance, should be by the Company Law Board. Offences which pre-suppose existence of *mens rea* and are punishable with imprisonment, fine or both should be retained with the Courts. (Para 16.16)

18.220 There should be right of appeal against all original orders of the Registrar of Companies imposing fine beyond certain limits to the Company Law Board and against all original orders of the Company Law Board imposing fine to the High Court. Penalties imposed by the Company Law Board should be recovered as if they were arrears of land revenue. (Para 16.17)

18.221 The Company Law Board may authorise any of its Regional Benches to hear the appeals. No appeal should be admitted unless the penalty imposed and against which appeal is filed is first deposited. Appellate authority shall have power to waive, enhance, reduce or compound the penalty. Appeal against order of the Company Law Board should only be on question of law. Non-payment of penalty accompanied by non-compliance of the directions should be a cognizable offence. Opportunity should be given to the party to be heard before any order is passed. No proceedings for default under any provisions of the Act shall be taken notice of after expiry of three years from the date of default. (Para 16.17)

Simplification and Overall Review of the Companies Act not Covered in other Parts of the Report (Capter XVII)

18.222 There has been criticism about some of the provisions of the present Companies Act, both from the point of view of their administration by the Government and in the context of day-to-day interpretation and practical working by companies. It is in the nature of things that a gap always remains between legislative intent and practical interpretation. All new legislations or modifications thereof are, therefore, an attempt to bridge this widening gap. It is with a view to (a) removing practical difficulties and problems which have been experienced in the actual implementation of the existing legislation for over two decades; (b) avoiding repetition and unnecessary verbiage; and (c) in the light of the structural changes suggested elsewhere in this Report by the Committee, that several of the existing sections call for modifications, some of substantial nature. The specific recommendations in this regard are accordingly contained in succeeding paragraphs. (Paras 17.1 and 17.2)

18.223 The present definition of 'subsidiary company' in Section 4 may be amplified to cover bodies corporate wherein more than half the nominal value of equity share capital is held either jointly or severally by a holding company and one on more of its subsidiaries. (Para 17.3)

18.224 Every company, along with its annual return, should state in the prescribed form whether it is a holding or a subsidiary company. (Para 17.4)

18.225 Sections 15A and 15B may be deleted and substituted by a general provision to give effect to the change in the name of any State or to the name of a new State by automatically substituting it in the existing situation clause of the memorandum. (Para 17.5)

18.226 No approval of the Company Law Board, or any other authority, should be necessary for alternation of the objects clause of the memorandum. Any member or members who hold not less than five per cent of the total voting power of the company and who are aggrieved by alteration of the objects clause may be given a right to apply to the Company Law Board. Such a right should also be given to the Registrar. (Para 17.6)

18.227 Section 20 should be amended so as to empower the Central Government to make rules and lay down the guideline currently followed by it relating to names of companies. (Para 17.7)

18.228 Reference to managing agents and secretaries and treasurers in clause (c) of sub-section (1) of Section 33 should be omitted and the clause should be modified to include agreement with managing or whole-time director. Sub-section (2) of Section 33 should be amplified to include a practising company secretary as a person competent to file the requisite declaration. (Para 17.8)

18.229 Sub-section (2) of Section 42 should be modified to provide that the restrictions under Section 42 shall not apply to receiving bonus shares by the holding company. Reference to unlimited company in sub-section (5) of Section 42 may be dropped. (Para 17.9)

18.230 Restrictions on interlocking of investments should be imposed to prevent one company from holding a large block of shares in another company. No company wherein more than twenty-five per cent of the share capital is held by another company shall be entitled to invest in excess of five per cent of the share capital of the other company. The present restrictions in Section 42(1) are applicable where the holding is in excess of fifty per cent. (Para 17.10)

18.231 The expression 'refusing permission' in Section 73 should be substituted by the expression 'refusing or not granting permission', so as to provide for an appeal being filed against delay in disposal of application by the Stock Exchange. (Para 17.11)

18.232 Sub-section (3) of Section 77 should be modified to provide that the loan which may be granted by a company to any person during his entire period of employment with the company should not exceed twelve months' salary or wages, or rupees twelve thousand, whichever is less. (Para 17.12)

18.233 Irredeemable preference shares as a class should be abolished. The existing irredeemable preference shares should be redeemable at the end of five years from the date of commencement of the Act with the option, to be exercised within six months from the date of commencement of the Act, to redeem them within a period of twelve years, and at the rate of interest of not less than ten per cent. No consent of any class of members should be necessary for such conversion. (Para 17.13)

18.234 No company, in future, should issue any preference shares which are not redeemable within a period not exceeding twelve years. At the time of redemption, the shares may be either renewed or paid off in cash to those who do not agree to renewal. No company can take recourse to Section 106 or Section 391 to have an arrangement by a majority decision, subject to Court's confirmation. Court's sanction for reduction of capital should not be made applicable to redemption of preference shares, so long as the total capital is not depleted. Shares may be redeemed either by issue of fresh shares or debentures or by crediting an equivalent amount to Capital Redemption Reserve Fund from out of profits. (Para 17.14)

18.235 A company which has failed to redeem its preference shares shall be prohibited from declaring any dividend on equity shares or transfer any of its profits to reserves until such time the preference shares are redeemed. (Para 17.15)

18.236 The suggestion that further issue of preference shares should be made to the existing preference shareholders only is not found to be acceptable. (Para 17.16)

18.237 Sub-section (3) of Section 81 may be amended to provide for conversion of loans issued prior to the coming into force of the

Amendment Act of 1963, into equity, if there is such a provision in the agreement. (Para 17.17)

18.238 All preference shares issued in future must be cumulative preference shares. All existing preference shares which are non-cumulative will be deemed to be cumulative with effect from the date of commencement of the Act. (Para 17.18)

18.239 In clause (c) of sub-section (2) of Section 87 the word 'equity' may be deleted. (Para 17.19)

18.240 Section 9 – The termination of excessive voting rights in existing companies be deleted as the eventuality has long passed. (Para 17.20)

18.241 Section 90 may be deleted. The existing provisions in private companies relating to disproportionate voting rights should be brought within the scheme of the Act within a period of three years. (Para 17.21)

18.242 In clause (a) of sub-section (1) of Section 94, the words 'issuing new shares' should be substituted by the words 'creating new shares'. Sub-section (3) of Section 94A may be deleted. (Para 17.22)

18.243 Reference to 'stock' in sections 94 and 95 is to be omitted, as there should only be two kinds of shares – equity and preference. (Para 17.23)

18.244 Section 98 may be deleted as unlimited companies are being proposed to be deleted. (Para 17.24)

18.245 Sections 108A to 108H may be transferred to the MRTP Act as these provisions pertain appropriately to the objects of that Act. (Para 17.25)

18.246 Sections 114 and 115 may be deleted as deletion of share warrants is being recommended. (Para 17.26)

18.247 The proviso to Section 125 may be amended to empower the Registrar of Companies to allow particulars relating to charges, etc., to be filed on payment of additional fees beyond the specified period.

Section 141 would apply only in case of failure to register the charge within sixty days. The Registrar should be empowered to refuse to register charge under certain circumstances. Appeal to the Company Law Board may be made for such refusal. The words 'requiring registration' may be substituted by the words 'as provided for registration under the Act'. (Para 17.27)

18.248 Sections 153, 153A, 153B and 187B need to be consolidated at one place. Reference to 'debentures' in these sections should bc omitted. The expression 'instrument in writing' should include constructive trusts. 'Paid-up value' should be the only criterion for determining the value of shares held by a trust. Aggregate value of shares held in a company by different rusts created by the same settler(s) should be taken into account. (Para 17.28)

18.249 The provisions of Section 187C may be deleted as they have not served any useful purpose. A provision on the lines of Section 12(3) of the Banking Regulation Act, 1949, may be incorporated in Section 155. (Paras 17.29 and 17.31)

18.250 Section 157 and 158 with regard to maintenance of foreign register may be deleted. (Para 17.33)

18.251 Sections 159 to 162 should be consolidated into a single Section to provide that the annual rcturns should be filed by different categories of companies as per the form set out in the Schedule. (Para 17.34)

18.252 The requirement of holding a statutory meeting (section 165) may be dispensed with. Particulars required to be incorporated in the statutory report should be sent to the shareholders within the pcriod under the Act and also placed before the first annual general meeting. (Para 17.35)

18.253 Annual general meeting should be allowed to be held on public holidays also. (Para 17.36)

18.254 Extra ordinary general meeting should be held only at the place where the registered office is located. (Para 17.37)

18.255 Minutes of the meetings of the Board and the Committees thereof should mandatorily contain certain particulars. Minutes of the meetings of the Committee should be circulated to all the members of the Board within a given period. (Para 17.38)

18.256 A new provision should be incorporated conferring on the High Court exclusive jurisdiction on applications for injunction in respect of holding of the meeting of the shareholders. This will help to reduce multiple legal proceedings. (Para 17.39)

18.257 Directors are to pay interim dividend only out of what they know are profits of the company. (Para 17.40)

18.258 The Companies (Transfer of Profits to Reserves) Rules, 1975, and the Companies (Declaration of Dividends out of Reserves) Rules, 1975, should be dispensed with. The substance of these Rules should be incorporated in the Act itself. Sub-section (3) of Section 205A may be deleted. (Paras 17.41 and 17.42)

18.259 Proviso (b) to sub-section (1) of Section 205 should be amended to ensure that a company does not distribute profits unless the entire loss, including depreciation, is completely made good. Reference to 'an amount which is equal to the amount provided for depreciation for that year or those years, whichever is less may be deleted. (Para 17.43)

18.260 References in Section 205 to Amendment Act of 1960 and proviso (c) to sub-section (1) of Section 205 may be deleted. (Para 17.44)

18.261 Section 205 should be recast to ensure that dividends are declared only out of true and fair profits of the company; to prohibit payment of dividend unless at least twenty-five per cent of the profits are transferred to the reserves; to provide for payment of dividend out of free reserves only; to empower the Board to pay interim dividend not exceeding half of the average rate of dividend declared for the last three years; to provide that a method of depreciation once followed should be adhered to and approval of the Central Government should be obtained for change in the method of calculating depreciation. Method for arriving at depreciation should be the same for all the purposes of the Act. (Paras 17.46 and 17.47)

18.262 Explanation be added to sections 198 and 309 to indicate what constitutes true and fair profits. (Para 17.48)

18.263 Sections 349 and 350 may be deleted. (Para 17.49)

18.264 Section 205A should be amended to provide for transfer to the Unpaid Dividend Account if dividend warrant not posted within seven days of expiry of forty-two days or if posted, not collected within ten days of expiry of six months. Sections 205A and 205B should be shifted to be placed after Section 207. (Para 17.50)

18.265 Section 208 may be deleted as it is improper to pay interest from capital. (Para 17.51)

18.266 Five copies of balance-sheets are to be filed under Section 220. (Para 17.52)

18.267 An Explanation is to be incorporated in Section 224(1) to indicate that an auditor holds the office from the date of an annual general meeting to the conclusion of the next annual general meeting. Consequential changes may be made in Section 224(4). (Para 17.53)

18.268 The Central Government's approval may be required under Section 259 only if the increase in number of directors is beyond fifteen in place of twelve at present. (Para 17.54)

18.269 Special resolution should be necessary under Section 293 for any proposal by which a company becomes a partner of a partnership firm or a participant in a joint venture. (Para 17.55)

18.270 Any reference to 'sole selling agent' in Section 294 should be substituted by "arrangement for distribution of companies' products". Selling arrangement by which not less than ten per cent of the goods of particular description are sold through any other person shall require approval by special resolution. The existing provisions requiring Central Government's approval in case of substantial interest in the company, will continue. (Para 17.56)

18.271 Prohibition against selling arrangement in notified industries may not be made applicable to small companies. (Para 17.57)

18.272 Parallel legislations in the field of marketing of products must be suitably strengthened. (Para 17.58)

18.273 Reference to 'private company' in sub-section (1) of Section 297 should be substituted by the expression 'body corporate'. Proviso to sub-section (1) may be deleted. In sub-sections (2) and (3), the words 'five thousand rupees' may be substituted by the words 'twenty-five thousand rupees'. (Para 17.59)

18.274 Proviso to sub-Section (1) of Section 309 should be amended to provide for services which are related to specified professions and to require approval of the Company Law Board in cases where the director does not possess the qualification for practice of the specified professions. (Para 17.60)

18.275 The monetary limit of five hundred rupees in clause (b) of sub-section (1) of Section 314 needs to be increased to one thousand rupees. Proviso to sub-section (1B) and sub-section (2C) may be deleted. The Words 'after the commencement of the Companies (Amendment) Act, 1974' in sub-section (2B) are to be dropped. (Para 17.61)

18.276 Sections 324 to 348, 351 to 369, 375 and 377 to 383 are to be deleted as they relate to managing agents, secretaries and treasurers, etc. (Para 17.62)

18.277 Section 376 should be shifted to appropriate place in sections 391 to 396, after deletion of reference to managing agents and secretaries and treasurers. (Para 17.63)

18.278 Sections 384 to 388A are to be deleted as a result of abolition of the office of 'manager'. (Para 17.64)

18.279 No change is necessary in the existing procedure relating to amalgamation and reconstruction in so far as MRTP undertakings are concerned. (Para 17.67)

18.280 The procedure in respect of other companies should be modified so as to reduce the delay on the suggested lines including making of only one application in the Court where the registered office of the transferee company is situated. (Para 17.68)

18.281 The Official Liquidator not to furnish a report in terms of the second proviso to Section 394(1) in the case of amalgamation. (Para 17.69)

18.282 In all cases of amalgamation of Government companies, the Central Government should exercise its powers under Section 396. (Para 17.70)

18.283 A scheme of amalgamation involving a sick unit and not involving an undertaking coming within the purview of the MRTP Act should be approved by the Central Government itself under Section 396 without Court's sanction. Section 396 may be modified to confer rule-making powers on the Central Government for the purposes of facilitating the exercise of such power. (Para 17.71)

18.284 Amalgamation or reconstruction involving small companies should be dealt with only by District Courts. (Para 17.72)

18.285 Section 416 may be deleted and suitable provision is to be made in Section 46 to the effect that any contract by or on behalf of a company in which the company is undisclosed principal should be void. (Para 17.73)

18.286 Provisions on the lines of Section 418 should be made in respect of gratuity fund or pension for employees. Each year's liability for gratuity should be provided and set apart. Contributions in respect of pending liabilities are to be made to the fund in seven equal annual instalments. (Para 17.75)

18.287 Sections 561 to 564 are to be deleted. All companies should henceforth be governed by the new Act. (Para 17.77)

18.288 Sections 565 to 581 are to be deleted. All existing companies should register under the new law and should be issued with new incorporation certificates on filing revised memorandum and articles of association. (Para 17.78)

18.289 In Section 610, fees payable for inspection of documents may be raised to rupees two. (Para 17.79)

18.290 A general provision as in clause (d) of Section 616 is sufficient. (Para 17.80)

18.291 Administration of *Nidhis*, Mutual Benefit Societies and Permanent Funds should be taken over by the State Governments or through a special Central Legislation. (Para 17.84)

18.292 Table A should consist of two parts – Compulsory Regulations and Optional Regulations. All companies should, by law, be deemed to have adopted the 'Compulsory Regulations'. Some of the existing Regulations of Table A as also certain specified sections of the Act should find place in Compulsory Regulations. A suitable provision in Part I of Table A may be made to the effect that proxies shall have the right to vote on show of hands as well as on a poll and shall also have a right to speak at the meeting. (Para 17.85)

18.293 Table C may be modified consistent with recommendations on guarantee companies. Tables D and E may be dispensed with. (Para 17.86)

18.294 Table F may be dropped. (Para 17.87)

18.295 Schedules VII and VIII are to be dispensed with. (Para 17.88)

18.296 Form of proxy in Schedule IX may be amended to incorporate suggestion in Chapter VII of the Report. (Para 17.89)

18.297 Schedule XI is proposed to be deleted and, instead, it is to be provided in Section 406 that provisions of Section 539 to 544 would apply, *mutatis mutandis*, subject to an application under Section 397 or 398. (Para 17.91)

18.298 Schedule XII will undergo change in the light of recommendations in Para 17.109 of Chapter XVII. (Para 17.92)

18.299 Schedule XIII may be transferred to the MRTP Act. (Para 17.93)

18.300 Government may undertake a review of the rules and forms in the light of the broad indications given by the Committee. (Paras 17.94 to 17.98)

18.301 The clarifications issued from time to time by the Central Government regarding availability of names for companies as per Rule 4A of the General Rules and Forms should be incorporated in the Rule itself so that the company promoters are informed about the criteria being followed by the Central Government in respect of names of companies. (Para 17.96)

18.302 Section 642 dealing with the rule-making power of the Central Government should contain an additional provision to the effect that approvals, sanctions, etc., accorded or granted by the Central Government are in accordance with the rules framed in this behalf. (Para 17.97)

18.303 In place of the existing system of charging fee for filing of each document, a consolidated annual fee for each company has been suggested to be prescribed. (Paras 17.99 to 17.101)

18.304 The first and second provisos to Section 611 are suggested to be deleted and suitable provisions made in the light of suggestions in Para 17.78. In sub-section (2), the words 'ten times the amount of fees so specified' may be substituted by 'the annual fee so specified'. Schedule X may be amended to incorporate the suggestion on 'Fees'. (Para 17.102)

18.305 A provision should be made authorising the refund of registration fees in certain circumstances. (Paras 17.103 to 17.105)

18.306 There are various areas in which corporate discipline cannot be achieved by mere amendment of the two Acts. The role of public financial institutions in regard to country's industrial growth has become very vital. It is, therefore, necessary that such institutions should play a more participative and purposeful role. (Para 17.106)

18.307 Consequential changes wherever necessary, are to be carried out in the light of the Report. (Para 17.107)

18.308 In order to prevent invalidation of the proceedings by reason of defects, irregularities or deficiencies in notice or time prescribed by the Act, a provision should be introduced empowering the Court to pass orders obviating the consequences that would flow from such invalidation. (Para 17.108)

18.309 Repeals and savings are to be provided for in the new Act. (Para 17.109)

Part B – MRTP Act

Concepts and Definitions under the MRTP Act (Chapter XIX)

23.1 The definitions of some of the economic concepts in the Act are not free from ambiguity. These expressions need to be redefined to make the intention clear and their working more effective. (Para 19.1)

23.2 As the scope of the Act is being enlarged to cover unfair trade practices, the title of the Act should be modified to read as "Monopolies and Trade Practices Act". (Para 19.2)

23.3 The definition of 'Commission' should accordingly be changed to read as "Monopolies and Trade Practices Commission". (Para 19.3)

23.4 Modern thinking on the test to determine dominance with reference to market share in respect of any goods or services favours a smaller percentage than one-third presently prescribed in the MRTP Act. Having regard to the vast size of our country, the level of industrial growth and the large number of entrepreneurial class available, the existing criterion of one-third share of market should be reduced to one-fourth for the purposes of determining dominance. (Para 19.4)

23.5 The concept of 'calendar year' as at present for determining dominance and other related issues is complex. The adoption of the 'lowest figure' of production, etc., for this purpose is unsound. The share of market for the purposes of dominance should be determined with reference to 'average annual production made or services rendered' during the three calender years immediately preceding, the preceding calender year in which "the question arises" rather than with reference to the year of the lowest production. (Para 19.5)

23.6 Reference to 'the number of workers employed' and 'price' as criteria for determining dominance should be deleted from Explanation III to Section 2(d). (Para 19.6)

23.7 The collection, maintenance and publication of up to date and correct data of goods produced or of services rendered is an immediate necessity for effective implementation of the Act and the Government should make necessary arrangements in this regard. At the same time, to ensure expeditious disposal of cases under the Act. Explanation IV in Section 2(d) should be modified to clarify that the data collected and published by an authority approved by the Central Government can form the basis for determination of dominance and for other purposes under the Act. (Para 19.7)

23.8 The definition of 'goods' in Section 2(e) should be revised so as to harmonise it with the definition of this term in the Sale of Goods Act, with a view to including stocks and shares within its ambit. This is to ensure that the investment companies will also come within the purview of the Act and thus a major lacuna would be plugged. (Para 19.8)

23.9 The definition of 'group' in Section 2(18A) of the Companies Act should be shifted to the MRTP Act with certain modifications as it has relevance to the purposes of this Act. The revised definition of this term has been suggested. (Paras 19.8 to 19.11)

23.10 The expressions 'inter-connected undertakings' and 'same management' should be re-defined on the lines suggested so as to remove obscurities and lacunae. (Paras 19.12 to 19.14)

23.11 Disputed questions relating to 'group', 'samc management' and 'inter-non-connected undertakings' should be referred by the Central Government to the Commission within a period of thirty days and the Commission shall pass final orders within a period of three months. Until the Commission finally decides the question, the concerned undertaking shall be deemed to be inter-connected for the purpose of the Act. (Para 19.15)

23.12 The definition of 'monopolistic trade practice' has to be combined with the provisions of Section 32 and should be amplified as suggested. (Para 19.17)

23.13 In view of the Committee's recommendation for the total prohibition of monopolistic trade practices, the concept of 'monopolistic undertaking' will not be relevant and its definition in Section 2(j) should be deleted. (Para 19.18)

23.14 The problem of restrictive trade practices needs to be tackled in more effective ways. The term 'restrictive trade practice' in Section 2(o) should be re-defined as suggested. (Para 19.19)

23.15 The term 'scheme of finances' in Section 2(q) should be amplified to include the sources of finance also. (Para 19.20)

23.16 The expression 'undertaking' in Section 2(v) should be re-defined as suggested since the present definition has been the subject-matter of considerable controversy and litigation. (Paras 19.21 to 19.23)

23.17 There is no justification for exempting Government and Government controlled/owned undertakings from the provisions relating to control and prohibition of monopolistic and restrictive trade practices (and the new provisions relating to unfair trade practices being suggested). The beneficiary of monopoly legislation is the consumer and it is only fair and reasonable that undertakings owned or controlled by the Government should be subject to same type of rigour and discipline as the private sector undertakings where the interests of the consumers are involved. Exemption to the Government companies will, however, continue from the applicability of Chapter III of the Act as there is no question of concentration of economic power in so far as the public sector is concerned. There will, however, be no exemption for an undertaking the management of which has been taken over by the Central Government in pursuance of any law because the basic characteristic of such an undertaking being in private sector is not changed by temporary takeover of the management by the Government. (Paras 19.24 to 19.27)

23.18 There is no justification for exempting the newspapers from the provisions of the MRTP Act. These provisions should continue to be applicable to newspapers as heretofore. (Paras 19.28 to 19.33)

Concentration of Economic Power (Chapter XX)

23.19 No change in the criterion of Rs. 20 crores as value of assets for applicability of Chapter III of MRTP Act is considered necessary at present. (Para 20.4)

23.20 During the period from 1-6-1970 to 31-12-1977, in about 74 per cent of the cases, approvals were granted by the Central Government. (Paras 20.8 to 20.12)

23.21 During the period from 1-6-1970 to 30-6-1978, about 92.6 per cent of such applications were disposed of by the Central Government without reference to the Commission. (Para 20.13 to 20.15)

23.22 There is no justifiable reason why the Central Government should not avail itself of the services of an impartial and expert body like the MRTP Commission in the disposal of applications dealing with matters falling pre-eminently within the latter's purview. The role of the Commission needs to be strengthened effectively. (Para 20.17)

23.23 Proposals under Sections 21 and 22, (a) from dominant undertaking for manufacture of goods or provision of services in which it is dominant; or (b) involving capital outlay exceeding Rs. 5 crores; or (c) where objections have been received or there is more than one applicant, should be compulsorily referred by the Central Government to the Commission (except under specified circumstances and for reasons to be recorded in writing) for inquiry as well as passing of final orders, instead of reporting back to Central Government as at present. The other cases can be referred to the Commission at the discretion of the Central Government as at present. However, once a reference has been made to the Commission, it should have power to pass final orders. (Paras 20.18 to 20.22)

23.24 Section 30 of MRTP Act should be amended to provide that reference of the disputed questions referred to in Para 23.11 and the proposals referred to in Para 23.23 will be made by Central Government within thirty days and that the Commission shall pass final orders on the proposals referred to it within a period of ninety days from the date of receipt of the reference by the Commission. (Para 20.19)

23.25 Where a scheme of merger or amalgamation of an undertaking covered by Section 20 of MRTP Act is approved by the Central Government in terms of Section 396 of the Companies Act in the national public interest, no further approval should be required under Section 23(2) of the MRTP Act. (Para 20.23)

23.26 Any proposal for acquisition under Section 23(4) where (a) it results in the control of $33^1/_3$ per cent or more of voting power; or (b) the cost of acquisition exceeds Rs. 3 crores; or (c) it is likely to result in the creation of a dominant undertaking, should be compulsorily referred to the Commission for final disposal. (Para 20.24)

23.27 The power to initiate action under Section 27 for division of an undertaking vests in the Central Government. This power has hardly been used. Power to order division of inter-connected undertakings under Section 27 is a matter of public policy for the Government to decide and is dependent on the circumstances of each case. No legal impediment under the Act comes in the way of Central Government to proceed under Section 27 if circumstances so justify in the public interest. While it is appropriate that the power to initiate action under Section 27 should continue to remain with the Central Government, once a reference has been made to the Commission, all further action should be taken by the Commission, including the final decision as to whether the undertaking should be divided or not and consequential arrangements. (Para 20.25 to 20.27)

23.28 Substantial expansion in the value of assets of an undertaking brought about by replacement or modernisation of plant and machinery without resulting in expansion of licensed/approved capacity by 25 per cent or more, or substantial expansion effected for fuller utilisation of existing licensed approved capacity by installation of balancing equipment, as approved by notified competent authority, should not require approval of the Central Government under Section 21. However, the person or authority proposing to effect such expansion should be required to furnish the prescribed details of such expansion to Central Government. (Para 20.29)

23.29 Establishment of a new inter-connected undertaking by dominant undertaking for the manufacture of the same type of goods or provision of services in which it is dominant should require prior approval of the Central Government under Section 22 of the Act. (Para 20.30)

23.30 It should be clarified that all proposals for diversification, whether at the same place or at a different place, amount to establishment of a new undertaking within the ambit of Section 22. However, proposals for manufacture of 'new articles' within the existing licensed capacity or by utilisation of waste-products/bye-products with the installation of balancing equipment, as approved by notified competent authority, should be exempted. (Para 20.31)

23.31 Section 23(4) may be modified to illustrate the expression 'or otherwise' by giving some specific instances like 'lease', 'licence', 'mortgage'. It should also be clarified that 'acquisition' would include purchase of shares, which, together with the shares, if any, already held, carry 25 per cent or more of the voting power at the generals meeting of the undertaking proposed to be acquired. This sub-section should further be modified to incorporate enabling provisions empowering the Commission/Central Government to pass final orders on the proposals for acquisition. (Para 20.32)

23.32 Sub-section (8) of Section 23 should be amended to clarify that it seeks to cover proposals for acquisition of undertakings to which Part A of Chapter III of the Act applies, by undertakings not covered by the MRTP Act. (Para 20.33)

23.33 The provisions contained in sections 108A to 108H of the Companies Act should be transferred to the MRTP Act. (Para 20.34)

23.34 The provisions of sections 108A to 108G should not apply to transfer of shares from one constituent of the group to another constituent of the same group as it does not lead to any further concentration of economic power. It should, however, be provided that an intimation will be given to the Central Government within two months of effecting the transfer. (Para 20.35)

23.35 The onus of giving notice under Section 21, or of making an application under Section 23, or for getting registration under Section 26 should be on the owner of the undertaking concerned. (Para 20.37)

23.36 The need for increase in production of goods, particularly those not being produced in the country or which are in short supply, should be specifically spelt out by adding clause (h) to Section 28. (Para 20.38)

23.37 Section 29 should be amended to specifically provide that the Commission shall give an opportunity of being heard to all interested persons before passing any order in respect of matters which are referred to it for final disposal. (Para 20.39)

Monopolistic, Restrictive and Unfair Trade Practices
(Chapter XXI)

23.38 Consumer protection legislation is lacking in the existing Act, as there is no protection of consumers against false or misleading advertisements or such other unfair trade practices. There is now greater recognition that the consumers need to be protected against such practices which are resorted to by the trade and industry to mislead and dupe the customers. The Committee has, therefore, proposed to specify certain unfair practices and prohibit them altogether. The Act will henceforward deal not only with monopolistic and restrictive trade practices but also with unfair trade practices. (Paras 21.2 to 21.19)

23.39 Section 10(b) empowers the Commission to initiate *suo moto* inquiries into monopolistic trade practices but there is no provision for follow-up action in Section 31. Similarly, it has no power to inquire into and pass final orders on any restrictive trade practice that may come to its notice during the course of inquiry into monopolistic trade practices under Section 37. This affects the functioning of the Commission. (Paras 21.2 to 21.7)

23.40 Consequent on the revised definition of 'monopolistic trade practices' and the Committee's recommendation to totally prohibit such practices, Section 32 will become redundant and should be deleted. (Para 21.8)

23.41 All monopolistic trade practices should be prohibited. Some of the restrictive trade practices which are destructive of competition should also be prohibited subject to certain general defences. The other restrictive trade practices should prohibited subject to certain specific defences in addition to the general defences. (Paras 21.9 to 21.11)

23.42 The Act should be amended to specifically empower the Commission to inquire into and pass appropriate orders in respect of such practices whether the relevant agreement was determined before or after the commencement of the inquiry proceedings before the Commission. (Para 21.21)

23.43 Consequential amendments to Sections 10, 31 and 37 of the Act have been suggested. (Para 21.23)

23.44 Collective agreements/arrangements and restrictive trade practices arising out of collective action relating to 'collective discrimination', 'boycott', 'collective bidding' and 're-sale price maintenance' should be prohibited subject to availability of certain general defences arising out of (i) defence requirements or security of the State, (ii) compliance with any of the conditions stipulated by the Government order, and (iii) any express authorisation of, or under any law made by, Central Government.

23.45 Bilateral agreements and restrictive trade practices relating to 'minimum re-sale price maintenance' and 'price discrimination' should also be prohibited subject only to the specified general defences. The other bilateral agreements and restrictive trade practices relating to:

(a) 'tie-up sales',
(b) 'exclusive dealings',
(c) 'production sharing', and
(e) 'conditional know-how'

should be prohibited subject to the availability of one or more of the general defences and also certain other defences enumerated in clauses (a) to (h) of Section 38 of the Act. (Paras 21.28 and 21.29)

23.46 All prohibited practices whether monopolistic, restrictive or unfair should be made actionable whether such a practice has been incorporated in the form of an agreement or not. (Para 21.29)

23.47 The requirement of compulsory registration of agreements relating to restrictive trade practices should be done away with as this requirement has only added to paper work. Out of 21,000 agreements registered, only 106 were brought before the Commission. It is felt that there are enough sources to proceed against prohibited practices without requiring all trade practice agreements to be registered. Section 33 should be deleted and suitable consequential amendments in sections 34, 35 and 36 of the Act should also be made. (Para 21.30)

23.48 In view of the recommended prohibition of the practice of maintaining minimum re-sale prices (subject only to general defences), it would be anomalous to retain the provisions of Section 41 empowering the Commission to exempt any class of goods from the operation of these provisions. This Section should, therefore, be deleted. (Para 21.31)

23.49 Unfair trade practices like:

(a) 'misleading advertisements and false representations',
(b) 'bargain sales',

(c) 'bait and switch selling',
(d) 'offering of gifts or prizes with intention of not providing them',
(e) 'conducting promotional contests',
(f) 'supplying goods that do not comply with safety standards', and
(g) 'hoarding and destruction of goods'.

should be prohibited subject to the specific exceptions indicated in respect of each. They should also be made punishable as an offence and any person guilty of contravention should be prosecuted before the Commission. (Paras 21.32 and 21.33)

23.50 The Act does not now contain any provision for recovery of damages for any loss suffered. It is only logical and equitable that a person who is affected by any prohibited practice should have a remedy to recover damages and compensation from the guilty party. It should, therefore, be provided that any person, authority, Central or State Government who has suffered loss or damage as a result of conduct of another person having indulged in any of the prohibited practices, viz., monopolistic trade practices, restrictive trade practices and unfair trade practices, will be entitled to recover the amount of loss or damage, including costs, suffered by him from the guilty party. (Paras 21.34 to 21.41)

23.51 Procedure for recovery of damages through 'class action' like a representative action should also be provided. Not to do so would be to deny them the benefit of consumer protection legislation. Such a provision is necessary to safeguard the interest of a large number of persons who may have suffered damages but being poor are not able to bring individual proceedings against the delinquent. (Para 21.42)

23.52 The Commission should be vested with power to grant interim injunction to suit the needs of each case. (Para 21.43)

23.53 In any proceedings for recovery of damages any conviction of a person a previously for an offence for having indulged in any of the prohibited practices, should, in the absence of proof to the contrary, be a proof that the person against whom the action is brought had engaged in the prohibited practices. (Para 21.45)

23.54 Any person may, on his own volition, apply for, and seek clearance from, the Commission in regard to any trade practice on the ground that such a practice falls under one or more of the exceptions or defence provided for in the Act. If the Commission does not give its decision within a period of three months, the party may proceed with the practice but his liability for civil action in damages would have arisen from the date of the practice was indulged in if ultimately the Commission refuses clearance. But the criminal liability would accrue only from the date of knowledge of the Commission's final order and if the party continues to indulge in that particular practice despite the Commission's decision. (Para 21.46)

23.55 All matters relating to recovery of damages or injunctions should be triable before the Commission and not the Magistrate as at present. Any person indulging in any of the prohibited practices for which no specific defence has been provided for, will incur not only civil liability but also criminal liability. Criminal proceedings for any violation thereof should be also brought before the Commission. The Chairman of the Commission or any Member of the Commission, so designated by the Chairman, may be authorised by law to hear and dispose of such matters by following the procedure of a warrant case under the Code of Criminal Procedure, 1973. Such a vesting of power in the Commission is considered necessary at least in the early stages of the development of this legislation, and in order to avoid conflict of views between the different Courts. (Paras 21.47 and 21.48)

Administrative Machinery under the Monopolies and Restrictive Trade Practices Act (Chapter XXII)

23.56 Where the person appointed to the office of Chairman of the Commission is a sitting Judge of a High Court, he should enjoy the same rank, status, pay and allowances and privileges as of the Chief Justice of a High Court since appeal from the Commission's order lies only to the Supreme Court. (Para 22.4)

23.57 A provision should also be made that where a vacancy in the office of a Chairman arises due to resignation, leave or otherwise, the senior most Member of the Commission may be appointed by the Government to act temporarily as the Chairman. (Para 22.5)

23.58 Provision should be made also for vacation of the office of a Chairman due to resignation or removal as now exists in the case of a Member. (Para 22.6)

23.59 In view of the enlarged functions envisaged for the Commission and the role the Registrar of Restrictive Trade Agreements and the Director of Investigation will have to play in future, the two offices should be combined into one and the post designated as that of Director-General of Trade Practices. (Paras 22.7 and 22.9)

23.60 Section 8 of the Act may be amended to provide for the appointment of the Director General of Trade Practices and the Commission should be empowered to appoint members of its own staff and determine their conditions of service subject to the rules made by the Central Government. (Para 22.8)

23.61 The proposed Director-General of Trade Practices should be vested with powers to search, seize and impound documents of evidentiary value for the purposes of investigation. The proposed Director-General should also have powers to initiate proceedings, or move for recovery of damages on behalf of the Central and State Governments and also to be joined as a party in the proceedings before the Commission. (Paras 22.10 and 22.11)

23.62 Section 12 dealing with the powers of the Commission should be amended to empower the Commission to provide for production before and examination by an officer of the Commission books of account and other documents and other information relating to any trade practice or business organisation. The Commission should also be made a Court of Record and be vested with powers to punish for contempt of itself. The Commission should also be empowered to issue injunction, interim or final. (Paras 22.12 and 22.14)

23.63 Section 13(3) of the Act may be modified to clarify that an order made by the Commission under the Section would cover any particular trader also instead of any particular class of trade practice or a particular trade practice only as at present. (Para 22.15)

23.64 Section 18 of the Act has to be amended to provide that the technical rules of the Indian Evidence Act, should not be applicable to the proceedings before the Commission, because such rules only weaken the powers of the Commission to deal with the matters under the Act effectively. The proceedings before the Commission should be conducted with as little formality and technicality and with as much expedition as the requirement of the Act and a proper consideration of the matters for the Commission permit. (Paras 22.16 and 22.17)

23.65 In order to remove any ambiguity, Section 16 of the Act has to be amended to clarify that the Chairman may constitute a Bench with one or more Members for exercising the powers and discharging the functions of the Commission. (Para 22.18)

23.66 Section 30 of the Act should be amended to include a reference to the several additional matters suggested for disposal by the Central Government and by the Commission and to which also the time limits in the Section would be applicable. (Para 22.19)

23.67 The penalty for failure to register an undertaking provided for in Section 48 should be made more stringent. Provision should also be made for permitting late registration of the undertakings on payment of a specified penalty not exceeding ten times the registration fee. (Paras 22.20 and 22.21)

23.68 Section 49 of the Act may be amended to provide for penalties for persons who fail to attend or produce the books of account or other documents in response to the summons issued by the Commission. The burden of proving reasonable excuse in such cases would be on the person alleging such excuse. (Para 22.22 and 22.23)

23.69 Sections 50 and 51 may be substituted by a new single Section 50 which will provide for punishment of persons contravening the provisions of sections relating to the monopolistic, restrictive and unfair trade practices, before the Commission. (Para 22.24)

23.70 A new provision for recovery of damages by persons who have suffered loss should be made in the Act on the lines suggested. The amount of damage recoverable should be equal to the loss or damage proved to have been suffered and include an amount for costs. The forum for recovery of damages will be the Commission. (Para 22.25)

23.71 Provision should be made for recovery of damages through 'class action' also, before the Commission. (Para 22.26)

23.72 The jurisdiction to try for offences under the Act should vest with the Commission instead of the Magistrate as at present. The Commission may, however, be given powers to transfer any of the proceedings to the Court of a Presidency Magistrate or Metropolitan Magistrate of the First Class if it considers expedient to do so. (Para 22.27)

23.73 The appeals against the final orders of the Central Government and the Commission should lie to Supreme Court only if it involves a substantial question of law of general public importance. (Para 22.28)

23.74 Absence of adequate and effective provisions prohibiting disclosure of confidential and secret information which might be received by the Commission or the Director-General of Trade Practices by way of complaints or otherwise would not only deter the informants from communicating such vital information about the prevalence of the prohibited trade practices, but may also inhibit the collection by the Commission and the DGTP of such information for purposes of proceedings under Section 10. Specific provision in the Act to the effect that complaints made or information supplied to the Commission or to the DGTP should not be liable to be disclosed if the Commission opines that it is not expedient and in the public interest to do so has therefore been recommended. (Para 22.30)

FINANCE COMMISSION (SEVENTH), 1977 — REPORT[1]

Chairman Shri J.M. Shelat, Former Judge of the Supreme Court of India

Members Dr. Raj Krishna; Dr. C.H. Hanumantha Rao; Shri H.N. Ray

M. Secy. Shri V.B. Eswaran

Appointment

The Commission was constituted by an Order dated 23rd June 1977 "In pursuance of the provisions of article 280 of the Constitution of India and of the Finance Commission (Miscellaneous Provisions) Act, 1951 (33 of 1951)".

Terms of Reference

The Commission shall make recommendations as to the following matters:

(a) the distribution between the Union and the States of the net proceeds of taxes which are to be, or may be, divided between them under Chapter I of Part XII of the Constitution and the allocation between the States of the respective shares of such proceeds;

(b) the principles which should govern the grants-in-aid of the revenues of the States out of the Consolidated Fund of India and the sums to be paid to the States which are in need of assistance by way of grants-in-aid of their revenues under article

---

1. Controller of Publications, Government of India, Delhi, 1978, 263 + 90 p.

275 of the Constitution for purposes other than those specified in the provisos to clause (1) of that article.

In making its recommendations, the Commission shall have regard, among other considerations, to:

(i) the resources of the Central Government and the demands thereon on account of the expenditure on civil administration, defence and border security, debt servicing and other committed expenditure or liabilities;

(ii) the existing practice in regard to determination and distribution of Central assistance for financing State Plans;

(iii) the revenue resources of those States for the five years ending with the financial year 1983-84 on the basis of the levels of taxation likely to be reached at the end of the financial year 1978-79 and the targets set for additional resource mobilisation for the Plan;

(iv) the requirements on revenue account of those States to meet the expenditure on administration and other non-Plan commitments or liabilities, keeping however in view national policies and priorities. In assessing such requirements, the Commission shall take into account:

(a) such provision for emoluments of Government employees, teachers and local body employees as obtaining on a specified date as the Commission deem it proper and with reference to appropriate objective criteria rather than in terms of actual increases that may have been given effect to; and

(b) commitments in regard to interest charges on their debt, transfer of funds to local bodies and aided institutions.

(v) adequate maintenance and upkeep of capital assets and maintenance of Plan schemes completed by the end of 1978-79, the norms, if any, on the basis of which specified amounts are allowed for the maintenance of different categories of capital assets and the manner in which such maintenance expenditure could be monitored being indicated by the Commission;

(vi) the requirements of States which are backward in general administration for upgradation of standards in nondevelopmental sectors and services with a view to bringing them to the levels obtaining in the more advanced States over the period covered by the Report of the Commission; the manner in which such expenditure could be monitored, being also indicated by the Commission;

(vii) the scope for better fiscal management and economy in expenditure consistent with efficiency; and

(viii) the need for ensuring reasonable returns on investments in irrigation and power projects, transport undertakings, industrial and commercial enterprises and the like.

The Commission may suggest changes, if any, to be made in the principles governing the distribution among the States of:

(a) the net proceeds in any financial year of estate duty in respect of property other than agricultural land;

(b) the net proceeds in any financial year of the additional excise duties leviable under the Additional Duties of Excise (Goods of Special Importance) Act, 1957, in replacement of the sales tax levied formerly by the State Governments on each of the following commodities, namely:

(i) cotton fabrics;
(ii) woollen fabrics;
(iii) rayón or artificial silk fabrics;
(iv) sugar; and
(v) tobacco including manufactured tobacco.

Provided that the share accruing to each State shall not be less than the revenue realised from the levy of sales tax for the financial year 1956-57 in that State;

(c) the grant to be made available to the States in lieu of the tax under the repealed Railway Passenger Fares Tax Act, 1957; and

(d) the grant to be made available to the States on account of wealth-tax on agricultural property.

In making its recommendations on the various matters aforesaid, the Commission shall adopt the population figures of 1971 in all cases where population is regarded as a factor for determination of devolution of taxes and duties and grants-in-aid.

The Commission may make an assessment of the non-Plan capital gap of the States on a uniform and comparable basis for the five years ending with 1983-84. In the light of such an assessment, the Commission may undertake a general review of the States' debt position with particular reference to the Central Loans advanced to them and likely to be outstanding as at the end of 1978-79 and suggest appropriate measures to deal with the non-Plan capital gap, having regard *inter alia* to the overall non-Plan gap of the States, their relative position and the purposes for which the loans have been utilised, and the requirements of the Centre.

The Commission may review the policy and arrangements in regard to the financing of relief expenditure by the States affected by natural calamities and suggest such modifications as it considers-appropriate, in the existing arrangements, having regard, among other considerations, to the need for avoidance of wasteful expenditure.

The Commission shall make its report by the 31st October, 1978 on each of the matters aforesaid and covering a period of five years commencing from the 1st day of April, 1979. The Commission shall indicate the basis on which it has arrived at its findings and make available the State-wise criteria adopted in making modifications, if any, in the States' forecasts of receipts and expenditure".

Contents

Introduction; Reassessment of the Forecasts of State Governments on Revenue Account; Reassessment of the Resource Forecast of the Central Government; Financing of Relief Expenditure; Estate duty in Respect of Property other than Agricultural Land; Additional Duties of Excise; Grant in Lieu of Tax on Railway Passenger Fares; Grant on Account of Wealth tax on Agricultural Property; Centre-State Financial Relations and our Scheme of Transfers to the States; Upgradation of Standards of Administration; Non-Plan Capital Gap of States; General Observations; Summary of Recommendations; *Notes:* Note by Shri H.N. Ray, Outlining his Views on the Returns from State Electricity Boards, etc., to be taken into Account for the Purposes of the Forecasts of the State Governments, and the Targets of Additional Resource Mobilisation, and not Thereon by Chairman and oher Members, Joint Note by Prof. Raj Krishna and Shri H.N.

Ray on Compensation to States for the Loss of Revenue Consequent on the Progressive Introduction of Prohibition, and Note thereon by Chairman and other Members, Note of Dissent by Prof, Raj Krishna Entitled "A More Equitable Distribution of Resources", and Note thereon by Chairman and other Members; Appendices from I to VI and Annexures from I to VII

Recommendations

Our recommendations to the President in regard to the devolution of taxes and grants-in-aid of the revenues of the States are set out below:

I. *Estate Duty*

(1) The net proceeds of Estate Duty in respect of property other than agricultural land attributable to Union territories in each of the years 1979-80 to 1983-84 should be determined in the same manner and on the same principles as for the determination of the shares of each State, taking the Union territories as one unit for the purpose.

(2) The balance of the net proceeds of Estate duty in each year should be distributed among the States in proportion to the gross value of the immovable property and property other than immovable property taken together located in each State and brought into assessment. For this purpose property located abroad should be deemed to be located in the State where it is brought to assessment.

(3) Sikkim will also be entitled to a share in the net proceeds of this duty, calculated in the same manner as for the other States, as from the date the duty may become leviable in that State in the period covered by our Report.

II. *Additional Duties of Excise in Lieu of Sales Tax*

(1) There is no need to set apart any guaranteed amounts to the States out of the net proceeds of additional duties of excise as in our view there is no risk of the share of any States falling short of the revenue realised in the financial year 1956-57 in a State from the levy of the sales tax on the commodities subject to additional duties of excise in lieu of sales tax;

(2) Sikkim should have a share in the net proceeds of these

duties except the duties on textiles on which the State levies sales tax;

(3) A sum equal to 3.271 per cent of the net proceeds of the additional duties of excise on sugar in each of the years from 1979-80 to 1983-84 should be retained by the Central Government as attributable to the Union territories and the balance of 96.729 per cent of the net proceeds should be distributed among the States in the percentages shown below:

	States	Percentages
1.	Andhra Pradesh	5.245
2.	Assam	2.408
3.	Bihar	5.933
4.	Gujarat	8.742
5.	Haryana	2.656
6.	Himachal Pradesh	0.860
7.	Jammu & Kashmir	0.831
8.	Karnataka	4.901
9.	Kerala	3.783
10.	Madhya Pradesh	6.019
11.	Maharashtra	17.082
12.	Manipur	0.143
13.	Meghalaya	0.029
14.	Nagaland	0.115
15.	Orissa	2.178
16.	Punjab	6.220
17.	Rajasthan	4.729
18.	Sikkim	0.057
19.	Tamil Nadu	6.449
20.	Tripura	0.172
21.	Uttar Pradesh	13.184
22.	West Bengal	8.254

(4) A sum equal to 2.192 per cent of the net proceeds of additional duties of excise on textiles and on tobacco in each of the years from 1979-80 to 1983-84 be retained by the Central Government as attributable to the Union territories.

(5) The balance of 97.808 per cent of such net proceeds of the additional duties of excise on textiles and tobacco be distributed among the States in the percentages shown below:

	States	Textiles	Tobacco
1.	Andhra Pradesh	8.020	8.018
2.	Assam	2.298	2.297
3.	Bihar	7.221	7.219
4.	Gujarat	6.015	6.013
5.	Haryana	2.790	2.789
6.	Himachal Pradesh	0.734	0.734
7.	Jammu & Kashmir	0.744	0.744
8.	Karnataka	6.083	6.081
9.	Kerala	4.020	4.019
10.	Madhya Pradesh	6.422	6.419
11.	Maharashtra	13.510	13.506
12.	Manipur	0.185	0.185
13.	Meghalaya	0.171	0.171
14.	Nagaland	0.084	0.084
15.	Orissa	3.457	3.456
16.	Punjab	4.270	4.268
17.	Rajasthan	4.366	4.365
18.	Sikkim	—	0.034
19.	Tamil Nadu	7.710	7.707
20.	Tripura	0.257	0.256
21.	Uttar Pradesh	12.549	12.544
22.	West Bengal	9.094	9.091

(6) In any year in which the State Government of Sikkim gives up its sales tax on textiles, it would be entitled to a share, as from the date such sales tax is given up, in the net proceeds of the additional duties of excise thereon. The State-wise percentage shares would then be as shown below:

	States	Percentage
1.	Andhra Pradesh	8.018
2.	Assam	2.297
3.	Bihar	7.219
4.	Gujarat	6.013
5.	Haryana	2.789
6.	Himachal Pradesh	0.734
7.	Jammu & Kashmir	0.744
8.	Karnataka	6.081
9.	Kerala	4.019
10.	Madhya Pradesh	6.419
11.	Maharashtra	13.506
12.	Manipur	0.185
13.	Meghalaya	0.171
14.	Nagaland	0.084
15.	Orissa	3.456

Contd.

	States	Percentage
16.	Punjab	4.268
17.	Rajasthan	4.365
18.	Sikkim	0.034
19.	Tamil Nadu	7.707
20.	Tripura	0.256
21.	Uttar Pradesh	12.544
22.	West Bengal	9.091

III. *Grant in Lieu of Tax on Railway Passenger Fares*

The grant to be made available to the States in each of the five years commencing from 1979-80, in lieu of tax under the repealed Railway Passenger Fares Tax Act 1957 be distributed among the States as under:

	States	Percentage shares
1.	Andhra Pradesh	6.99
2.	Assam	2.46
3.	Bihar	9.50
4.	Gujarat	5.28
5.	Haryana	1.97
6.	Himachal Pradesh	0.13
7.	Jammu & Kashmir	0.74
8.	Karnataka	3.21
9.	Kerala	2.61
10.	Madhya Pradesh	5.84
11.	Maharashtra	15.87
12.	Manipur	—
13.	Meghalaya	—
14.	Nagaland	0.26
15.	Orissa	1.73
16.	Punjab	3.81
17.	Rajasthan	5.48
18.	Sikkim	—
19.	Tamil Nadu	6.85
20.	Tripura	0.04
21.	Uttar Pradesh	18.58
22.	West Bengal	8.65

IV. *Grant on Account of Wealth Tax on Agricultural Property*

The grant to be made available to the States in each of the years

1979-80 to 1983-84 should be an amount equivalent to the net collection in that State in each year. Sikkim will become entitled to a grant in each year on the same basis if and when the levy of the wealth tax is extended to that State in the period covered by our Report.

V. *Income-Tax*

In respect of distribution of the net proceeds of income tax in each of the financial years from 1979-80 to 1983-84:

(1) Out of the net proceeds of taxes on income in each financial year a sum equal to 2.19 per cent thereof should be deemed to represent the proceeds attributable to Union territories;

(2) The percentage of the net proceeds of taxes on income, except the portion representing the proceeds attributable to Union territories, to be assigned to the States, should be eighty-five; and

(3) The distribution among the States *inter-se* of the share assigned to the States in respect of each financial year should be on the basis of the following percentages:

(Percentages)

	States	Without Sikkim	With Sikkim (if the income-tax becomes leviable in that State)
	1	2	3
1.	Andhra Pradesh	8.023	8.021
2.	Assam	2.522	2.521
3.	Bihar	9.540	9.536
4.	Gujarat	5.959	5.957
5.	Haryana	1.819	1.819
6.	Himachal Pradesh	0.595	0.595
7.	Jammu & Kashmir	0.818	0.818
8.	Karnataka	5.442	5.440
9.	Kerala	3.950	3.948
10.	Madhya Pradesh	7.356	7.354
11.	Maharashtra	10.953	10.949
12.	Manipur	0.188	0.188
13.	Meghalaya	0.178	0.178
14.	Nagaland	0.085	0.085

Contd.

	1	2	3
15.	Orissa	3.739	0.738
16.	Punjab	2.714	2.713
17.	Rajasthan	4.364	4.362
18.	Sikkim	—	0.035
19.	Tamil Nadu	8.050	8.048
20.	Tripura	0.258	0.258
21.	Uttar Pradesh	15.429	15.422
22.	West Bengal	8.018	8.015

VI. *Union Excise Duties*

(1) During each of the years 1979-80 to 1983-84 the entire net proceeds of the Union Excise duty on generation of electricity should be paid out of the Consolidated Fund of India to each State in an amount equal to the collection in or attributed to that State; and

(2) Forty per cent of the balance of the net proceeds of the Union duties of excise on all other articles levied and collected during each of the years 1979-80 to 1983-84, excluding cesses levied under Special Acts and earmarked for special purposes, should be paid out of the Consolidated Fund of India to the States and distributed among them on the basis of the following percentages:

(Percentages)

	States	Excluding Sikkim	Including Sikkim (if and when Union excise duties become leviable in that State)
	1	2	3
1.	Andhra Pradesh	7.698	7.691
2.	Assam	2.793	2.793
3.	Bihar	13.025	13.021
4.	Gujarat	4.103	4.101
5.	Haryana	1.177	1.177
6.	Himachal Pradesh	0.521	0.521
7.	Jammu & Kashmir	0.839	0.839
8.	Karnataka	4.877	4.876
9.	Kerala	4.036	4.035

Contd.

	1	2	3
10.	Madhya Pradesh	8.727	8.725
11.	Maharashtra	6.633	6.632
12.	Manipur	0.218	0.218
13.	Meghalaya	0.200	0.200
14.	Nagaland	0.097	0.097
15.	Orissa	4.682	4.682
16.	Punjab	1.226	1.226
17.	Rajasthan	4.813	4.813
18.	Sikkim	—	0.028
19.	Tamil Nadu	7.641	7.637
20.	Tripura	0.373	0.373
21.	Uttar Pradesh	18.293	18.290
22.	West Bengal	8.028	8.025

VII. *Grants-in-Aid*

The following States be paid the sums specified against each of them as grants-in-aid of their revenues in the respective years indicated in the table below under the substantive part of Clause 1 of Article 275 of the Constitution:

Grants-in-aid to States over 1979-84

(In Rs. crores)

State	1979-80	1980-81	1981-82	1982-83	1983-84	Total amount to be paid in five years
1. Himachal Pradesh	37.60	40.54	41.63	43.00	44.30	207.07
2. Jammu & Kashmir	41.06	40.82	39.20	39.40	39.08	199.32
3. Manipur	26.19	28.00	29.27	30.76	32.10	146.32
4. Meghalaya	16.97	17.67	18.44	19.48	20.05	92.61
5. Nagaland	38.29	41.34	43.65	46.48	48.59	218.35
6. Orissa	41.55	37.74	29.03	19.16	9.44	136.92
7. Sikkim	6.32	6.70	7.11	7.54	8.05	35.72
8. Tripura	24.36	25.75	27.29	28.85	30.32	136.57
Total	232.34	238.56	235.62	234.67	231.93	1173.12

Our Recommendations on Other Terms of Reference

I. *Financing of Relief Expenditure*

In the light of review of the existing policy and arrangements in regard to the financing of relief expenditure and after considering the expenditure incurred by the State Governments in providing gratuitous relief and on repair and restoration works of public properties after natural disasters. We recommend the following annual provisions (margins) under the head of account 289 – Relief on account of natural calamities for different States:

	State	(Rs. lakhs)
1.	Andhra Pradesh	858
2.	Assam	346
3.	Bihar	1308
4.	Gujarat	956
5.	Haryana	147
6.	Himachal Pradesh	51
7.	Jammu & Kashmir	130
8.	Karnataka	200
9.	Kerala	159
10.	Madhya Pradesh	183
11.	Maharashtra	457
12.	Manipur	8
13.	Meghalaya	7
14.	Nagaland	14
15.	Orissa	871
16.	Punjab	268
17.	Rajasthan	774
18.	Sikkim	1
19.	Tamil Nadu	859
20.	Tripura	18
21.	Uttar Pradesh	1080
22.	West Bengal	1360
	Total	10055

In our view the present policy and arrangement of Central assistance to States for relief expenditure should be modified. For drought relief expenditure in excess of the margin we have provided, the State Government should make a contribution from its Plan for providing relief employment. The extent to which the State Government should contribute from its Plan in this manner should be assessed by a Central Team after consultation with the State Government and approved by the Central Government. This contribution should not exceed about 5 per cent of the Annual Plan outlay. This Plan contribution of the State Government should be treated as an addition to the Plan outlay in that year and covered by advance Plan assistance as in the present scheme. The adjustment of the advance Plan assistance against a ceiling of the Central assistance for the Plan of the State should be effected within five years following the end of the drought. If the expenditure requirement, as assessed by the Central Teams and the High Level Committee cannot be adequately met in a particular case after the State Plan contribution is taken into account, the extra expenditure should be taken as an indication of the special severity of the calamity which would justify the Central Government assisting the State to the full extent of the extra expenditure, half as grant and half as loan. In regard to the expenditure on relief and repairs and restoration of public works following floods, cyclones and other calamities of this nature. Central assistance should be made available as non-Plan grant, not adjustable against the Plan of the State or against Central assistance for the State Plan, to the extent of 75 per cent of the total expenditure in excess of the margins. Where a calamity is of rare severity, it may be necessary for the Central Government to extend assistance to the States concerned even beyond the scheme/s we have suggested.

II. *Non-plan Capital Gap of the States*

We have made an assessment of the non-plan capital gap of the States on a uniform and comparable basis for the five years ending with 1983-84. The methodology adopted by us and the State-wise non-Plan capital gaps so assessed by us are indicated in Chapter II and Appendix VI. 2.

In the light of the non-Plan capital gaps of the States as assessed by us, we have reviewed the States' debt position with particular reference to the Central loans advanced to them and likely to be outstanding as at the end of 1978-79. Having regard *inter alia* to the overall non-Plan gap of the States, their relative position and the purposes for which the loans have been utilised and the requirements of the Centre, we have recommended the following measures for dealing with the non-Plan capital gap of the States:

(i) The existing terms of repayment of Central loans advanced to Orissa for Hirakud Project Stage I and to all States for rehabilitation of displaced persons, repatriates, etc., and outstanding at the end of 1978-79, may remain undisturbed;

(ii) Short-term loans, if any, by the Central Government to the States that may remain outstanding at the end of 1978-79 may be recovered according to the existing terms applicable to such loans;

(iii) Central loans advanced to State Governments by way of share out of net collections of small savings, and outstanding at the end of 1978-79, may be converted into loans in perpetuity, in respect of which the States need make no repayment of principal from 1979-80 but should continue to pay interest at the existing rate;

(iv) The balance of the Central loans outstanding against the State Governments at the end of 1978-79 may be consolidated, in respect of each State, into one loan as on 1st April, 1979;

(v) A portion of the Central loans so consolidated equivalent to the percentage shown against the respective State in column 3 of the table in paragraph 25 of Chapter 11 may be written off;

(vi) A further portion of the loans so consolidated equivalent to the percentage shown against the respective State in column 4 of the table in paragraph 25 of Chapter 11, may be converted into 30-year loan, recoverable in equal annual instalments commencing from 1979-80, together with interest at the rate of 4.75 per cent per annum;

(vii) The balance of the Central loans so consolidated equivalent to the percentage shown against the respective State in column 5 of the table in paragraph 25 of Chapter 11, may be converted into 15-year loan, recoverable in equal annual instalments commencing from 1979-80, together with interest at rate of 5 per cent per annum; and

(viii) While making financial assistance available to the States from 1979-80, whether for Plan or for non-Plan purposes, the Government of India and the Planning Commission should determine the loan and the grant components with due regard to the end-use of the assistance and, having so determined the loan component, prescribe the terms of repayment thereof consistently with the terms that we have recommended in relation to the loan that may be outstanding against the States at the end of 1978-79.

Note by Shri H.N. Ray, outlining his views on the returns from State Electricity Boards, etc., to be taken into account for the purposes of the forecasts of the State Governments, and the targets of additional resource mobilisation

1. I have not been able to agree with the decision of the majority of the Commission that in projecting the returns from State Electricity Boards, a rate of 6 per cent per annum on the total investment should be stipulated, *including* the revenue obtained from the electricity duty levied by the State Government and the Central excise duty levied by the Central Government on the generation of the State undertaking. It has been further decided by the majority of the Commission that the return should be calculated on the total investment of the State Government till the end of 1976-79, and ignoring any fresh investments during the period of our Report.

2. Annex (1) to this note prepared by the Secretariat of the Commission [except the percentage calculations in Columns 4(b) and 5(b)] shows separately the electricity duty and the Central Excise duty for 1978-79 collected from "own generation" as a percentage of the total Government investment in the undertaking for each State.

3. I find it difficult to accept the proposition that the amounts collected by the Central Government as an excise duty should be set off against the stipulated return of 6 per cent. In law, the Central excise duty accrues to the Central Government. When imposing the duty, the Finance Minister in his Budget Speech of February 1978 stated as follows:

> "I feel that with our enormous investment in power, there is ample justification for claiming a contribution from those who benefit from these investments. I am, therefore, proposing to levy a duty of 2p. per Kilowatt hour on electricity generated".

The intention, presumably, was to levy the duty so as to increase the return from the investments in electricity undertakings and to realise a higher amount from the consumers, so that the overall resources of the Central and State Governments would increase, and would be available for developmental and other essential purposes. Our information is that most of the States have taken steps to pass on the Central excise duty burden to the consumer. Whatever justification there might or might not be for setting off the electricity duty (which accrues to the State Government), there appears to be no justification for setting off the Central excise duty accruing by law to the *Central Government* from the *returns* which the State Government is assumed to derive during the forecast period from its investments in electricity undertakings. In fact, setting off the amounts collected as Central excise duty from the stipulated return, as decided by the majority of the Commission, would frustrate the purpose for which the duty was imposed in the first instance. That the Central Government has recently decided to make over the non-shareable portion of the duty from 1979-80 onwards to the various State Governments and that we are recommending the transfer of the entire Central Excise duty levied on electricity generated to the concerned States does not, in my view, vitiate the legal point. This money is now undoubtedly available to the State Government for various purposes – but this factor by itself would not absolve the State Electricity Board from earning a reasonable cash return on the State Government's investment through efficient operation of the system.

4. The combined effect of setting off both the electricity duty and the Central excise duty is somewhat anomalous in respect of the following States as the aggregate set off is in excess of 6 per cent:

States	Percentage of total investment		
	Electricity duty	Central excise duty	Total percentage
Gujarat	4.922	2.512	7.434
Kerala	3.444	4.297	7.741
Orissa	3.325	3.011	6.336

This would mean that according to the Commission's decision, no further return as such need be expected from the State Electricity Boards of these States as the stipulated return and more is already being earned by way of electricity duty and Central excise duty. On the contrary, the excess amounts over 6 per cent have been set off against the *other receipts* of these three States, so as not to "penalise" them for their better management compared to the other States. For some other States, the set off of these duties against the stipulated return of 6 per cent would be quite significant as shown below:

States	Percentage of total investment		
	Electricity duty	Central excise duty	Total percentage
Haryana	3.59	1.92	5.51
Karnataka	1.88	2.25	4.13
Madhya Pradesh	2.35	1.65	4.00
Maharashtra	0.93	2.51	3.44
Punjab	1.84	1.01	2.85

5. My distinguished colleagues have argued that the Central Excise duty on electricity generation, has inhibited tariff revisions, and additional resource mobilisation in this sector. Central excise duties are levied on a vast number of commodities, and it could be similarly argued that these duties have inhibited State Governments from levying Sales tax, etc., at higher rates, and generally hindered their additional resource mobilisation efforts. For all other commodities also, the Central excise duty is being shared with the States. Nevertheless, it is *not* the practice, whether in a public sector enterprise or in the private sector, to set off the Central Excise duty paid to the Central Government, when computing the return on the investment in a commercial organisation (which the State Electricity Board is meant to be). What is really sought is a genuine cash return from the investments made. The principle implicit in the majority recommendation of the Commission, if conceded, could lead to unsound practices in various undertakings both in the Central and the State spheres for determining returns on the investments made. The principle adopted may thus blur the line of demarcation between what is a cost of production, and what is a return on the investment made. Taking the case of the State Electricity Boards a step further, there is no logical reason why the arrangement should cover only the Central Excise duty on electrical energy, and not the excise duty on coal (levied in the same budget) or the duty on furnace oil, which also raised the cost of generation to a corresponding extent. It is sig-

nificant that inclusion of the Central excise duty in the stipulated return would have widely disparate results so far as different States are concerned. Even if we were to omit the atypical States, the incidence of the Central excise duty is only 0.84 per cent in Assam and 1.03 per cent in Uttar Pradesh, but is as high as 4.30 per cent in Kerala. Thus, in making the projections, although the stipulated rate of return taken as a whole is 6 per cent. Kerala would have a substantial advantage as compared with Assam or Uttar Pradesh. Such discrimination to my mind appears to be unjustified. Again, it is open to the Government of India to withdraw or modify the rates of the Central Excise duty on electricity. There is no assurance that this will not be done in the next 5 years. Any such decision would thus cause deviations from the State forecasts, beyond the control of the State Government. This consideration would suggest that the recommended linkage is wrong in principle and should be avoided.

6. A return of 6 per cent without adjustment of duty, to be achieved in gradual stages by 1983-84 does not appear to be too onerous a task. In Cols. 1 and 2 of the table below are given some figures* showing the net surplus for certain State Electricity Boards as a percentage of the cumulative *block capital* in completed works at the middle of the year for 1977-78 and 1978-79. The net surplus has been arrived at from the gross operating surplus by deducting subsidy from the Government, interest to institutional creditors, and transfers to Depreciation Reserve Fund and General Reserve Fund. For the same Boards/Mysore Power Corporation, the return on *Government's investment* for 1978-79 have been tabulated in Col. 4.

(in percentages)

States	1977-78	1978-79	Return on Govt. investment in 1978-79
1	2	3	4
Andhra Pradesh	2.90	2.93	4.7
Gujarat	2.02	0.81	1.3
Karnataka	2.75	15.19	4.2
Maharashtra	5.09	4.44	5.0

---

* *Source*: Secretariat compilations.

Our Report shows that the World Bank has obtained undertakings that the Electricity Board concerned should achieve a return of 9-1/2 per cent on what was termed as the average capital base. While this concept, of course, took note of the *net* value of assets in use, it also added 1/6th of the operation and maintenance expenditure (excluding depreciation). This return, *exclusive* of electricity duty, was more than achieved in several States during 1976-77, e.g., Assam, Gujarat, Karnataka, Madhya Pradesh and Maharashtra, was detailed in the body of our report. The Venkataraman Committee laid down a norm of 6 per cent interest, 3 per cent profit and 1/2 per cent appropriation to reserve – *exclusive* of a notional 1-1/2 per cent on account of electricity duty.

7. For road transport undertakings, we are stipulating a return of 6.5 per cent on the capital as a general rule, though lower rates have been adopted for the weaker units. The point worth emphasising is that for these undertakings we have *NOT* taken note of either the motor vehicles tax or the tax on passengers and goods, which also accrue to the State Government. By the same token, we should treat electricity undertakings similarly. Again, we are stipulating that over and above the interest on the loan component, other State Government enterprises should earn by 1983-84 a return of 5 per cent on the equity capital as it stood at the end of 1978-79. This return has been adopted despite the fact that in 1976-77 the return on share capital was only 1.15 per cent averaged out for the enterprises of all States. The return for all State Electricity Boards was higher at 1.5 per cent. Further, out of 434 State Government enterprises, as many as 121 were promotional enterprises and therefore could not be reasonably expected to yield high profits. All State Electricity boards by statute are meant to be commercially viable. It may be recalled that we are stipulating a return of 7.5 per cent on equity investments by the Central Government in its undertakings, besides interests on loans, again to be achieved during the last year of our forecast period.

8. Having regard to the returns already achieved by the better-run State Electricity Boards as indicated above, the recommendations of the Venkataraman Committee, the undertaking to earn a return of 9-1/2 per cent given in the World Bank, and its over fulfilment in some cases, and the returns we ourselves are stipulating for Central and State enterprises. I am of the view that an *unadjusted* 6 per cent rate of return on the massive capital sunk in electricity undertakings is not an unfair proposition. I would also suggest that for

the relatively weak units, the stipulated return need be achieved in gradual stages only during the final year, 1983-84. The financial effects of doing so are indicated in Annex 2 prepared by the Secretariat of the Commission at my instance. If a 6 per cent rate of return on Government investments is stipulated for each year, the credit to be given to the State Government budgets in the aggregate would be Rs. 2211 crores over the forecast period (col. 2 of Annex 1 X 5). If, however, State Electricity Boards are gradually expected to achieve a return of 6 per cent in the final year with progressive improvement in their working, then the contribution in aggregate terms during the forecast period would be Rs. 1449 crores (Annex 2). According to the majority recommendations of the Commission, however, after setting off the electricity duty and the Central Excise duty, the total contribution to the State budgets by these undertakings would be Rs. 1101 crores (Col. 7 of Annex I). This would suggest that the return proposed by me is feasible, calling for only a moderate improvement over what the majority has assumed but with the advantage that unsound practices for computing returns need not be introduced. It will be recalled that these investments *do not* include fresh investments during the forecast period, and also have a fair proportion of investments made when prices of plant and equipment were such lower.

9. My impression is that there is enormous scope for improving the efficiency of most State Electricity Boards and certain reports on the functioning of particular bodies are highly disconcerting. There is also scope for fixing tariffs in a more business – like manner, specially in the agricultural sector where heavy losses are being incurred. The increases in procurement prices of first wheat and now paddy and coarse grains should enable revisions to be undertaken without causing hardship. The nation is entitled to a proper return from the massive investments made in the power sector, which will continue to grow rapidly, specially when such a return is achievable with more efficient management and economic tariffs. The assumption made by a body such as the Finance Commission, and its general attitude in financial matters, has effects spreading well beyond the transfer of funds from the Centre to the States. Having regard to the overall national interest, this Finance Commission should not, in my view, adopt too relaxed an approach to the question of the rate of return expected from investments in State Electricity Boards.

10. In making these comments, I would like to clarify that the intention is not to modify in any way the existing terms and conditions

as between the State Government and the State Electricity Board. The purpose of laying down a particular rate of return is merely to arrive at a *notional* figure of the likely returns during the forecast period and thereafter to assess the financial position of the State Government on a uniform basis and in a normative manner.

11. Our terms of reference require us to have regard amongst other considerations to the revenue resources to the States for the five years ending with 1983-84 on the basis of the levels of taxation likely to be reached at the end of 1978-79 and the targets set for additional resource mobilisation for the Plan. In arriving at these targets, it has been decided by the majority of the Commission that the revenue from the Central excise duty on electricity generated by the State Electricity Boards and by the departmental undertakings of the State Government should be *excluded* also from this target. This has resulted in a reduction of the target for all the States combined from Rs. 452.17 crores to Rs. 326.84 crores after adjusting the Central excise duty on electricity amounting to Rs. 125.33 crores per annum. In my view, the preceding arguments for not adjusting the Central excise duty against the stipulated return, have equal validity for not making a corresponding adjustment in the target of additional resource mobilisation adopted by the State Government. This tax having been imposed by the Centre should not count as a resource mobilisation effort by the State Government. When the target was initially fixed in consultation with the State Government concerned, and accepted by it. Even if it is contended that the levy of a Central Excise duty on electricity generation has inhibited State Governments from raising additional resources, this consideration would apply only with respect to a very limited field, namely, the electricity tariff, and not over the entire field of State taxation. Further, as pointed out in paragraph 5 above, the Government of India can withdraw or modify the Central Excise Duty on electricity at any time. This would effect the State budget, but not the target of additional resource mobilisation adjusted for *present* rates of duty. Thus, an element of uncertainty is injected by the linkage into the State forecasts, over which the State Government has no control. Finally, I would add that the decision of the majority to set off the Central Excise duty on electricity generation once against the stipulated return of 6 per cent on the capital invested by the State Government in its State Electricity Board, and again by lowering the target of additional resource mobilisation by an amount equivalent to the duty, confers a

double benefit on the State. This arrangement appears to me to be unduly liberal, especially when the Government of India and the Finance Commission are transferring the *entire* proceeds of the Central Excise duty on electricity back to the States, as against the general ratio of about 40 per cent for the devolution of Central Excise duties.

20

TASK FORCE ON PROJECTIONS OF MINIMUM NEEDS AND EFFECTIVE CONSUMPTION DEMAND, 1977 – REPORT[1]

Chairman Dr. Y.K. Alagh, Adviser (PP) Planning Commission, New Delhi

Members Dr. D. Coondoo; Dr. D.B. Gupta; Prof. N.S. Iyengar; Dr. L.R. Jain; Shri G.V.S.N. Murty; Prof. R. Radhakishna; Dr. S.D. Tandulkar; K.C. Majumdar

Alterations Prof. P.V. Sukhatme of the Maharashtra Association for the Cultivation of Science who was abroad at the time of constitution of the Task Force, was subsequently included as Member of the Task Force on his return to India.

Appointment

A number of useful research studies on consumer demand-behaviouristic/effective and normative — have been and are being conducted both at the national and regional levels as well as for certain occupational groups, etc., by research institutions like the Indian Statistical Institute, Calcutta; Institute of Economic Growth, Delhi; Sardar Patel Institute of Economic and Social Research, Ahmedabad and by research workers in individual capacities. In this context, it was felt that if the results of these studies could be brought together at one place, it should be possible to develop ideas to articulate a private consumption model — at national as well as regional levels for the next Five Year Plan. To this end, it was decided by the Government of India, Planning Commission to set up a Task Force on Projections of Minimum Needs and Effective Consumption

---

1. Prospective Planning Division, Planning Commission, Government of India, New Delhi, 1979, iii + 54 p.

Demands to serve as a focal point vide resolution No. 4/3/77/PP.

Terms of Reference

To examine the existing structural studies on consumption patterns and standards of living and the minimum needs with particular reference to the poorer sections of the population for the nation as a whole, and its different regions separately by rural and urban areas; on the basis of the above studies, to forecast the national and regional structure and pattern of consumption levels and standards for the end of the Sixth Plan and subsequent perspective plan taking into consideration the basic minimum needs as well as effective consumption demand.

Contents

Task Force — Terms of Reference and Composition; Methodological Framework; Demand Systems; Projection of Private Consumption by Input-Output Sectors; Recommendations and Future Direction of Work; Appendices I and II; and Annexures I and II

Recommendations

5.1 During the course of discussions, the Task Force suggested the following recommendations:

(a) To estimate the average calorie requirement for an individual separately for rural and urban areas taking into consideration the distribution of age, sex and activity;
(b) To estimate the poverty line corresponding to the calorie requirement using the NSS data of the 28th round (1973-74);
(c) To estimate commodity-wise private consumption effective/behaviouristic and normative for the Sixth Plan 1978-1983. It was recommended that the commodity-wise private consumption may be estimated by considering Linear Expenditure System (LES) for maximum number of groups of commodities and best fitting Engel curves within each LES group;

The Committee further recommended that the views expressed by Prof. N.S. Iyengar in his letter to the convenor and the reactions of Dr. R. Radhakrishna be appended to the

Report; and

(d) As for calculating the calorie requirement, it is preferable to consider the minimum rather than average required for biological existence taking into consideration that there is considerable variation in calorie requirement. In view of this, it is recommended that 75 per cent of the poverty line may be considered as appropriate cut off point which has been rightly considered in the Draft 1978-1983 Plan Document.

Future Directions of Work

5.2 It was agreed that the following aspects may be taken up as task ahead for estimating the private consumption vector of the input-output model. These are:

(i) Methodological framework of consumption model;
(ii) Concomitant data problems; and
(iii) Related operational issues.

5.3 *Methodological Framework*

This relates to normative as well as effective/behaviouristic and other alternative aspects of the consumption model.

(i) *Normative Consumption*

5.3.1 In constructing the weighting diagram for determining the all-India calorie requirements separately for rural and urban areas, certain assumptions have been made. In this connection, it seems useful from operational angle to firm up some of these, particularly the one related to classification of workers as heavy, moderate and sedentary. To this end, a quick survey of existing literature on the subject, coupled with some exercises based on available data, may commend.

5.3.2 Since daily calorie requirements for the same person category are likely to vary over space because of climatic factors difference in body weights, etc., it appears desirable, at least in the long run, to develop regional calorie norms. Regions having formed, as much as possible, on the basis of homogeneity criterion consistent with similarity of climatic factors, uniformity of body weights, etc. As a corollary to this, a refinement to the procedure adopted at present to work out all-India calorie requirements seems in order. First overall region-level caloric requirements will have to be worked out and then an all-India figure arrived at by weighting these regional figures; the weights being the regional population figures.

5.3.3 A comparison of two series of private consumption expenditure one based on NSS household consumption expenditure-data and the other brought out by the CSO as a part of their National Accounts Statistics — shows that they differ perceptibly with the NSS series invariably tending to be on the low side. The reasons behind these differences and how to reconcile them is obviously a matter for further research and investigation. In this connection, it may be added that if, for instance, in actuality food items are correctly reported and non-food items alone are under-reported, then evidently, poverty line as calculated by us is understated and so also the population below it. On the contrary, converse holds good if non-food items are correctly reported and food items are under-reported.

5.3.4 Food component of the poverty line could alternatively be obtained by LP model* resulting in a minimum cost balanced diet compatible with locally available food-stuffs and satisfying, as far as possible, local tastes and preferences. Minimum cost figures thus arrived at for various person categories could be aggregated into an overall region-level or all-India figure by using an appropriate weighting diagram. This, when added to the food component of the original poverty line, would result in an alternative poverty line estimate. This may be more realistic *vis-a-vis* the original poverty line inasmuch as it food component is based on observational data rather than interview-based data which, in no small measure, may be affected by various biases and errors attributable to this method. In fact, norms for non-food component could also be suitably modified and moderated in the light of the observations made by various distinguished study groups in connection with their recommendations on minimum wage or need-based wage, etc., and allied materials available on the subject as well as through independent studies.

---

* Some work in this area as a part of district level food and nutrition studies is being undertaken by Department of Food.

Effective Consumption

5.3.5 Effective/behaviouristic demand in the present work has been analysed within the framework of LES-cum-consumption functions model. In the ensuring discussion we will take up the LES followed by its integration with demand functions.

5.3.6 Leaving aside the limitations of the LES to satisfactorily handle price effects-cross as well as own-pragmatic considerations suggest that certain modifications could be introduced in it while largely retaining its original structure and simplicity to allow greater sophistication in income response. The simplest way to achieve it is, as already tried out by some researchers in the field, to introduce time trends in the LES parameters preferably in this only, to allow for steady changes in tastes and preferences.

5.3.7 To judge the relative performance of LES, it may be instructive to compare its results with those of alternative models.

5.3.8 The consumption model for demand projections is intended to capture essentially the inter-temporal variations in consumer behaviour which is essentially of a short-run nature. As against this parameter of LES estimated in the present work tend to be a 'mongrel' reflecting both the short-term and long-term consumption behaviours. This is because the time series of cross-section data used in the model not only include intertemporal variations but inter-cross section variations also. Inter-temporal variations could probably be disentangled by using dummy variables for cross-sections in the regression analysis.

Problem of Integration

5.3.9 Integration of demand functions with LES tantamounts to assuming that both the systems reflect the same behaviour pattern of the consumer. But, as is well known, cross section analysis relating to a single point of time essentially reflects long-term consumption behaviour. In a situation like this, it may be argued whether integration is at all warranted. A way out of these theoretical complications relating to specification and interpretation of the model, of course within the LES framework, may be to estimate LES on the basis of regression analysis using dummy variable applied to time series of cross-section data on the one hand and estimating demand functions on time series data for finer classification of broad consumption estimates yielded by the LES on the other hand. As far as the latter is concerned, this will necessitate availability of house-hold consumption data in as much detail as contained in 28th Round of the NSS for a series of rounds.

(ii) *Data*

5.4.1 National Sample Survey household consumption data are collected, both in value and quantity wherever relevant, at a fairly disaggregative level. In order that the data may be useful for the purpose of consumption model building they should also be available both for the previous rounds and for the up-coming rounds in as detailed a manner as is the case with the 28th round of the NSS. In the case of States, in order to get tolerably realistic estimation of the model, the relevant tabulations would have to be based on Central sample data and State sample data combined to overcome the problem of small sample size. Wherever State sample is not collected, the same would have to be collected in future or Central sample would have to be of adequate size. As regards index number problem, the implicit deflator, if worked out regularly, based on National Sample Survey (NSS) value and quantity data would probably resolve it. In the case of such items where only value figures are available, appropriate unit prices will also have to be collected or compiled.

5.4.2 Closer examination and scrutiny of concepts, definitions, coverage and related aspects needs no emphasis to throw light on the disparity between the NSS and CSO series of private consumption expenditure. In this connection, surveys like Food and Nutrition studies being conducted by Food and Nutrition Board, Ministry of Agriculture and Irrigation, Department of Food, could provide an independent check on the two sets of data in question.

(iii) *Related Operational Issues*

5.5 This section broadly re-capitulates area of further work:

(i) Preparation of a paper surveying the existing literature on consumption functions and demand projections;
(ii) Discussion regarding the norms that should be adopted in respect of non-traded public goods like housing, primary

education, drinking water and medicines. In this connection, Appendices 15.1 and 15.2 give certain norms and coefficients. This information has been gleaned from a recent note entitled 'Minimum Needs Programme and its Commodity Composition', prepared by the Perspective Planning Division;

(iii) Views should be expressed on the distribution policy that should be adopted regarding food, sugar, clothing, housing, education, health and miscellaneous civil services in the final report;

(iv) Regional focus in the estimation of demand for various essential commodities should be brought out; and

(v) For estimation of private consumption for the new plan model, studies comprising the following should be carried out:

(a) re-estimation of the linear expenditure system considering more number of commodity groups preferably comparable with the input-output classification using the latest NSS data,

(b) estimation of linear expenditure system for different groups of expenditure classes taking into consideration the change in the expenditure classes over different rounds due to price changes,

(c) estimation of different Engel curves for as many number of commodities as possible using data of various NSS Rounds,

(d) estimation of regional specific norms of minimum needs both for essential traded goods and non-traded public goods, and

(e) consideration of alternative consumption model.

DIRECT TAX LAWS COMMITTEE, 1977 – REPORT[1]

Chairman Shri C.C. Chokshi
Members Shri S.P. Mehta; Shri Harnam Shankar; Shri C.C. Ganapati; Shri T.S.R. Narasimhan
M. Secy. Shri T.S.R. Narasimham; D.N. Pathak

Appointment

The Direct Tax Laws Committee constituted pursuant to the statement of the Honorable Minister of Finance in June 1977, vide Government of India Resolution No. A 11019/70/77-Ad VII dated June 25, 1977.

Terms of Reference

"To examine and suggest legal and administrative measures for simplification and rationalisation of Direct Tax Laws".

Contents

Part I: Introduction; Definition; Basis of Charge; Taxation of Non-residents on Income Deemed to Accrue in India; Exemptions; Computation of Income under the Head 'Salaries'; Interest on Securities; Income from House Property; Profits and Gains of Business or Profession; Capital Gains; Income from other Sources; Income of other Persons included in Assessee's Total Income; Set Off and Carry Forward of Losses; Deductions to be made in Computing total Income; Incomes Forming Part of Total Income on which no Income-tax is Payable and other Provisions of the Act; The Com-

1. Ministry of Finance, Government of India, New Delhi, 1978, 253 p., 3 Pts.

panies (Profits) Surtax Act, 1964; Wealth-tax; Gift-tax; Valuation of Assets; Conclusion; Summary of Observations and Recommendations. **Part II**: Introductory; Preliminary; Administration; Pre-assessment Payment of Taxes; Assessment Procedure; Penalties; Appeals; References and Revisions; Settlement of Cases; Payment and Refund of taxes; Recovery of Taxes; Liability in Special Cases; Registration of Firms, Associations of Persons and Bodies of Individuals; Offences and Prosecutions; Miscellaneous Provisions; Approvals under the Tax Laws; Conclusion; Summary of Observations and Recommendations. **Part III**: Introductory; Definitions; Basis of Charge of Estate Duty; Exceptions from Charge; Other Exemptions and Rebates; Value Chargeable; Deductions and Reliefs; Assessment, Penalties and Prosecutions; Appeal Rectification and Revision; Recovery of Duty; Settlement of Estate Duty Cases; Rates of Estate Duty; Summary of Observations and Recommendations

Recommendations

PART I

Introduction

1. The problem of simplification and rationalisation of tax cannot be considered in the abstract and divorced from the background of the economic activity in which the tax laws are required to operate. (Para I-0.5)

2. The administration is in a position to ensure fair play and justice as also equity in the tax laws. (Para I-0.7)

3. Tax laws cannot be reduced to a plane of total or absolute simplicity. (Para I-0.8)

4. Artificial distortions lead to complexities in the law as well as increased administrative difficulties. (Para I-0.9)

5. The errant taxpayer should not expect nor be shown any indulgence under the law. (Para I-0.13)

6. A climate of mutual trust and fair-play should be fostered so as to make for better voluntary compliance with the tax laws on the part of the tax-payers.

There is need for a clear statement that measures like disclosure scheme would not be repeated and that errant taxpayers would necessarily be dealt with in accordance with the due process of law. (Para I-0.14)

7. The need for continuous fiscal research embracing various aspects of thc tax provisions need no emphasis. (Para I-0.6)

8. Continuous fiscal research undertaken by an independent autonomous body will be to public finance what a well established scientific research institution is to technology. (Para I-0.7)

9. There is no particular merit in or necessity for clothing the budget proposals relating to the tax laws with an undue air of secrecy. (Para I-0.8)

10. In the circumstances prevailing in our country at present, where the requirement of rapid economic development is paramount, an experiment in restructuring the base for levy of tax, from income to consumption would be unwise and the cost of the nation would be incalculable and unjustifiable. It would be more prudent to extend the area of saving out of income qualifying for tax relief, than change the fundamental yardstick of income as the base for charge of tax. (Para I-0.21)

11. The concept of income as a base for tax cannot be artificially confined to a single accounting year and there should be a reasonable flexibility in the law to take into account adjustments which are not necessarily or strictly confined to a single year. (Para I-0.22)

12. If the phenomenon of inflation had continued unabated and the value of the rupee further eroded we would have examined the need for introducing the concept of indexation in our taxing statutes. (Para I-0.25)

Definitions (Chapter 1)

13. It would be appropriate that the amendments arising out of our recommendation are all brought into force at one and the same time and that too with effect from a specified assessment year, say, assessment year 1980-81. (Para I-1 1)

14. The expression 'amalgamation' may be defined to mean the merger of one or more companies with another company, or the merger of two or more companies to form one company, under a scheme sanctioned by the court under Section 394 of the Companies Act, 1956, or ordered by the Central Government under Section 396 of the said Act. (Para I-1.5)

15. An amendment may be made in the definition of capital asset to expressly include therein self-generated assets like goodwill.

The recommendation in this regard is, however, conditional upon the acceptance of the other recommendation contained in Chapter 9 of allow the cost of acquisition of such asset determined in the manner explained in that Chapter. (Para I-1.7)

16. The definition of a "company in which the public are substantially interested", should be simplified in the manner suggested. (Para I-1.12)

17. It is appropriate that sub-clause (e) of clause 22 of Section 2 is excluded from operation in cases where the payment in question is made in such circumstances or for such a brief duration that it cannot in substance be treated as falling within the intent of that sub-clause. (Para I-1.17)

18. An explanatory definition of the term "education" should be introduced with retrospective operation to the effect that "education shall not be restricted to scholastic instruction only". (Para I-1.21)

19. The artificial definition of "interest" in Section 2(28A) is unnecessary and not called for and may hence be deleted. (Para I-1.24)

20. Sub-clause (v) of Section 2(31) defining "person" should be divided into two parts as follows:

"(v) an association of persons whether incorporated or not;

(va) a body of individuals whether incorporated or not but not including a combination of individuals who merely receive income jointly without anything further." (Para I-1.26)

21. Sub-clause (i) of the definition of "person" in Section 2(31) should refer to "an individual including individuals who do not fall within sub-clause (v) or (va)". (Para I-1.27)

22. The definition of "relative" in Section 2(41) should apply for all the provisions of the Income-tax Act and the extended definition in other provisions, viz., Section 13 and Section 80B, should be deleted. (Para I-1.30)

23. A definition of a new expression "scheme of reconstruction" should be enacted in Section 2. (Para I-1.31)

24. The following recommendations are made in relation to "Previous year":

(1) The general rule that previous year means the financial year immediately preceding the assessment year should continue with regard to taxpayers who do not have income from a busi-

ness or profession and those who do not maintain accounts. This will not unduly disturb revenue collections and will also facilitate the assessment of the salary-earner class.

(2) In respect of companies, including statutory corporations, there should be a uniform previous year coinciding with the calendar year which should be applicable to all cases. Banks and insurance companies already maintain accounts on the calendar year basis as required by law. This recommendation would necessitate a change in the accounting period by those companies which follow periods other than the calendar year. In the case of companies which now follow the financial year, i.e., year ending 31st March, the transition year will consist of only 9 months, while those which follow accounting periods ending on 'Diwali', 30th September, 30th June, etc., will have the transition year covering a period longer than 12 months. There should be no special method of computation of the tax liability in such cases in order to compensate for the variation in the length of the transition year from a period of 12 months.

(3) A non-corporate tax-payer who carries on a business or profession, who maintains accounts for any source of income and claims the benefit of the exception to the normal rule in regard to previous year, should be required to choose one previous year according to his individual requirement, which would, then, be the previous year in respect of his income from all sources other than share from a firm dealt with in item (5) below.

(4) In the case of taxpayer who has chosen, under recommendation (3) above, a year other than the calendar year or the financial year to be his previous year, any change in the previous year in future should be allowed only if he wishes to adopt the calendar year or the financial year and not any other period. Any such change should be allowed without any condition.

(5) In the case of a partner of a firm, his share of income from the firm will continue to be assessed on the basis of the previous year of the firm as at present. This could result in such a taxpayer having a previous year for his share of income from the firm or as many different previous years as the number of firms in which he is a partner, assuming that these firms choose different previous years for the closing of their ac-

counts and a separate previous year for his other income.

(6) The operation of the new provisions based on the above recommendations may be reviewed in due course. If it is observed that the medium of firms is being resorted to with the objective of perpetuating the multiplicity of previous years in the case of non-corporate taxpayers, the previous year for firms in general could also be standardised at a later stage as in the case of companies. (Para I-1.40)

Basis of Charge (Chapter 2)

25. The rates of income-tax should be specified in a schedule to the substantive enactment imposing the tax, instead of being laid down from year to year in a separate Act of Parliament. (Para I-2.2)

26. The rate structure of income-tax should provide for a maximum marginal rate of tax of 60 per cent which should be applicable on income exceeding Rs. 2 lakhs, with an appropriately smooth and even progression at all levels below Rs. 2 lakhs. (Para I-2.9)

27. Surcharges on income-tax should be abolished and in any event, the maximum marginal rate of income-tax of 60 per cent should be inclusive of surcharges if any. (Para I-2.10)

28. The revenue presently being derived by the Centre through the scheme of integration of agricultural income with non-agricultural income should not be forgone and the scheme should continue to operate. (Para I-2.20)

29. If the consensus arising out of the dialogue and discussion between the Central Government and the State Governments is that agricultural income-tax should also be imposed under a Central Act, it would be more appropriate to do so by a direct amendment of the Constitution than by amending the definition of 'agricultural income' in the Income-tax Act or by resorting to the provisions of Article 252(1) of the Constitution. (Para I-2.32)

30. If the Centre is not to levy income-tax on agricultural incomes the following measures are suggested for the consideration of the Government:

(a) States which do not have any law for taxation of agricultural income at present may be advised by the Central Government to introduce such legislation at an early date;

(b) The pattern of the legislation may as far as possible be uniform in all the States;

(c) The uniformity should extend to the levy of the tax on all categories of agricultural income, whether from plantations, cash crops, or food crops;

(d) As far as possible, the principle of progressions, with a graded rate structure, should be adopted, broadly conforming to the minimum exemption limit and the maximum rate under the Central income-tax law;

(e) With a view to facilitating administration and eliminating the process of elaborate determination through books and records, the law could provide for a scheme of composition of the tax. This composition scheme could provide for a flat determination of the income having regard to the category of the land and the nature of agricultural activity carried out thereon. The composition scheme contained in Section 67 of the Karnataka Agricultural Income-tax Act could provide a useful model. Needless to say, the composition scheme should not be available to organised bodies like companies and co-operative societies which are required by law to maintain proper books of account; and

(f) The scheme of integration of agricultural income for determining the tax on non-agricultural income under the Finance Act should have a complementary provision incorporated in the State laws for the determination of the tax on agricultural income. In other words, the State law should provide for taking the non-agricultural income of a taxpayer into account for determining the rate of tax applicable to his agricultural income. This will be a necessary ingredient of the progression in the rate structure of agricultural income-tax. (Para I-2.33)

31. No change is required in the concept of "not ordinarily resident" or in the tests for determining whether a person is "not ordinarily resident". (Para I-2.38)

32. The test in Section 6(1)(b) for determination of residence with reference to the maintenance of a dwelling house should be deleted. (Para I-2.39)

33. Section 6(1)(c) should be amended and the words 'sixty days' be replaced by the words 'ninety days'. The Explanation to Section 6(1) should be deleted. (Para I-2.40)

34. No basic change in the scope of tax liability, by linking

residential status with citizenship, is necessary. (Para I-2.41)

35. No change is necessary in regard to the scope of total income as contained in Section 5 of the Act. (Para I-2.42)

Taxation of Non-Residents on Income Deemed to Accrue in India (Chapter 3)

36. The threat of an assessment based upon business connection of every foreigner dealing with India has to a large-extent been reduced as a result of the tests laid down by the Supreme Court. (Para I-3.2)

37. Clause (v) of Section 9(1) should be deleted and income by way of interest should be deemed to accrue or arise in India in the circumstances specified in Section 9(1)(i) prior to its amendment in 1976. (Para I-3.4)

38. It is eminently in the national interest that some machinery should be devised for making the incidence of tax on foreigners both certain and foreseeable, and at the same time, equitable. (Para I-3.6)

39. The tax sought to be imposed on the non-resident collaborator in industrial ventures in India, in effect, falls on the Indian participant and ultimately, enters into the cost of products manufactured under such collaboration. (Para I-3.11)

40. In giving the prior determination about taxability of payments under collaboration arrangement, Government would take into account the guiding principles already enunciated namely:

(1) consideration for transfer of know-how outside India against payment outside India will not attract any tax in India;
(2) payment for engineering and technical services performed outside India will not attract tax in India;
(3) services rendered in India will result in income accruing or arising in India which will be liable to tax in India but only after deduction of all expenditure wholly and exclusively incurred for the purpose of earning such income;
(4) royalties paid in consideration for the use of know-how in India will be liable to tax in India subject to deduction of expenditure incurred for the purpose of earning such royalties; and
(5) where composite services are rendered, partly in India and partly outside, the income deemed to accrue or arise in India shall be only such part of the income as is reasonably at-

tributable to the operations carried out in India. (Para I-3.13)

41. Clauses (vi) and (vii) of Section 9(1) should be deleted and the deeming of royalties and technical service fees as income in India should be restored to the position obtaining prior to the amendments of 1976. At the point of time when collaboration arrangements are approved by the Central Government a determination should be made by the Central Government of the quantum of fee which is deemed to accrue or arise in India and the quantum of income component therein (that is to say fees less expenses attributable thereto). (Para I-3.16)

42. Section 44D should be deleted and in its place a provision should be made for allowance of expenditure against royalties and fees for technical services of only such amount and in such manner as may be determined by the Central Government while approving the terms of collaboration. (Para I-3.18)

43. The provisions of Section 44C should be amended to allow a uniform deduction of 5 per cent of the adjusted total income as defined in the Explanation thereto in respect of head office expenditure in the case of non-residents. (Para I-3.21)

Exemptions (Chapter 4)

44. The various exemptions and exclusions contained in Section 10 may be rearranged as follows:

(a) all exclusions relating to computation of income under the head "Salaries" should be grouped together; exemptions which are merely designed to spell out the diplomatic immunities and privileges enjoyed under international law by citizens of a foreign country rendering services to their Government in India, should be placed together as at present;
(b) exemptions applicable to institutions of various kinds, either in respect of their entire income or in respect of only specified items of their income, should be grouped together distinctly and separately from other exemptions which are operative without reference to the status of the recipient; and
(c) the remaining exemptions, which are either based on the nature of the receipt or which are of a miscellaneous character not capable of a rational classification, may be enumerated

separately from the exemptions relating to institutions referred to in item (b).

Exemptions which are now scattered over the Finance Acts and other enactments, (exempting from tax for all time or for limited periods) the income of certain corporations and other bodies such as the Unit Trust of India, the Industrial Development Bank of India, etc., or which make special provisions (short of total exemption), as in the case of the Industrial Finance Corporation of India, State Financial Corporations and the Agricultural Refinance Corporation, may also be incorporated in the Income-tax Act either *in extenso* or by way of reference to the relevant provision of the concerned enactment in a schedule, in future, it should be ensured that, whenever any such exemption or special provision is enacted, it is specifically mentioned in the Income-tax Act. (Para I-4.5)

45. Appropriate instructions should be issued by the Board to the officers not to deny any exemption or deduction which an assessee may claim merely on the basis that it is open to him to claim exemption under some other provisions of the Act. (Para I-4.6)

46. The exemption under Section 10(4A) in respect of interest on Non-resident (External) Accounts should be made available to all assessees who are non-residents for the purposes of the Foreign Exchange Regulation Act and not only to "non-residents" under the Income-tax Act. (Para I-4.7)

47. The lay may be amended to vest power in the Central Government to extend the period of 90 days mentioned under Section 10(6) (vi) in appropriate cases. (Para I-4.8)

48. The stipulation in Section 10(6)(viia) that the technician should be employed in a capacity in which his specialised knowledge and experience are actually utilised, in order that he may be entitled to the exemption under that provision, is a superfluity and this requirement should be deleted. (Para I-4.10)

49. It should be clarified that the exemption from tax under Section 10(6) (viia) will be available even if the foreign technician is employed in connection with a business to be commenced later. (Para I-4.11)

50. The condition under Section 10(6)(viia), that the technician should not have been resident in India in any of the four financial years immediately preceding the year of his arrival in India, should be deleted. (Para I-4.12)

51. A clarificatory amendment should be made to the effect that "remuneration", for the purpose of Section 10(6)(viia), shall not include allowances, such as daily allowance or travelling allowance, which are eligible for exemption from tax under any other provision of the law. (Para I-4.13)

52. Payments of the nature of contributions towards retirement and social security benefits made by the foreign employer in the home country of the foreign technicians should be specifically excluded from liability to tax in India. (Para I-4.14)

53. The Period of full exemption from tax of the remuneration of a foreign technician under Section 10(6)(viia) may be raised to 36 months, with exemption for a further period of 36 months where the employer pays to Government the tax on the technician's salary. (Para I-4.15)

54. Daily allowance paid by Indian concerns to foreigners working in India for temporary periods, as in the case of technician referred to in Section 10(6) (vi) or Section 10(6) (viia), should not be liable to tax and should be exempted under Section 10(14) if such daily allowances have been approved by the Reserve Bank of India or the Central Government. (Para I-4.16)

55. The provision in Section 10(7) exempting allowances and perquisites paid or allowed as such outside India from liability to Indian tax, should be extended to all Indian citizens whether they render services to Government or to any public sector corporation or other Indian employer. (Para I-4.17)

56. No useful purpose would be served by having a specific clause in Section 10 of the Act to exempt receipts under life policies which by their very nature are capital receipts and not income. (Para I-4.18)

57. Section 10(14) may be amended to exempt from tax city compensatory allowances up to the maximum monetary limit applicable in the case of employees of the Central Government as specified stations. (Para I-4.21)

58. Approval granted by the Central Government to the agreement relating to the borrowing of money abroad for industrial development in India should be adequate for the purpose of the exemption from tax of the interest payable thereon, under Section 10(15)(iv). The further requirement, under that provision, of approval of the rate of interest should be deleted. (Para I-4.22)

59. The approval of a scientific research association, for the pur-

pose of various tax concessions, should have a currency of only three years at a time. (Para I-4.24)

60. Section 10(21) may be clarified to provide, firstly, that in the case of a scientific research association approved for the purpose of Section 35(1)(ii) which has scientific research as its only object, the whole of its income will be exempt from tax and, secondly, that in the case of an institution which has scientific research as one of its several objects, and which is approved for the purposes of Section 35(1)(ii), its income will be eligible for exemption from tax to the extent it is applied for the purposes of scientific research or set apart for application to such purposes. (Para I-4.25)

61. The exemption in clause (23A) of Section 10 may be extended to cover all income, from whatever source derived, in the case of an association or institution referred to therein. (Para I-4.27)

62. The condition under Section 10(23B) that the institution referred to therein should not exist for the purpose of profit should be deleted. (Para I-4.28)

63. Section 296 may be suitably amended to require notifications issued by the Central Government under Section 10(23C)(v) also to be laid before Parliament. (Para I-4.29)

64. Section 10(29) may be amended to make it clear that it applies specifically to State Warehousing Corporations. (Para I-4.30)

Computation of Income Under the Head 'Salaries' (Chapter 5)

65. The various provisions relating to the computation of income under the head "Salaries" and deductions therefrom should be grouped together in the Sections dealing with computation of income under the head "Salaries". (Para I-5.4)

66. Amending the definition of salary so as to have a uniform definition for different purposes, is not desirable as the benefit of simplification would be more than off-set by the complications and inequities that would result by adoption of a single norm for different objectives. (Para I-5.6)

67. The standard deduction under Section 16(i) may be calculated at the uniform rate of 20 per cent at all levels of salary and the monetary ceiling may be increased from Rs. 3,500 to Rs. 5,000. (Para I-5.9)

68. In the case of an employee having the use of a conveyance, the limit over the deduction under Section 16(1) should be raised to

Rs. 2,500 from the present limit of Rs. 1,000. Further, in the case of an employee who is in receipt or a conveyance allowance, the ceiling should be fixed at Rs. 5,000 as reduced by the amount of conveyance allowance not qualifying for exemption under Section 10(14) or Rs. 2,500, whichever is higher. (Para I-5.10)

69. The standard deduction should be allowed also to a person in receipt of a pension from a former employer, at half the normal rate, i.e., at the rate of 10 per cent subject, however, to a ceiling of Rs. 1,000 per year. (Para I-5.11)

70. Section 16(1) which provides for the standard deduction should give an option to the salary-earner to claim, in place of the standard deduction, a deduction of the actual expenditure incurred out of the remuneration wholly, necessarily and exclusively for the purposes of employment. (Para I-5.12)

71. Though Section 16 may empower a salary-earner to claim the actual expenditure in lieu of the standard deduction, deduction of tax at source should be effected by the employer after allowing only the standard deduction. (Para I-5.13)

72. In determining the perquisite value of residential accommodation under the Rule 3 of the Income-tax Rules, the addition in respect of the excess of the fair rental value over 20 per cent or 30 per cent, as the case may be, of the salary, should be subject to a limit of 15 per cent of the employee's salary. This limit should, however, not apply in respect of residential accommodation where the annual cost to the employer is not less than Rs. 36,000 per annum. The annual cost should necessarily include not only the direct cost of the accommodation but also incidental costs such as interest, maintenance, depreciation, etc. (Para I-5.15)

73. No requisite value should be attributed to the provision of a mere transport facility to an employee from his residence to the office and back. (Para I-5.16)

74. The existing administrative instructions regarding the perquisite value of domestic help should continue where the employer directly meets the costs of such services. Where, however, such services are engaged by the employee and in turn the employer pays the employee a cash amount by way of reimbursement, the perquisite value should be determined at 50 per cent of the amount paid by the employer, without any upper monetary limit. (Para I-5.17)

75. Despite the observations of the Madras High Court in some cases, no attempt should be made to tax employees on an imputed

benefit by virtue of loans granted by the employer under the schemes of loans to employees. The present practice of not taxing any imputed benefit should continue. If necessary, administrative instructions may be issued to that effect. It would, however, follow that where loans or advances made show abuse of power, the Department should, of course, be entitled to take appropriate action in bringing to tax the value of the benefit enjoyed. (Para I-5.18)

76. As long as expenditure on medical benefits to employees is within the reasonable bounds of commercial expediency, no attempt should be made to draw any distinction between ordinary medical treatment and other medical treatment and consequently no attempt should be made to bring to tax any such facility in the hands of the employees as perquisites. In other words, the administration should continue to be liberal in the matter of determination of perquisite in relation to medical facilities. (Para I-5.19)

77. Section 89(1) should be recast so as to allow that Section to be applied at the time of calculating the tax to be deducted at source from payments of salary in the circumstances referred to in that Section. The provision of Section 192, relating to deduction of tax at source from salary payments, should also be amended to enable the employer to take into account the provisions of Section 89(1) while calculating the tax to be deducted as source. (Para I-5.25)

78. For the purpose of the relief under Section 89 (1), wherever the arrears of salary relate to a period exceeding 5 years, the arrears should be spread equally over five years inclusive of the year of payment. The amount so included should be added to the total income of each of these years and the tax determined accordingly. A provision on these lines should be incorporated in Section 89 itself. (Para I-5.27)

79. For the purpose of the relief under Section 89(1), payments of gratuity, compensation, etc., may be spread over the last 5 years equally including the year of retirement. The amount allotted to each year may be added to the total income of such year and tax determined accordingly. This formula should likewise be incorporated in the Act itself and not left to the Income-tax Rules. (Para I-5.29)

80. Rule 6 in Part A of the Fourth Schedule should be amended to provide that only contributions of the employer in excess of 10 per cent of the salary of the employee will be deemed to be employee's income and that no part of the interest credited to the employee's account shall be deemed to be his income. (Para I-5.30)

81. Provisions of a substantive nature, at present, contained in the rules in the Fourth Schedule in so far as they relate to the taxation of certain amounts as income of the employer should be included in the Sections of the law dealing with the computation of income under the head "Salaries". (Para I-5.34)

82. The provisions for bringing to tax non-exempt portions of payments from an approved superannuation fund should be clearly enacted. (Para I-5.35)

83. Provisions of Rule 72 of the Income-tax Rules should find their place in the substantive law and not in the rules framed by the Board. (Para I-5.36)

Interest in Securities (Chapter 6)

84. The category of income at present assessable under a separate head "Interest on securities" should more appropriately be assessed either under the head "Profits and gains of business or profession" where the income partakes of the character of business income or under the residuary head "Income from other sources" where it is not derived from a business activity. The existing provisions in Sections 18, 19, 20 and 21 will, then, no longer be necessary. (Para I-6.4)

85. Section 57 is wide enough to cover the two items of deductions at present allowable under Section 19 of the Act. (Para I-6.5)

86. Interest on securities should be subjected to tax in accordance with the method of accounting regularly employed by the taxpayer and, in the absence of accounts, such interest should be subjected to tax as income of the year in which it is received. (Para I-6.7)

87. It is not necessary to continue the provisions of Section 89(2) for allowing relief where interest on securities is received in arrears. (Para I-6.8)

88. The provisions of Section 96 should be continued. (Para I-6.9)

Income from House Property (Chapter 7)

89. The concept of owner under Section 22 should be consistent with the observations of the Supreme Court and should not be unduly strictly construed in the manner done by the Calcutta and Bombay High Courts. In other words where actual income is received by a

person other than the legal owner then he alone should be assessed and no concurrent assessment should be made on the legal owner under Section 22 of the Act. In all such cases, the beneficial owner should be assessed on such income under the head "Income from house property". (Para I-7.5)

90. One house property used by the taxpayer for his own residence should be exempt from tax under Section 22 of the Act. (Para I-7.11)

91. The recommendation made in para I-7.11 should be in addition to the concession available to the taxpayer under Section 23(3). (Para I-7.13)

92. The condition connected with the allowance for the first five years in respect of new residential units under Section 23(1) that the income of such units is in no case a loss should be deleted. (Para I-7.14)

93. Amounts recovered from its members by a Co-operative Housing Society to meet various charges should be expressly allowed as a deduction in the computation of income from property in the hands of the members, so however, that where any part of such amounts is already allowable in the computation under any specific provision of the law, no double deduction of the same item should be made. (Para I-7.15)

94. The income under the head "Income from house property" should be computed after allowance in respect of repairs on the basis of 1/6th of the annual letting value under Section 24(1)(i) as at present, with a right to the taxpayer to claim the actual expenditure if it is in excess of the deduction on the basis of 1/6th. To determine such excess, the comparison should not be limited to a single previous year but should extend to the previous year relevant to the year of assessment and the five previous years immediately preceding it. (Para I-7.16)

95. Section 24 should expressly provide for a residuary item of deduction in respect of other expenditure (not being in the nature of capital expenditure) laid out or expended wholly and exclusively for the purpose of making or earning income under the head "Income from house property". (Para I-7.17)

96. If the rents are in arrears for a period of two years, the taxpayer should be entitled to the deduction of the same under Section 24(1)(x) without any further requirements as at present stipulated in Rule 4 of the Income-tax Rules. (Para I-7.18)

97. A provision should be made for bringing to tax amounts subsequently realised out of amounts allowed as deduction under Section 24(1)(x) in the year of realisation, so that the relaxation in the conditions for allowance does not result in an undue benefits to taxpayers. (Para I-7.18)

98. The fiction in Section 27(iii) of treating each member of a co-operative society as the owner of a portion of the property, should be extended to the members of a limited company owning house property possession of which is divided among the several members. (Para I-7.19)

Profits and Gains of Business or Profession (Chapter 8)

99. The distinction between an adventure in the nature of trade and a capital or casual transaction has, to some extent, lost its significance in the context of the present scheme of the Income-tax Act where income from casual transactions as well as gains from certain capital transactions are brought to tax. (Para I-8.3)

100. The law should recognise the peculiar nature of income derived from professional activity by the exercise of intellectual skill which should be encouraged by suitable incentives in the computation of the chargeable income. (Para I-8.5)

101. The Supreme Court has laid great emphasis on the computation of business profits and gains in accordance with the ordinary principles of commercial accounting. (Para I-8.6)

102. Section 28 should be extended to cover income of a business or profession which is discontinued, which is, at present dealt within Section 176(3A) and Section 176(4). All the deductions as available to a continuing business should be allowed to the closed business in the computation of the income as discussed in Para I-8.11. (Para I-8.7)

103. Expenditure incurred in the course of the trade, which is unremunerative is, none the less, a proper deduction as expenditure wholly and exclusively incurred for the purposes of the trade. (Para I-8.8)

104. The general provision in Section 37(1) should have primacy in the scheme of computation of income from business or profession and should come immediately after Sections 28 and 29. (Para I-8.9)

105. The sole test for allowance of business expenditure should be that laid down in Section 37(1), namely, whether the expenditure

is laid out or expended wholly and exclusively for the purposes of the business or profession, not being in the nature of capital expenditure or personnel expenses. (Para I-8.9)

106. All expenditure incurred wholly and exclusively for the purposes of the business or profession, other than personal expenditure of the taxpayer, should be allowed as a deduction in computing the profits and gains. If the expenditure is in the nature of revenue expenditure it should be allowed in the year in which it is incurred or actually met, in accordance with the method of accounting followed by the taxpayer. If the expenditure is of the nature of capital expenditure, it should still be allowable in the process of computation of taxable profits through allowances such as depreciation or amortisation as explained in the Interim Report, Paras 3.30 and 3.31. (Para I-8.10)

107. Expenditure which would have been allotable had the business continued should be allowed even after the closure of business and profit or loss should be computed accordingly. The expenditure arising out of the closure of the business should also be regarded as expenditure incurred for the purposes of the business. (Para I-8.11)

108. At least for the future, artificial disallowance of business expenditure should be kept at the minimum and the Government should accept the concept of real income as evolved by courts of law over the years. (Para I-8.12)

109. Where any incentive or extra deduction for a particular expenditure is desired to be granted, the intention should be expressly and clearly spelt out in the law. (Para I-8.13)

110. Where the Income-tax Officer disallows an item of expenditure in the assessment for any year as not pertaining to that year, he should simultaneously be required to determine the year to which such expenditure relates. If it relates to a past year then he should be required to simultaneously revise the assessment of the past year and allow the deduction. If it relates to a future year, the assessment order should record a findings in regard to the year to which it relates and such a finding should be binding on the Income-tax Officer or his successor in so far as the assessment for such subsequent year is concerned. (Para I-8.14)

111. All situations warranting deduction of business expenditure cannot be legislated upon and much would depend upon an enlightened approach in the administration of the law based on considerations of equity and justice. (Para I-8.17)

112. Where the asset qualifying for investment allowance under

Section 32A is acquired or installed in one previous year but brought into use in any subsequent previous year, not necessarily the previous year immediately following the year of acquisition/installation of the asset, the investment allowance should be granted in the year in which the asset is first put to use for the purposes of the business. (Para I-8.19)

113. Provisions corresponding to those in sub-sections (6) and (7) of Section 32A entitling the successor to the investment allowance should be made also in the following types of cases involving a change of ownership of assets qualifying for inverstment allowance:

(a) where an individual proprietor of a business expires and his successor inherits the business;
(b) where the change in ownership takes place as a result of partition of the property of a Hindu undivided family which is carrying on the business; and
(c) where a sole proprietor converts his business into a partnership and continues as a partner for the unexpired portion of the mandatory holding period of asset. (Para I-8.20)

114. The Explanation to Section 32A(4) should suitably clarify that it covers not merely cases of inadequacy of the reserve but also absence of any reserve under similar circumstances. (Para I-8.21)

115. In the case of assessees engaged in the business of operation of ships or aircraft, investment allowance should also be granted in respect of any new plant and machinery installed for the purposes of such business. (Para I-8.22)

116. In the circumstances mentioned in Section 33B of the Income-tax Act, the taxpayer should be entitled to carry backward business losses and other admissible allowances and deductions to the three years immediately preceding the year in which the business was disrupted, to be set off against the profits assessed for those years. If there is still any loss or other amount which remains unabsorbed by such set off, such loss, etc., may be allowed to be carried forward for future set off in the same manner as at present. Such right to carry backward and set off losses should, however, be allowed only if the taxpayer satisfies the Income-tax Officer at the time of assessment that he has taken adequate steps for the revival, re-establishment or reconstruction of the disrupted business. (Para I-8.25)

117. In the case of patents and copyrights, the cost of acquisition should be amortised over a ten-year period. (Para I-8.26)

118. The first proviso to Section 36(1)(ii), which limits the allowance in respect of bonus paid to employees to the amount payable under the Payment of Bonus Act should be deleted. (Para I-8.27)

119. In regard to the allowance for bad, doubtful or irrecoverable debts, the law should be amended on the following lines:

(i) The allowance in respect of debts estimated to be bad, doubtful or irrecoverable should be with reference to the amount written off by the assessee in the profit and loss account of the relevant previous year. Where such write off relates to debts which fell due within a period of two years preceding the date of the write off the taxpayer may be called upon to justify the write off. In any case, the taxpayer should be entitled to freely write off debts which are not recovered for a period of two years from their original due date;
(ii) The existing provisions for subjecting to tax any recovery out of the amounts written off should continue as a necessary safeguard in the interests of revenue; and
(iii) The write off of the debt by the debit to the profit and loss account may be made balanced either by a corresponding credit entry to the debtor's account or by passing a credit entry in another appropriate account, such as "Provision for bad and doubtful debts account". (Para I-8.31)

120. The *Explanation* appearing after sub-section (4) of Section 41 should be placed either at the end of the entire Section of after sub-section (3) and should, with the necessary change in language, cover sub-section (2), sub-section (2A) and sub-section (3). (Para I-8.32)

121. In clauses (iv) and (v) of Section 36(1), relating to deduction of amounts paid by the employer by way of contributions to a recognised provident fund, approved superannuation fund or approved gratuity fund, a specific provision should be made that, if the contributions are not paid within a period of three months from the end of the previous year, thc deduction shall not be allowed in the computation of the business profits of that year. However, in cases of delayed payments, the deduction should be allowed in the year of actual payment. (Para I-8.33)

122. The ceiling for allowance of entertainment expenditure may be raised to Rs. 1 lakh from the existing Rs. 30,000. This may be achieved by suitably increasing, the rates and the length of the slabs so as to arrive at the ceiling of Rs. 1 lakh where the profits and gains of the business exceed Rs. 2.80 crores, on the following lines:

(i)	on the first Rs. 20 lakhs of the profits and gains.	at the rate of 1% or Rs. 10,000 whichever is higher;
(ii)	on the next Rs. 60 lakhs of the profits and gains	at the rate of 1/2%;
(iii)	on the next Rs. 2 crores of the profits and gains.	at the rate of 1/4%;
(iv)	on the balance	Nil

(Para I-8.35)

123. The ceilings of Rs. 100 and Rs. 50 mentioned in Rule 6D may be increased to Rs. 250 and Rs. 125 respectively. These monetary ceilings should be revised periodically having regard to the tariffs of hotels run by the India Tourism Development Corporation. (Para I-8.36)

124. The provisions in sub-clauses (i) and (iii) of clause (a) of Section 40 should be deleted. (Para I-8.37)

125. The nature of the arrangements that would be considered as effective for the purposes of Section 40(a)(iv) should be spelt out in the rules. (Para I-8.38)

126. A specific provision should be made to the effect that the monetary ceiling laid down in Section 40(c) and in Section 40A(5) will not apply in any case where the salary and perquisites of the director or other person, etc., have been approved by the Government of India in the Department of Company Affairs, and that the test of whether the payment is excessive or unreasonable will also not apply in such cases. The provisions of Section 40(c) should operate in a mutually exclusive area from those of Section 40A(5) and accordingly Section 40A(5) should be rendered inapplicable to cases of persons who are covered by Section 40(c). The items of expenditure like provident fund contributions, etc., which are excluded from disallowance under Section 40A(5), should continue to be excluded from disallowance under Section 40(c). (Para I-8-39)

127. Any payment by way of gratuity to retiring employees (computed in accordance with a scheme applicable to all the

employees) should be excluded from the scope of 'salary' for the purposes of the limit specified in Section 40A(5) and in Section 40(c). (Para I-8.40)

128. The provision in Section 40A(3) should be kept on the statute book with a view to encouraging transactions through banks, but the limit of Rs. 2,500 may be raised to Rs. 10,000. (Para I-8.41)

129. The provision in Section 40A(8) should be deleted along with the Tenth Schedule to the Income-tax Act, which pertains to those provisions. (Para I-8.45)

130. The proviso to clause (b) of Rule 5 of the First Schedule should be deleted. (Para I-8.47)

131. The view that the deductions under Chapter VIA are not to be allowed in the computation made under the First Schedule is clearly opposed to the express terms of Section 44. The clear position in law should be reiterated by suitable instructions to the assessing officers. (Para I-8.50)

132. Suitable instructions may be issued to the assessing officers clarifying the position in law and setting at rest the needless controversy based upon the erroneous construction of Section 44 regarding credit for taxes deducted at sources. (Para I-8.51)

Capital Gains (Chapter 9)

133. In relation to transfer of immovable property by way of sale, where the agreement to sell is evidenced by an instrument in writing, where possession of the immovable property has been handed over to the purchaser and the whole or substantially the whole of the consideration has been received by the transferor, the capital gains should be chargeable at such point of time when these requirements are fulfilled. Where the gain is brought to charge in these circumstances it should not again be deemed to arise in the previous year when the instrument of conveyance is executed and registered. (Para I-9.11)

134. The provisions of law should be suitably amended to as to expressly include self-generated assets within the meaning of "capital assets" and thereby bringing to tax the capital gains on the transfer of such assets. This recommendation is conditional upon the further recommendations for determination of cost of acquisition of such asset. (Para I-9.12)

135. The cost of acquisition of self-generated assets may be

deemed to be a percentage of the sale proceeds as under the following formula:

(1) Where the asset is held by assess for not more than five years before its transfer	20% of the sale proceeds.
(2) Where the assets is held for more than five years but not more than ten years	40% of the sale proceeds.
(3) Where the asset is held for more than ten years but not more than fifteen years	60% of the sale proceeds.
(4) Where the asset is held for more than fifteen years	80% of the sale proceeds.

(Para I-9.13)

136. In case of self-generated assets, the taxpayer should not have the right of substitution of the fair market value for the cost of acquestion. (Para I-9.14)

137. Distribution of capital assets in payment of his share to a partner on his retiring from a firm should be brought within the the purview of Section 47(ii) and Section 49(1)(iii)(b). (Para I-9.15)

138. Where a partner introduces capital assets into a partnership firm, it should be deemed to be a transfer under Section 2(47) of the Act, subject to the recommendation inthe next paragraph. (Para I-9.17)

139. The fiction of transfer on introduction of capital assets into a partnership by a partner should apply in the year when the taxpayer concerned realises the consideration for such introduction, in money or the equivalent of money, or when the firm transfers such assets, whichever is earlier. (Para I-9.18)

140. Where an asset which was at any time a capital asset is subsequently realised as a trading asset, the element of capital gains should be brought to tax. For this purpose, the consideration realised at the point of ultimate transfer less the amount assessable as profits and gains of business should be deemed to be the full value of the consideration for determination of the capital gains. In other words, the difference between the value at which the asset is taken into the business as a trading asset and the cost of acquisition would represent the capital gains liable to tax at the point of time when the asset

is actually transferred. (Para I-9.19)

141. The exemptions under Section 47(i) and (v) should be deemed to be wrongly allowed where within a period of 5 years after the transfer:

(a) the relationship of holding company and wholly-owned subsidiary is altered, or
(b) the transfer company does not or ceases to hold the transferred asset as a capital asset. (Para I-9.23)

142. The cost of acquisition of an asset under a gift or by way of inheritance should be the cost to the previous owner as increased by the proportionate amount of gift-tax or estate duty attributable to such asset, so however that such increase does not result in the cost exceeding the value adopted for the purposes of gift-tax or estate duty. (Para I-9.14)

143. The cost of improvement, as defined in Section 55(1)(b) and referred to in Sections 48 and 49, should include all expenditure incurred by a taxpayer in obtaining possession of the asset and establishing or completing full title thereto. (Para I-9.25)

144. The assurance given by the Finance Minister in the Lok Sabha at the time of insertion of Section 52(2) should be incorporated in the Section itself. Section 52(2) should apply to cases of understatement of the consideration which actually passed and should not apply to cases where nothing more than the declared consideration is received or accrues to the taxpayer. (Para I-9.27)

145. Where evidence of a gift or a deemed gift is available in relations to the transfer of a capital asset, the question of applying the provisions of Section 52(2) should not arise. (Para I-9.28)

146. The provision for allowing deduction of a portion of the long-term capital gains under Section 80T should be applied both to corporate taxpayers and non-corporate taxpayers and no separate rate of tax on long-term capital gains in the case of companies need be specified in Section 115. (Para I-9.31)

147. The limits of Rs. 25,000 and Rs. 50,000 specified in Section 53 should be doubled to Rs. 50,000 and Rs. 1,00,000 respectively. (Para I-9.32)

148. The following amendments should be made to Section 54:

(1) the house property in respect of the transfer of which exemp-

tion from tax on the capital gains is provided should be required to be used by the taxpayer or his parents for his or their residence throughout the period 365 days preceding the date of the transfer. The condition of user for residence should not require physical occupation throughout the year but it should suffice if the property is retained for occupation in contradistinction to its being let out;

(2) it should be clarified that the benefit under the Section is not to be restricted only to individuals but is available to Hindu undivided families as well;

(3) it should be clarified that residential units in co-operative societies also qualify for the benefit under Section 54 and the fiction in Section 27(iii) extended to cover members of companies, as recommended in Chapter 7, should be made applicable for the purpose of Section 54; and

(4) the new acquisition may be made either for the taxpayer's own residence or for that of his parents;

(5) the period within which the new asset has to be constructed or acquired may be allowed to be extended by the Commissioner in appropriate cases where he is satisfied that the delay was caused by factors beyond the control of the taxpayer. (Para I-9.35)

149. The Commissioner should have the power to extend the time-limit for acquiring the new asset for the purposes of the exemptions provided in Sections 54B and 54D as well. (Para I-9.36)

150. The requirement of reinvestment under Section 54E should be with reference to the full value of the consideration *less* expenditure incurred wholly and exclusively in connection with the transfer. (Para I-9.37)

151. Assets specified in Section 54E for the purpose of reinvestment should included one residential house for the use of the taxpayer or his parents. (Para I-9.38)

152. Where realisation of the assets acquired in conformity with the requirements of Section 54E is made for the purposes of payment of estate duty on the death of the taxpayer, it should not entail liability to tax on capital gains as a breach of the Section. Further, it may be suitably clarified that realisation of a part of the new asset (otherwise than as stated above) would entail taxation of only the proportionate amount of capital gains originally exempted from tax.

(Para I-9.39)

153. The passing of the specified assets to the legal heirs in the case of the death of the taxpayer should not entail consequences under sub-section (2) of Section 54E, provided such legal heirs continue to fulfil the same condition of holding the specified assets as would have applied to the taxpayer were he alive. (Para I-9.40)

154. The Commissioner should be given discretion to extend the time-limit for reinvestment in the specified assets where the receipt of the consideration for the transfer of the original assets is deferred or delayed. (Para I-9.41)

155. The right of substitution of the market value for the cost of acquisition should not be with reference to the market value as on 1-1-1964 but should be with reference to the market value on the day ten years preceding the last day of the previous year in which the transfer takes place. (Para I-9.42)

156. A specific provision should be made to secure that, when an asset which fell outside the definition of capital asset when it was acquired by the assessee but which later came within the scope of the definition, is transferred, the cost of acquisition of the asset to the taxpayer should be taken to be the fair market value of the asset as on the date when it came within the definition. For determining whether the asset is a short-term or long-germ asset, the period of holding should be reckoned from the point of time when the asset came within the definition of capital asset. (Para I-9.43)

157. A clarificatory amendment should be made in Section 2(42A) to include the contingencies contemplated in Section 55(2)(v) for determining the period for which such capital assets are held by the taxpayer. (Para I-9.44)

158. The provision for grant of tax credit certificates under Section 280ZA may be discontinued and the capital gain arising in the circumstances mentioned therein be accorded treatment similar to that under Section 54D of the Act. (Para I-9.45)

59. Additional compensation or consideration received with reference to compulsory acquisition of capital assets should be deemed to be the income of the year in which it is received and not of the year of transfer of the capital asset. The taxpayer should be entitled to the exemption under Section 54E with reference to the date of receipt of such additional compensation. These provisions should likewise apply to cases where the consideration originally determined by the Central Government or the Reserve Bank is subsequently

enhanced. (Para I-9.47)

160. Where compensation for the compulsory acquisition of a capital asset is subsequently reduced, specific provision should be made to rectify the relevant past assessment. (Para I-9.48)

161. Provisions broadly corresponding to the removal of obstacles in relation to amalgamation of companies under the Income-tax Act should be extended to schemes of reconstruction as defined under the Income-tax Act. Accordingly, in relation to such schemes of reconstruction the law should expressly provide that there should be no tax liability of any kind and that the relevant allowances shall continue. (Para I-9.50)

Income from other Sources (Chapter 10)

162. It is only in cases where dividend does not constitute business income that it should fall to be assessed under the residuary head. The provision in Section 56(2)(i) bringing dividends to tax under the head 'Income from other sources' in all cases should be deleted. (Para I-10.2)

163. Dividend income other than interim dividends should be taxable in the year in which the dividend is distributed or paid. (Para I-10.5)

Income of other Persons Included in Assessee's Total Income (Chapter 11)

164. It is not advisable to substitute the present provisions for clubbing of incomes under Section 64(1) by the adoption of the family as a unit of assessment. (Para I-11.2)

165. Where a minor receives income as a beneficiary under a trust and such income is derived from the profits and against of a business carried on by the trustees in partnership with others, such income of the minor should be added to the income of the parent. The clubbing provisions in Section 64 should be extended to cover such cases. (Para I-11.4)

166. If the spouse is a beneficiary under a trust and the trustees joint in partnership with the individual the clubbing provisions at present contained in Section 64(1) (i) and *Explanation* 1 thereto should become applicable. (Para I-11.5)

167. Income referred to in Section 64(1) of the Act should in-

clude loss. (Para I-11.6)

168. Section 64(2) should apply to all cases of conversion of individual property into joint family property by a member otherwise than for adequate consideration whether by the act of impressing the property with the character of family property or by throwing it into the common stock of the family or by gift. (Para I-11.7)

Set off and Carry Forward of Losses (Chapter 12)

169. Losses relating to any source under any head should qualify for the benefit of carry forward and set off against income of subsequent years. (Para I-12.3)

170. The carry forward and set off of business losses should be allowed without any condition that the business or profession in which the loss was sustained should continue to be carried on by the taxpayer in the subsequent years. (Para I-12.5)

171. Losses relating to salary, house property, business or profession, other sources, and short-term capital assets (but excluding losses in speculation business, long-term capital losses and losses referred to in Section 74A) should be allowed to be carried forward to subsequent years and set off against income of those years under the same head of any other head in the eight years following the year in which the loss is incurred. (Para I-12.6)

172. Provision of a general right to carry back business losses is not favoured. (Para I-12.7)

173. During such time as a separate tax is levied on registered firms, the losses incurred by a registered firm should be carried forward and set off against the firm's income in the subsequent years, only for the purpose of ascertaining the tax payable by the firm. The existing provisions regarding apportionment of the loss amongst the partners with the corresponding rights of the partners to set off such loss or carry forward such loss in their personal assessments should continue. It would follow that the apportionment of the share of income/loss of the firm (as reduced by the registered firm's tax) among the partners in the subsequent year would have to be of the income/loss without the set off of the past losses because such losses would have been already apportioned among the partners in the earlier years. (Para I-12.8)

174. There is no need to make any further specific provision in the law in regard to the order of set off of various allowances and

losses. (Para I-12.9)

175. The Board's instructions regarding the order of set off of speculation losses and other losses against profits from speculation business may be suitably clarified in the Act itself. (Para I-12.10)

176. Return of loss field after the 30th of June or such extended time as may be allowed by the assessing authority or the Commissioner should not confer on the taxpayer the right of carry forward of losses under the provisions of Chapter VI of the Act. (Para I-12.11)

Deductions to be made in Computing Total Income (Chapter 13)

177. The following types of savings should be included for the purposes of the deduction under Section 80C:

(a) Deposits or cumulative time deposits with public sector banks for a period of not less than 10 years with facilities in the matter of borrowings and encashment, broadly comparable to those available in the case of 10-year or 15-year cumulative time deposits accounts in post offices;
(b) Single premium paid or a policy of insurance on the life of the taxpayer where the duration of the policy is for a minimum period of 10 years or life, without any option to obtain a cash payment by surrender or commutation, in the intervening period. (Para I-13.6)

178. The ceiling of Rs. 2400 and Rs. 600 laid down in Section 80D should be doubled to Rs. 4800 and Rs. 1200 respectively. (Para I-13.7)

179. Taxpayers who are not otherwise eligible to medical facilities provided by an employer should be entitled to a deduction of actual medical expenses incurred on themselves and members of their family, dependent on them upon a limit of 10 per cent of the gross total income or Rs. 5,000 per annum, whichever is lower. (Para I-13.8)

180. The benefit of Section 80E should be extended to all taxpayers rendering professional services mentioned therein. The monetary limit of deduction should be increased to Rs. 10,000 per annum. The condition that the unearned income referred to in sub-Section (6) should not exceed Rs. 10,000 to qualify for the benefit, should be deleted. (Para I-13.9)

181. The limit of Rs. 12,000 in respect of the gross total income in Section 80FF should be increased to Rs. 25,000. The limits of Rs. 1,000 and Rs. 500 in the said Section should also be increased to Rs. 2,000 and Rs. 1,000 respectively. (Para I-13.10)

182. The quantum of deduction under Section 80G should be raised to 100 per cent of donations of funds of a national character as specified at present in the Section or as may be notified by the Government from time to time. (Para I-13.12)

183. *Explanation* 3 to Section 80G should be deleted and thus charitable purpose for the purposes of Section 80G should not exclude religious purposes. (Para I-13.13)

184. Certificates under Section 80G should be issued by the Income-tax Officer having jurisdiction over the charitable trust. The certificate should be granted within a period of three months from the date of application. The grant of the certificate should continue to be merely a measure of administrative convenience and not be made a pre-condition for grant of the deduction under Section 80G. The order of the Income-tax Officer refusing to grant the certificate should be made appealable in the normal course. Once a certificate is granted its withdrawal or cancellation should not disqualify donations made prior to the withdrawal or cancellation for the purpose of the deduction under the Section. (Para I-13.14)

185. A new Section should be inserted after Section 80G to allow full deduction of contributions which any taxpayer may make to approved scientific research institutions. The deduction under this Section should only be available to assesses who do not have any income under the head "Profits and gains of business or profession." (Para I-13.15)

186. The new Section as recommended in para I-13.15 should cover also contributions by taxpayers to institutions referred to in Section 35CCA. (Para I-13.16)

187. The limit of Rs. 300 in Section 80GG should be raised to Rs. 400. The deduction should not be denied where the residential accommodation owned by the individual, his spouse, minor children or the Hindu undivided family is situated at a place other than the one where the taxpayer resides or conducts his business or profession. (Para I-13.17)

188. Section 80V should be extended to cover interest up to a limit of Rs. 10,000 per year paid by a taxpayer on borrowings from banks or financial institutions for acquiring, constructing, repairing,

renovating or reconstructing one residential house property used for the purposes of the taxpayer's own residence. (Para I-13.18)

189. Reference to Section 80VV in Section 37 should be omitted. The deduction under Section 80VV should operate in the case of assessees having on income chargeable under the head "Profits and gains of business of profession". (Para I-13.19)

190. The monetary limit of Rs. 5,000 referred to in Section 80VV should be removed. (Para I-13.20)

191. Deductions pertaining to income under specific heads should be placed along with the computation Sections relating to the relevant head of income. (Para I-13.21)

192. Where, however, the deductions under Chapter VIA are designed to reduce the effective rate of tax applicable to the income, such provisions should continue in the same Chapter. (Para I-13.22)

193. The deduction under Section 80J should be extended to aircraft in like manner as in the case of a ship. (Para I-13.25)

194. The provisions of Section 80J should be continued without any time limit and the condition regarding commencement of operations before a prescribed date should be deleted. (Para I-13.26)

195. In regard to the deduction under Section 80J, the percentage should be applied in full for each assessment year irrespective of the days of operations of the industrial undertaking, etc., and directions to this effect should be issued by the Board. (Para I-13.27)

196. The method of computing the capital employed for the purpose of the deduction under Section 80J should be laid down in the Section itself. (Para I-13.28)

197. The provisions for determination of capital employed for the purpose of the deduction under Section 80J should be so devised as to approximate closest to the concept of capital employed from the rational accounting point of view. In order to facilitate the work of the Income-tax Officer the capital employed in the industrial undertaking should be certified by an accountant as defined in the *Explanation* below Section 288(2) of the Act. (Para I-13.34)

198. Where the determination of the capital employed in a separate undertaking for the purposes of the deduction under Section 80J presents undue difficulty, it may be ascertained on a *pro rata* basis by ascertaining the proportion of the net fixed assets of the new undertaking to the total net fixed assets of the taxpayer and by applying such proportion to the total capital employed in the business. (Para I-13.35)

199. The quantum of the deduction under Section 80J should be increased to 10 per cent per annum of the capital employed, and this rate should be correspondingly adjusted as and when the bank rate is changed upwards or downwards. All the recommendations contained in Paras I-13.26 to I-13.36 apply equally to ships, hotels and to aircraft as recommended in Para I-13.25. (Para I-13.36)

200. The deduction under Section 80JJ should be specifically confined to cases where the activities referred in that Section are carried on in a rural area as defined in Section 35CC. (Para I-13.37)

201. The grant of tax concession under Section 80JJ in regard to the profits and gains of the business of live-stock breeding involving race horses should be restricted to only such of the race horses as are sold at public auctions. (Para I-13.38)

202. Deduction under Section 80M should be allowed with reference to the net income from dividends coming within the scope of this Section (i.e., after allowing expenses which are actually incurred for earning and realising the dividend income). (Para I-13.39)

203. Income exempt under Section 80MM should be the net income (i.e., after deduction of expenses incurred for the earning of that income) which is included in the gross total income, and not the gross receipts. A clarificatory amendment should be made in the Section to secure that the deduction will be allowed even where the technical know-how or services are supplied or rendered in connection with the setting up of the business. (Para I-13.40)

204. The Board's refusal to a grant approval under Section 80MM should be made appealable to the Central Tax Court recommended in Part II of this Report, and pending the establishment of the Central Tax Court the appeals against Board's order should lie to the Delhi High Court. The Board should have the power to admit an application for approval after the first day of October where sufficient reason is shown for the delay. (Para I-13.41)

205. The deduction under Section 80N should also be allowed only with reference to the net income by way of dividend referred to in that Section and not the gross amount. The deduction should not be confined to dividend on the shares originally allotted to the Indian company as mentioned in that Section but should cover also the dividends pertaining to any bonus shares subsequently allotted with reference to the original holding. There should be a provision for condonation of delay in the making of the application to the Board for the purpose of Section 80N and for appeal to the Central Tax

Court of the Delhi High Court against the Board's order refusing such approval. (Para I-13.42)

206. As in the case of Section 80MM and Section 80N, there should be provision for condonation of delay in making the application to the Board for approval of the agreement for the purpose of Section 80-O and for appeal to the Central Tax Court or the Delhi High Court against the Board's order refusing approval. The deduction under this Section should also be allowed only with reference to the net income and not the gross receipts. (Para I-13.43)

207. Where the income of co-operative societies is wholly exempted from tax under the provisions of Section 80P (2) (a) in relation to the activities of the society *vis-a-vis* its members, the same exemption should also be extended to an apex society which itself consists of a group of co-operative societies whose income is exempt under this Section. (Para I-13.44)

208. Section 80RR should be extended to members of learned professions as referred to in Section 10(23A) as also persons engaged in such cultural activities of the nature notified by the Central Government. (Para I-13.45)

Incomes Forming Part of Total Income on which no Income-tax is Payable and Other Provisions of the Act (Chapter 14)

209. Clause (iii) of Section 86 should be deleted and share of profit of a partner in an unregistered firm should not be included in the total income of the partner in his assessment. As under the existing law share of loss of a partner in an unregistered firm should not be apportioned to him and should not be available for set off against his other income. (Para I-14.4)

210. An association of persons should not be separately taxed on its income where it registers particulars of its constitution and the profit-sharing ratios of the members under a procedure similar to that of registration of firms outlined in the Interim Report. In circumstances where a firm would have been treated as an unregistered firm, an association of persons should be separately assessed and be taxed on its income at the flat rate of 60 per cent. As a corollary the provision in sub-clause (v) of Section 86 should be deleted. The loss of an association of persons which is registered and the loss of one which is separately assessed should, likewise, be treated similarly to the loss of a registered firm and the loss of an unregistered firm,

respectively. (Para I-14.8)

211. A body of individuals should not be taxed as a unit on its income where it registers particulars of its constitution and profit-sharing ratios of the individuals constituting the body, under a procedure similar to that recommended in thc case of an association of persons. In circumstances similar to those where an association of persons would be separately assessed and taxed at the flat rate of 60 per cent, a body of individuals should be separately assessed as a unit but not at the flat rate of 60 per cent but at the appropriate slab rates of tax. The loss of the body of individuals which is registered and the loss of one which is separately assessed as a unit should likewise be treated similarly to the loss of an association of persons which is registered and the loss of one which is assessed as a unit, respectively. Where a body of individuals is assessed as a unit, the individual members should not be again assessed in respect of any income falling to their hare in the income of the body. (Para I-14.10)

212. Where property is held in trust, and the trustees carry on a business, if an assessment is made in the status of body of individuals, taking the beneficiaries of the trust collectively. The recommendation made in the preceding paragraph would ensure that the tax is appropriately charged in the hands of the respective beneficiaries rather than on the body of individuals as a single independent entity. If the assessment is made on the trustees, they would only be representative assessees and thus be assessed in like manner and to the same extent as the beneficiaries in relation to their respective shares. (Para I-14.11)

213. The right to declare the constitution of the body of individuals and seek separate assessments of the members should not extend to the members of the body of individuals consisting only of husband and wife governed by the system of community of property in force in the Union Territories of Dadra and Nagar Haveli and Goa, Daman and Diu, if they are otherwise assessable as a body of individuals. (Para I-14.12)

214. An express statutory provision should be made that once a firm, association of persons or body of individuals is assessed, the income in question cannot again be assessed in the hands of the constituents of the firm, association of persons or body of individuals. However, if the individual members are first assessed, it should not be construed that the formalities of registration are automatically complied with and the Department should not be prevented from

framing an assessment on the firm, association of persons or body of individuals, as the case may be, in the circumstances where such an assessment would lie. However, in such a situation the prior assessment that may have been made on any of the individual members should be appropriately rectified as a mistake apparent from the record, and the tax, if any, collected should be duly refunded. In other words, the procedure of assessment ceases to be matter of choice for the Department and it is only according to the clear circumstances as outlined earlier that assessment would be made either on the firm, association of persons or body of individuals as a unit of assessment on the one hand or the individual members thereof on the other. (Para I-14.15)

215. Apart from such a specific provision to prevent double assessment, a general provision to prevent double assessment should be enacted, preferably in the charging Section itself. (Para I-14.16)

216. The provisions for clubbing incomes of the spouse of an individual and of a minor child of the individual, as obtaining in relation to a firm under Section 64(1)(i) and (iii), should be enacted correspondingly in relation to an association of persons which is engaged in a profit earning activity but not in relation to a body of individuals. (Para I-14.17)

217. The flat rate of tax to be charged under Section 164 should be 60 per cent in place of 65 per cent. As this rate of 60 per cent is the maximum rate recommended, the question of applying the alternative higher rate applicable to an association of persons would not arise. (Para I-14.25)

218. Sections 236 and 236A should be deleted. (Para I-14.27)

The Companies (Profits) Surtax Act, 1964 (Chapter 15)

219. The levy of surtax should not be merged with the income-tax on companies. The levy of surtax under the Surtax Act may be continued. (Para I-15.5)

220. The deductions to be made from the total income under Rule 1 of the rules for computing chargeable profits in the First Schedule should necessarily be restricted to the net amounts, if any, which remain included in the total income as computed under the Income-tax Act. (Para I-15.9)

221. Clause (xii) should be deleted from Rule 1 of the First Schedule. (Para I-15.10)

222. The provision in sub-clause (b) of clause (i) of Rule 2 of the First Schedule is redundant and this provision should be deleted. (Para I-15.11)

223. Rule 3 of the First Schedule should be deleted. (Para I-15.12)

224. The two terms, "reserve" and "provision", should be defined under the Surtax Act by adopting for that purpose the definitions in Part III of Schedule VI to the Companies Act, 1956. (Para I-15.14)

225. Rule 2 of the Second Schedule should be amended to secure that:

(a) the adjustment with reference to assets the income whereof is excluded is made on the basis of the book value of the said assets;

(b) Rule (2)(ii) refers only to amounts excluded in computing the capital under Rule 1(ii) and items (5), (6) and (7) referred to in the *Explanation* to Rule 1;

(c) Rule 2(ii) relates to the position as on the 1st day of the previous year. (Para I-15.18)

226. *Explanations* 1, 2 and 3 appearing after rule 2 of the Second Schedule should be placed at the end of the Second Schedule, expressly clarifying that they apply to all the rules of the Second Schedule. (Para I-15.19)

227. The application of Rule 3 of the Second Schedule in cases of amalgamation of two companies should entitle the amalgamated company to reckon the increase in the paid up share capital as from the date from which the amalgamation is effected and not only from the date of actual allotment. (Para I-15.20)

228. An *Explanation* should be added to Rule 4 of the Second Schedule clarifying that no diminution under Rule 4 is to be made with reference to the items of income in relation to which the company has been allowed deductions under Chapter VIA of the Income-tax Act. (Para I-15.24)

229. The deficiency in chargeable profits with reference to the standard deduction relating to a year should be allowed to be carried forward and set off in the following three years before the determination of the chargeable profits which attract surtax liability. (Para I-15.27)

230. The statutory deduction under the Surtax Act should be in-

creased from 15 per cent to 20 per cent of the capital. (Para I-15.29)

231. Surtax should be levied at the flat rate of 40 per cent on the amount by which the chargeable profits exceed the standard deduction. (Para I-15.30)

232. Continuation of any artificial condition about the composition of the capital as computed for surtax for the purposes of the proviso in the Third Schedule, is not favoured; the third condition in the said proviso, that paid-up capital subscribed in cash should be not less than 25 per cent of the 'capital', for applying the ceiling of 70 per cent, should be deleted. (Para I-15.31)

233. The provision for a ceiling on the total incidence of surtax and income-tax should be amended as under:

(a) a ceiling of 70 per cent on the total incidence should apply in the case of domestic companies which are widely-held (Section 108);
(b) a ceiling of 75 per cent on the total incidence should applying in the case of all other companies;
(c) the ceiling should not be made conditional upon fulfilment of any requirement about the composition of the capital as computed for the purposes of surtax. (Para I-15.32)

Wealth-Tax (Chapter 16)

234. Debts which are utilised for acquiring property on which wealth-tax is not charged either because such property falls outside the definition of 'assets' or it is specifically exempted from charge by virtue of Section 5 should alone be disqualified from deduction in determining the net wealth. (Para I-16.4)

235. Disputed demands for tax, penalty or interest under direct tax laws should be allowed as a debt on the valuation date so, however, that if the demand is altered as a result of appellate proceedings or otherwise, the assessment in question shall be appropriately rectified under Section 35 of the Act. (Para I-16.5)

236. The provision in item (b) of sub-clause (iii) of clause (m) of Section 2 should be deleted and the restriction on allowing tax demands remaining outstanding for more than 12 months should be removed. (Para I-16.6)

237. Suitable administrative instructions should be issued so as not to treat as an asset, claims for enhanced compensation which are

not finally decided as at the valuation date. In the alternative a clarificatory *Explanation* may be inserted in Section 2(m) of the Act. (Para I-16.7)

238. Sub-Section (1A) of Section 4 should be amended to cover property gifted by the individual to the Hindu undivided family. (Para I-16.8)

239. Sub-Section (3) of Section 4 may expressly be made applicable to assets included in the net wealth of the taxpayer under Section 4(1A) to allow deduction of debts refereable to such assets. (Para I-16.9)

240. The provision in sub-section (5A) of Section 4 regarding gifts by book entries should correspondingly be reflected in the Gift-tax Act as well, where also such a transaction should not be regarded as a gift. On the delivery of money or money's worth, the gift-tax and to warrant exclusion from the net wealth of the donor, subject to the other clubbing provisions. Such amendment should be made with retrospective effect from 1st April, 1976, when sub-section (5A) came into force. (Para I-16.10)

241. An express provision against double assessment should be made in the charging Section. (Para I-16.11)

242. Reliefs under the Wealth-tax Act should be by way of straight deductions and not by way of rebate at the average rate of tax. (Para I-16.12)

243. Exemptions left to notifications should be consolidated in a schedule to the Wealth-tax Act which may be altered by the Central Government under a specific authority conferred by the Act. (Para I-16.13)

244. Section 5(a)(xa) should be amended as under:

> "The amount of any outstanding fee in respect of professional service rendered by the assessee as a lawyer, solicitor chartered accountant, architect, engineer, medical practitioner or such other professional service as may be notified in this behalf by the Central Government in the Official Gazette, where the books of account are regularly maintained on the cash system of accounting". (Para I-16.24)

245. Such a provision should be made operative retrospectively from the date the Wealth-tax Act came into force, as it is largely clarificatory and it is also intended to settle the controversies in a

larger number of assessments which are unsettled. (Para I-16.25)

246. A specific provision should be introduced in Section 5 of the Wealth-tax Act to exempt from tax the net wealth of all such bodies, associations or institutions as enjoy exemption from income-tax on their income under the provisions of Section 10 of the Income-tax Act. (Para I-16.26)

Gift-Tax (Chapter 17)

247. Treating gifts as income under the Income-tax Act is not favoured; the Gift-tax Act should continue in its present form. (Para I-17.3)

248. Concepts which are common to the direct tax laws should, as far as possible, bear the same connotation under all the laws. The definition of 'company' as contained in the Income-tax Act should be made applicable for the purposes of the Gift-tax Act. (Para I-17.4)

249. An *Explanation* should be added at the end of Section 2(xii) clarifying that where there is *bona fide* change in the constitution of a firm engaged in one of the learned professions, it shall not be regarded as a gift. (Para I-17.6)

250. Another *Explanation* should be added at the end of Section 2(xii) clarifying that where a *bona fide* change in the constitution of a firm carrying on any business is made on grounds of commercial expediency, it shall not be regarded as a gift. (Para I-17.7)

251. No part of the premium paid on a life insurance policy effected under the Married Women's Property Act should be regarded as a gift. (Para I-17.8)

252. A transfer by way of gift by an individual to the Hindu undivided family of which he is a member should be treated in like manner as property impressed with the character of joint family property or thrown into the common stock of the family under Section 4(2) of the Gift-tax Act. (Para I-17.9)

253. Section 18 of the Gift-tax Act should expressly permit the taxpayer to compute the advance gift-tax by taking into account the rebate on stamp duty under Section 18A. (Para I-17.12)

254. The provisions of Section 18A should be amended to allow full credit for the stamp duty paid on an instrument of gift against the gift-tax payable in every case without any limitation. (Para I-17.13)

Valuation of Assets (Chapter 18)

255. There is no reason why the value of assets by and large should be determined differently under the Wealth-tax Act from that under the Gift-tax and Estate duty Acts. There is need for evolving, as far as possible, a uniform system of valuation, as far as possible, a uniform system of valuation under these laws in view of the fact that the basic concept of price in the open market is common. (Para I-18.2)

256. Any rules which may be framed for determining the market value of assets should as far as possible be made applicable to all the direct tax statutes. (Para I-18.5)

257. For the purposes of valuation of unquoted equity shares of companies:

(a) Rule 1D of the Wealth-tax Rules should be deleted and in its place fresh rules should be notified by the Government after consultation with the Institute of Chartered Accountants of India who may evolve guidelines for valuation;

(b) the rules/guidelines should be framed separately for companies in four different categories, viz., (i) industrial, (ii) investment, (iii) trading, and (iv) others, including service companies;

(c) the auditors of the companies whose shares are not quoted should be required to furnish a statement, to be attached to the audited statements of accounts, showing the valuation of the shares of the company as at the balance-sheet date with a certificate to the effect that the value has been determined in accordance with the rules framed under the direct tax laws;

(d) the statement of valuation should be reasonably explicit so that the figures adopted on the statement are readily verifiable with reference to the audited statements of account and the process by which the value of the share determined is reasonably clear; adjustments which may be made by the auditor should be clearly reflected in the statement;

(e) the value as determined in the statement of valuation by the company's auditor should be adopted by the assessing officer for all the direct tax laws unless the officer is of the opinion that the value needs to be modified to the extent the valuation is not in conformity with the rules notified under the Act;

(f) the value to be adopted on the basis of the aforesaid statement should relate to the date of the balance-sheet either coincident with of immediately preceding the valuation date. (Para I-18.12)

258. Rules 10(2) and 10(4) of the Gift-tax Rules should be deleted. (Para I-18.13)

259. Rule 1C(1) of the Wealth-tax Rules should be amended to provide for the normal yield on preference shares to be one per cent over the rate notified by the Controller of Capital Issues under the Capital Issues (Exemption) Order. (Para I-18.14)

260. The rate of interest under clause (c) of the *Explanation* to Rule 1B(1) of the Wealth-tax Rules should be equivalent to the rate of interest allowed by public sector banks on long-term fixed deposits of more than 5 years duration. (Para I-18.15)

261. Agricultural lands including plantations may be valued by capitalisation of the income therefrom at rates to be notified by the Board. (Para I-18.18)

262. House property should be valued on the basis of capitalisation of income as recommended in the Interim Report, for all direct tax laws. No separate valuation of development potential of the property should be made. However, open land and surplus land should be separately valued on the basis of estimation of the open market value. (Para I-18.20)

263. Rules 2A to 2F of the Wealth-tax Rules should be substituted by rules which provide for the valuation of a business concern as a whole on the basis of the balance-sheet drawn up in accordance with the method of accounting and the determination of the excess of assets over liabilities as per such balance-sheet. The only adjustments which need be made should be those which the circumstances of the case may require, such as adjustments for any departure from the method of accounting, or straight write offs of assets, like capital assets for scientific research or excessive write off of depreciation beyond that permitted under the tax laws. No adjustments of hypothetical nature or adjustments to individual items as at present contemplated in Rules 2A to 2F should be made. The taxpayer should also not be entitled to deductions for liabilities like gratuity, bonus, etc., which remain unprovided in accordance with the method of accounting. In particular, no adjustments which amount to a change in the method of accounting with reference to which income

is computed should be made. However, assets which do not really pertain to the business should be separately valued as under Rule 2G. (Para I-18.24)

264. Recommendations in the preceding paragraph should be regarded as applicable to the case of the learned professions as well and the global valuation as contemplated in Section 7(2)(a) should likewise be expressly made applicable to such professions. (Para I-18.26)

265. The valuation of interest in business for the purposes of gift-tax and estate duty should be on the basis of capitalisation of the income. The value should be determined on the global valuation basis by capitalisation of the income of the business leaving the actual computation of the income as well as the rate of capitalisation to the valuer and the assessing officer. In no case, however, the value of the business should be taken at a figure below the value of the net tangible assets as shown in the balance-sheet, the justification being that in making the valuation, negative value of intangibles should be ignored. (Para I-18.27)

266. Rule 2 of the Wealth-tax Rules should clarify that in allocating the net wealth of a firm among the partners, the interest of each partner would be deemed to comprise of the assets qualifying for exemption under Section 5(1) of the Wealth-tax Act and other assets on a proportionate basis. The some procedure should also apply in allocating the net wealth of an association of persons or body of individuals among its members. (Para I-18.29)

267. Rule 10(1) of the Gift-tax Rules which prescribes the cash surrender value as the value of a policy of insurance is fair and reasonable. (Para I-18.30)

268. Where the period for which a gift is not revocable is less than one year, the actual income for the period up to the date of revocation should be discounted for determining the present value of the gift. (Para I-18.31)

PART II

Introduction

1. A consolidated code should be enacted laying down uniform procedures for the management and administration of the four direct taxes, viz., income-tax, wealth-tax, gift-tax and surtax on company

profits. Estate duty legislation should, however, continue to remain separate as a self-contained statute. (Paras II-0.1 to 0.3)

2. Integration of the procedural and administrative provisions of direct tax laws does not mean that there should be common proceedings for the levy of these taxes in any given case. While the proceedings for the assessment and collection of these taxes in any given case should remain separate, they should as far as possible be taken up and completed simultaneously, so as to save the time of the Department as also of the taxpayer. (Para II-0.6)

Preliminary (Chapter 1)

3. The title of the proposed enactment consolidating the procedural provisions of the direct tax laws should be "The Direct Taxes Management and Administration Act". (Para II-1.2)

4. When the Indian Income-tax Act, 1922 was replaced by the Income-tax Act, 1961, the transitional provisions led to considerable problems and litigation which could not be totally obviated or resolved even by the exercise of the power to remove difficulties vested in the Central Government under Section 298. To avoid such difficulties, the old law should continue upto and inclusive of a specified assessment year, say, assessment year 1979-80. The new provisions should apply for and from the immediately following assessment year, i.e., 1980-81. Whenever the Government desires to adopt the new procedure even for old proceedings, e.g., provision of appeal to the Central Tax Court, this should be achieved by appropriate amendments to the old law. (Paras II-1.3 to 1.5)

5. There should be a specific provision in the Management Act spelling out the scope of the Act and making it applicable to the assessment and collection of the following direct taxes, namely:

(1) Income-tax;
(2) Wealth-tax;
(3) Gift-tax; and
(4) Surtax on company profits.

If, in future, the Government considers it necessary to levy any other direct tax, the procedure for the assessment and collection of such tax should also be governed by the Management Act. (Para II-1.6)

6. The preliminary chapter of the Management Act should contain definitions of various terms having relevancy for the purposes of the procedural provisions of the tax laws. There should also be a specific provision that words which are not defined in the Management Act, but are defined in the substantive enactment would have the same meaning for the purposes of the Management Act and, correspondingly, there should be a similar provision in the substantive enactment to the effect that words which are defined in the Management Act but not in the substantive enactment will have the same meaning for the purposes of the substantive enactment also. (Para II-1.7)

Administration (Chapter 2)

7. In the context of integrating the procedural provisions of the different tax laws, redesignation of the authorities administering them has become inevitable. This is the opportune time for rationalising the designations of the various direct taxes authorities. The existing cadre of Assistant Commissioners should be redesignated as Deputy Commissioners and Income-tax Officers, Class-I, in the Senior scale, should be designated as Assistant Commissioners. Suitable provisions should be made in the law so as to enable Assistant Commissioners (new designation) to perform all the functions and exercise all the powers of the assessing authorities. (Paras II-2.4 and 2.5)

8. The classification of assessment charges into senior-scale charges and other charges should be brought about and where a Class-II Officer is required to hold a senior-scale charge, he should be appropriately compensated for the higher responsibility that he is required to shoulder. (Para II-2.6)

9. The association of the Inspecting Assistant Commissioner in the process of assessment, through all its stages, is necessary not only in important cases, but also in all scrutiny cases. The appeals arising from all such cases are bound to raise important issues of law and fact, meriting consideration by more experienced and senior officers. Appeals against orders of the Direct Taxes Officer, Assistant Commissioner and Deputy Commissioner (new designations) should lie to the Commissioner (Appeals). (Para II-2.7)

10. Deputy Commissioners should be deployed exclusively on supervising, guiding and directing the work of assessing officers.

(Para II-2.9)

11. It is not necessary to retain the cadre of Additional Commissioners as one of tax authorities. (Para II-2.10)

12. A cadre of Regional Commissioners should be created having the status of Additional Secretary to the Government of India. Regional Commissioners will be responsible for administratively controlling, coordinating and supervising the work of Commissioners in their respective regions and accountable to the Board for the overall performances of their regions. They should also perform the functions of the Director of Inspection and control the activities of the officers of the intelligence wing for the Region. (Para II-2.11 and 2.12)

13. The Chairman of the Central Board of Direct Taxes should have the status of a Secretary to the Government of India. The Board should have adequate staff assistance and should be provided with personnel having necessary technical background and experience. (Para II-2.16)

14. The institution of Valuation Officers as statutory authorities under the direct tax laws should be done away with. If necessary, the services of Valuation Officers may be utilised by the Government in a purely advisory capacity in suitable cases. (Para II-2.19)

15. The executive cadre of the Income-tax Department should comprise the following authorities:

(1) Central Board of Direct Taxes,
(2) Regional Commissioners,
(3) Directors of Inspection,
(4) Commissioners of Direct Taxes,
(5) Commissioners (Appeals),
(6) Deputy Commissioners of Direct Taxes,
(7) Assistant Commissioners of Direct Taxes,
(8) Direct Taxes Officers,
(9) Inspectors of Direct Taxes.

(Para II-2.20)

16. The manpower assistance to the officers at various levels in the Department should be adequately augmented and they should be provided with adequate office space, storage space, equipments and aids. (Para II-2.21)

17. When an advance ruling is given by the Board in the case of any assesses, the Board should have the power to issue instructions to

the subordinate authorities to ensure compliance with such advance ruling. This will necessitate the omission of clause (a) of the proviso to Section 119(1). (Para II-2.22)

18. The law should be amended, if necessary, to enable the Board to issue directions to subordinate authorities for granting relief even after the expiry of the statutory time limit in cases where the claim for any exemption, deduction, refund or any other relief is made by the assessee within the specified time limit. (Para II-2.23)

19. The Central Government and the Board should have the power to condone the delay in making an application to them for approval, etc., under various provisions of the tax laws. (Para II-2.24)

20. It is not desirable to make any radical change in the existing pattern of jurisdiction so as to vest in the Board the overall jurisdiction for assessment and collection following the pattern obtaining in USA and Canada. (Para II-2.26)

21. No major changes are necessary in the powers of tax authorities. (Para II-2.27)

22. The Commissioner's power to delegate the functions of the Income-tax Officer should be limited so as to restrict such delegation to an Inspector of Income-tax only and not to any members of the ministerial staff. Further, the Commissioner should have no power to delegate functions under Sections 131, 132, 132A and 132B even to Inspectors. (Para II-2.28)

23. The provision enabling the Board do delegate the power to authorise a search to a Deputy Director of Inspection or an Inspecting Assistant Commissioner should be deleted. (Para II-2.29)

24. The powers of search should not be extended for the purpose of gift tax. (Para II-2.30)

25. There should be a time limit of, say, six months for the disposal of applications under Section 132(11) by the notified authority. (Para II-2.31)

26. The provisions relating to the power of calling for information under Section 133, powers of survey under Section 133A and powers of inspection under Section 134 may be incorporated in the Management Act. (Para II-2.33)

27. The provisions of Section 135 authorising the superior authorities to exercise the power of making enquiries vested in the Income-tax Officer duplicate provisions in other Sections and need not be retained in the Management Act. (Para II-2.34)

28. Section 136 deeming proceedings before the Income-tax

authorities as judicial proceedings for certain purposes and Section 138 relating to disclosure of information may be included in the Management Act so s to apply uniformly to all direct taxes. (Para II-2.35)

29. Sections 285A and 285B of the Income-tax Act, prescribing certain information returns may be incorporated in the chapter — "Administration" in the Management Act. (Para II-2.36)

30. All penalties such as those under Sections 285A and 285B should be dealt with in the Chapter on penalties and, further, the designated officer, to whom such information is required to be furnished, should be empowered to levy the penalty. (Para II-2.37)

31. The material date for the purposes of Section 285B should be the date of expiry of 30 days from the end of the financial year to which the information relates or 30 days from the date of grant of the certificate of fitness for public exhibition of the film by the Board of Film Censors, whichever is earlier. (Para II-2.38)

32. Information under Section 285B should be required to be furnished in respect of expenses debitable to the cost of production of the film. The limit of Rs. 5,000 should be raised to Rs. 10,000 and information should be required to be furnished of all payments in respect of such expenses, aggregating to Rs. 10,000, made to any person during a financial year. (Para II-2.38)

33. The format of the statement required to furnished under Section 285B, prescribed under the 121A (form No. 52A) should be changed to make the requirements of the Section clearer. (Para II-2.39)

34. Once the several statements required at present to be furnished by persons responsible for paying interest or dividends are replaced by a consolidated provision in the Chapter dealing with deduction of tax at source, it will not be necessary to include the provisions of Sections 285 and 286 in the chapter—"Administration". (Para II-2.40)

35. Publication of names of assesses on whom penalties have been imposed should be made only after the penalty has been upheld by the Tribunal or it has otherwise become final, and not earlier. (Para II-2.41)

36. The provision in Section 294A may be omitted if it no longer necessary to retain it for rescinding any exemption of modification already made. If it is considered necessary to retain the provision it may be included in the Chapter—"Administration" in the Manage-

ment Act. (Para II-2.42)

37. A consolidated provision authorising the Board to frame rules for the various purposes of the direct taxes may be incorporated in the Management Act. Care should be taken, while drafting the rules having substantive implications, to ensure that they apply only prospectively. Frequent amendments to the Income-tax Rules unsettle the smooth administration of the Act. All amendments to the rules should be made only once in a financial year and notified by the September so as to operate from the first April of the following year. Where an interim amendment becomes unavoidable, it should be fully justified with adequate reasons as to why the change could not be made part of the annual amendments to the Rules. (Paras II-2.43 and 2.44)

38. Section 298 dealing with the power of the Central Government to remove difficulties should be placed in the Chapter—"Administration". (Para II-2.45)

Pre-Assessment Payment of Taxes (Chapter 3)

39. The provisions for deduction of tax at source already cover a wide area and it is not necessary to extend the area of their operation any further. (Para II-3.2)

40. Where salary is paid in arrears, specific provision should be made enabling the employer to take into account the relief to which the employee is entitled while deducting tax at source from payments on account of arrears of salary. (Para II-3.3)

41. The administrative practice of taking into account the deduction under Section 80C and that under Section 80G, with reference to contributions to certain specified funds, while deducing the tax at source from salaries, should be given statutory basis by suitably amending the relevant provision. (Para II-3.4)

42. The element of salary income referred to in Rule 6 in Part A of the Fourth Schedule, as modified in the light of the suggestions in Part I of the Report should be clearly brought within the purview of deduction of tax at source by making an appropriate provision in Section 192. (Para II-3.5)

43. The limit for deduction of tax under Section 194C should be raised from Rs. 5,000 to Rs. 25,000. (Para II-3.6)

44. Deduction of tax from payments by way of insurance commission should be required to be made only where the payment to

any one person during a financial year exceeds Rs. 1,500. (Para II-3.7)

45. The time limit for remittances of the tax deducted at source to the credit of the Central Government may uniformly be prescribed as one month following the end of the month in which the deduction is made, without linking it to the date of obtaining the challan for making the remittance. In cases where interest payments to residents, payments to contractors and payments by way of insurance commission are credited to the account of the payee in the books of the payer, being a person carrying on a business or profession, the existing provision permitting remittance of the tax deducted within two months of the close of the payer's accounting year, may be allowed to continue. The facility now allowed in certain cases to remit the tax deducted at source at quarterly intervals should be withdrawn. (Para II-3.8)

46. Credit for tax deducted at source in respect of any income should be allowed in the assessment year in which such income is subjected to tax. In a case where deduction of tax is made in a year later than that in which the income is subjected to tax, the credit should be allowed by rectification of the assessment within the normal period of limitation or within one year from the end of the financial year in which the tax is deducted, whichever is later. (Para II-3.9)

47. The existing arrangements for keeping a watch over deductions from various categories of payments and the remittance of the amounts deducted to the credit of the Central Government need improvement to make them more effective. Central monitoring should be expended to cover all deductions of tax at source. Statutory returns including those required under Sections 285 and 286, should be required to be submitted only at yearly intervals on the existing pattern of salary returns and the necessary changes should be made in the law to require such returns to be submitted to a designated Income-tax Officer instead of to the several Income-tax Officers assessing the payers. Suitable arrangements should be made for Government departments, both at the Centre and the State, to submit returns of tax deducted at source from payments of salaries payments to contractors, payment of interest, lottery winnings, etc., and arrangements should be made for checking these centrally as in the case of returns furnished by payers other than Government. (Para II-3.10)

48. Suitable provision should be made in the law to enable the

person responsible for deducting tax at source to obtain refund of any excess payment made by him to Government on this account from the Income-tax Officer dealing with this subject, independently of his own assessment, subject to necessary safeguards. (Para II-3.11)

49. The law should bc properly amended to bring out the real intention behind the recommendations relating to the provisions for payment of advance tax, contained in the Interim Report, which is to simplify the procedures relating to payment of such tax and elimination of unproductive work. (Para II-3.12)

50. The provision in the Gift-tax Act for payment of tax in advance within 15 days of the taxpayer's making the gift may be included in the Management Act without change. (Para II-3.13)

Assessment Procedure (Chapter 4)

51. By integrating the procedures for assessment and refund under the different direct tax laws, any variations in the procedure would get eliminated and a uniform procedure will become applicable for the purposes of all the direct taxes. (Para II-4.1)

52. In the Management Act, a tax return should be defined as referring to a return of income or a return of wealth or a return of gifts or a return of chargeable profits or any combination of two or more of such returns. (Para II-4.2)

53. There should be a single provision in the law requiring the filing of a tax return if the total income/net wealth/taxable gifts/chargeable profits of a person exceeded the maximum amount which is not chargeable to tax or if a person desires to have an assessment made of his total income, net wealth, taxable gifts, or chargeable profits or to have any loss, unabsorbed allowance or deficiency computed and carried forward to future years or to avail of the exemption provided in the case of charitable or religious trusts or to claim refund of any pre-assessment tax paid by him or on his behalf. (Para II-4.3)

54. Statutory time limits are important inasmuch as their non-observance entails certain consequences by way of interest, penalty, prosecution, etc. While the taxpayer should suffer these consequences if he fails to furnish the return within the time limits specified in the statute, the non-observance of the time limit should not by itself invalidate the return. The law should make the following provisions in regard to filing of tax returns:

(1) In order to ensure uniformity, tax returns should be required to be filed by 30th of June in each year.

(2) The law should specifically provide that returns filed after 30th June will nevertheless be valid in law. Subject to the consequences laid down in the law, the taxpayer should have the right to file a tax return at any time before an assessment is made for the relevant year without any outer time limit.

(3) For delays in filing the tax return beyond the 30th of June and until 30th of September, the taxpayer should be required to 'buy time'. The cost of buying time should be calculated with reference to the net tax and the rate of interest should be one per cent per month.

(4) Where a return is field after 30th September of the assessment year, the assessment should not ordinarily be made without scrutiny of accounts. However, such a return may be accepted as correct without scrutiny if the Commissioner so directs provided the return is filed before the last day of the assessment year. If a return is filed after the close of the assessment year, it should invariably be subjected to scrutiny.

(5) Where the return is delayed beyond the 30th September of the assessment year, the tax payer should become liable to pay penalty in the circumstances stated in the Chapter on Penalties.

(6) If the return is not furnished before the close of the assessment year, the assessee should also become liable to prosecution in the circumstances stated in the chapter 'Offences and prosecutions'.

(7) The assessee should forfeit the right to carry forward of loss, unabsorbed allowances, deficiency, etc., if the return is not furnished before the expiry of the assessment year. Similarly, an assessee claiming exemption from tax available to charitable or religious trusts, etc., should also be rendered ineligible for such exemption if the return is not field before the expiry of the assessment year. The Commissioner should, however, the empowered to relax this condition in appropriate cases.

An exception will have to be made in the case of a return for the purpose of surtax where the company wants to claim the set-off of a deficiency against the chargeable profits for a subsequent year.

The company should be required to file a return of such deficiency only when it makes sufficient profits which attract liability to surtax in a subsequent year and not earlier.

(8) An assessee who claims refund of pre-paid taxes should be eligible for such refund only if the return is field within a period of two years from the end of the relevant assessment year. The existing powers of the Board to authorise admission of belated claims should continue. (Para II-4.4)

55. Sub-Section (1A) of Section 139 exempting certain categories of salaried taxpayers from the obligation to file returns should be deleted. (Para II-4.5)

56. The working of the system of permanent account numbers should be improved. Numbers should be allotted to all taxpayers who have so far applied for them and there should be arrangement for prompt allotment of such numbers to those who apply for them in future; the directories of taxpayers should be updated; the Department should ensure that all communications sent to the taxpayer carry his permanent account number; and, lastly, the penalty for non-compliance should not attach to minor defaults such as failure to quote the permanent account number on routine correspondence like reminders, etc., sent by the taxpayer to the Department. (Para II-4.6)

57. The existing provisions of Section 140 should be modified to permit the tax return in the case of a company being signed by the holder of a power-of-attorney in a case where there is no managing director or other director stationed in India or by the liquidator in the case of a company in liquidation. (Para II-4.8)

58. Suitable alternative provisions should be made to permit the return being signed by any other person who manages the affairs of a Hindu undivided family in a case where there is no adult member of the family. (Para II-4.9)

59. Return forms pertaining to a particular assessment year should be used only for that assessment year and not for any earlier assessment year, and the assessment year to which the particular form pertains should be printed in bold figures on the first page of the form so as to facilitate easy identification. (Para II-4.12)

60. Provisions for payment of tax on self-assessment before the furnishing of the return should be extended to gift-tax and surtax and

the existing provisions in the Wealth-tax Act and Surtax Act for the making of a provisional assessment should be deleted. In all cases, the challan for payment of taxes on self-assessment should be required to be attached to the relevant tax return, in the absence of which the return should be considered to be invalid. Further, as recommended in the Interim Report (Para 7.18) interest payable for delay in furnishing the tax return beyond 30th June should be required to be paid along with the tax on self-assessment. (Para II-4.14)

61. Interest on excess payment of advance-tax should be calculated with reference to the tax payable on the basis of the income returned and only up to the date of furnishing the return or 30th June of the assessment year, whichever is earlier. At the same time, with a view to expediting the refund of excess advance-tax paid, for any delay in granting the refund beyond three months from the end of the month in which the return is field or 1st October of the assessment year whichever is later, interest at 12 per cent per annum should be allowed up to the end of the month preceding the month in which the refund voucher is actually issued to the assessee. (Para II-4.15)

62. The provisions of Section 142 of the Income-tax Act should be incorporated in the Management Act and made applicable on a uniform basis to all direct taxes. (Para II-4.17)

63. The process of assessment by acceptance of returns should be extended also for the purpose of wealth tax and gift-tax subject to guidelines to be issued by the Board. (Para II-4.18)

64. The procedure for examination of accounts and other materials before completion of an assessment should apply uniformly to all the taxes. (Para II-4.19)

65. The provisions relating to *ex parte* assessments should be incorporated in the Management Act. (Para II-4.20)

66. The provision for the reopening of an *ex parte* assessment by the Income-tax Officer on the application of the assessee need not be incorporated in the Management Act. (Para II-4.22)

67. The provisions of Section 144A should be made uniformly applicable to all direct taxes. (Para II-4.24)

68. The provisions of Section 144B should be deleted. (Para II-4.25)

69. The Valuation Officer should not function as a statutory authority under the Wealth-tax Act or the other direct tax enactments but his role, wherever, necessary, should be merely advisory. The provisions of Section 16A of the Wealth-tax Act and connected

provisions in the other direct tax laws should be deleted. (Para II-4.26)

70. The assessing officer should be empowered to issue a notice calling for a return for the purpose of income-tax, wealth-tax and gift-tax in cases where such return has not been furnished by the assessee by 30th September of the assessment year. Such a notice may be issued at any time up to the expiry of eight years from the end of the relevant assessment year, without the need to obtain the approval of the Commissioner in this behalf. (Para II-4.27)

71. The assessing officer should have the power to call for a return for the purpose of income-tax, wealth-tax or gift-tax even after the expiry of eight years, but before the expiry of sixteen years, after obtaining the Board's approval for the purpose. The minimum limit for the issue of such notice after the eight year period should remain at Rs. 50,000 for the purposes of income-tax and it may be placed at Rs. 5 lakhs for the purpose of wealth-tax and Rs. 50,000 for the purposes of gift-tax. (Para II-4.28)

72. The assessing officer should have the power to call for a return for the purposes of surtax at any time before the expiry of eight years from the end of the relevant assessment year or one year from the end of the financial year in which the assessment or reassessment of the company for the purposes of income-tax is completed or such assessment is modified as a result of appeal, revision or rectification whichever is later. The monetary limit of Rs. 50,000 and the requirement of the Board's approval should not apply even in a case where the notice is issued after the expiry of eight years from the end of the relevant assessment year. (Para II-4.29)

73. The time limits for initiating action for reopening of completed assessments should on the pattern of the existing provisions in the Income-tax Act and should uniformly apply to wealth-tax and gift-tax as well. (Para II-4.31)

74. While incorporating the existing provision in Section 14 of the Surtax Act in the Management Act it should be extended to cover a case where the surtax assessment needs modification in consequence of a reassessment of the company for the purposes of income tax. The period of four years for such modification should in all cases, be reckoned from the last day of the financial year in which the event necessitating the modification of the surtax assessment happened. The provisions for reopening a surtax assessment independently of the income-tax assessment should be on par with the cor-

responding provisions applicable in respect of other direct taxes. (Para II-4.32)

75. The provisions in Section 143(2) of the Income tax Act which enable the Income-tax Officer to reopen an assessment, completed by accepting the return, with the approval of the Inspecting Assistant Commissioner or on the request of the taxpayer should be deleted. A suitable *Explanation* may be added to the provision dealing with the reopening of completed assessments on the basis of information, clarifying the scope of the word "information". (Para II-4.33)

76. The existing provision, requiring the approval of the Commissioner for reopening a completed assessment under the Income-tax Act after the expiry of four years but within eight years from the end of the assessment year, on the ground that there was failure on the part of the assessee in disclosing fully and truly all material facts necessary for the assessment of his income, should continue and apply uniformly for wealth-tax and gift-tax as well even though at present, there is no such provision for the purposes of those taxes. (Para II-4.34)

77. There should be a provision for initiating proceedings for reassessment of escaped income, wealth or gifts beyond eight years up to a period of 16 years, on the ground of the taxpayer's failure to disclose fully and truly all material facts necessary for assessment subject to the approval of the Board and also subject to the minimum monetary limit of Rs. 50,000 in respect of escaped income or taxable gifts and Rs. 5 lakhs in respect of escaped wealth. (Para II-4.35)

78. In cases where proceedings are initiated for reassessment of escaped income, wealth, etc., there should be no insistence on the submission of a fresh return but the assessee should be given the right to file a return at any time before the reassessment is completed if he so wishes. Further, the assessing officer should intimate to the assessee clearly the reasons for reassessment and give the assessee a reasonable opportunity to state his objections, if any, to the reopening of the assessment. The assessee should, for this purpose, be allowed a minimum time of 30 days. (Para II-4.36)

79. For initiating action for assessment or reassessment in the circumstances mentioned in Section 150, there should be a time limit of one year from the end of the financial year in which the order in appeal, reference or revision is received by the assessing officer. (Para II-4.37)

80. The provision in Section 152(1) need not be repeated in the Management Act. (Para II-4.38)

81. The provisions of Section 152(2) should be made applicable to all types of reassessments under all the four Acts on a uniform basis. The right under this Section should be available to the assessee not withstanding that the might have field an appeal against the original assessment provided that such appeal has since been disposed of and the matter has become final. (Para II-4.39)

82. A uniform time limit of two years for completion of assessments should be laid down in the Management Act for all the taxes. In respect of surtax, however, an alternative time limit of one year from the end of the financial year in which the income-tax assessment is completed, if later, will have to be provided. To obviate undue burden on the Department in having to deal with a large number of pending assessments under the Wealth-tax Act and Gift-tax Act getting barred by time in one year, the reduction of the time limit from four years to two years should be staggered suitably. Similarly, in respect of surtax where there is no time limit at present for completion of assessments, suitable staggering should be provided while imposing the time limit recommended. (Para II-4.40)

83. For all the four direct taxes, extended time limit with reference to the date of filing the return should be available up to the last day of the financial year following that in which the return is filed. Such extension should be available only with reference to the date of filing the first return and not any revised return. There should be no extension of the time limit with reference to the consideration whether or not the case attracts penalty for concealment. (Para II-4.41)

84. For completion of assessment, reassessment or recomputation in pursuance of proceedings initiated by issue of a notice under Section 148 on the basis of fresh information, without there being any default on the part of the assessee in furnishing the return or in disclosing material facts, the extending period of the year from the date of service of the notice should be counted from the last day of the financial year in which the notice is served. (Para II-4.42)

85. The time limit under Section 153(2A) for completing assessments/reassessments in consequence of or to give effect to any finding or direction contained in any order in appeal, revision, etc., should remain as at present. For completing a partner's assessment on the basis of the assessment of the firm under Section 147 there

should be an extended time limit of one year from the end of the financial year in which the assessment of the firm was made instead of there being no time limit as at present. (Para II-4.43)

86. Where the assessee claims in writing that the whole or any part of the proceedings should be reopened and he should be reheard by the successor in office because of the change in incumbent, the limitation under clause (i) of *Explanation* 1 to Section 153, should expire on the last day of the financial year following that in which such claim is made by the assessee. (Para II-4.44)

87. In a case where the assessment proceeding is stayed by an order or injunction of any court, the limitation under clause (ii) of *Explanation* 1 to Section 153 should expire on the last day of the financial year following that in which the stay order is vacated. (Para II-4.45)

88. In the light of the recommendation for the deletion of Section 144B, the provision in clause (iv) of *Explanation* 1 to Section 153 should be deleted. The time limits under clauses (iii) and (v) of the said *Explanation* should get extended up to the last day of the financial year next following that in which the report of audit is furnished by the assessee or, as the case may be, the decision of the Settlement Commission rejecting the application, etc., is received by the Commissioner. (Para II-4.46)

89. The assessment of deficiency for surtax purposes should be made simultaneously with the surtax assessment in which the deficiency is required to be set off. (Para II-4.47)

90. Persons carrying on a profession should be required to maintain only certain basic records such as a professional case diary, a fee register, a cash book (which may not necessarily be balanced daily), a journal, if the accounts are maintained on mercantile basis, and a ledger. In conjunction with the bank pass book, etc., these records should provide quite sufficient material for the computation of their income for purposes of assessment. (Para II-4.49)

91. Books of account and other documents relating to any business or profession coming within the scope of Section 44AA should be required to be retained for a minimum period of eight years. (Para II-4.51)

92. The procedural provisions of Chapter XI of the Income-tax Act relating to levy of additional income tax on a closely-held company should be incorporated in the Management Act in the Chapter dealing with assessment procedure. (Para II-4.51)

93. The Management Act should provide for the issue of a notice by the assessing officer to the company before starting the proceedings for the levy of additional tax. Such notice should be issued by the assessing officer soon after the completion of the relevant assessment or reassessment of the company. (Para II-4.52)

94. In the light of recommendation in the Interim Report (Para 6.11) that provisions relating to levy of additional income-tax should be restricted in their application to closely-held investment companions only, the provisions of Section 107A will be otiose and may be omitted. (Para II-4.53)

95. The powers of rectification of all tax authorities and the Tribunal should be made uniform and apply to all orders passed by them. The existing provisions laying down the time limit for rectificatory action at four years from the date of passing of the order sought to be rectified, should in the interest of uniformity, certainty and erase in keeping track of dates of limitation, be amended so as to permit rectification within a period of four years from the end of the financial year in which the order sought to be rectified was passed. (Para II-4.54)

96. The extended time limit of four years provided in the various sub-sections of Section 155 should be made to expire at the end of the four years from the last day of the financial year in which the event which attracts the amendment happened. (Para II-4.55)

97. Penalties for different types of default should be dealt with in separate Sections of the Management Act. (Para II-5.2)

98. Any delay in furnishing the tax return beyond 30th September of the assessment year should attract penalty at the rate of one per cent of the gross tax, i.e., tax determined on assessment without giving credit for prepaid taxes, for every month of default. There should also be no ceiling on the amount of penalty payable for delaying the tax return so that a person who fails to furnish the tax return for several years may be required to pay an adequate price for his delinquency. The penalty provisions should apply uniformly to all the four direct taxes. (Para II-5.3)

99. In view of the recommendations that there should be no time limit, as such, for furnishing a return on the taxpayer's own volition, and also that there should be no upper limit on the penalty for default in furnishing a tax return. *Explanation* 3 to Section 271 may be deleted. (Para II-5.4)

100. Considering the increased emphasis on voluntary com-

pliance by taxpayers and acceptance of returns, the provision in Section 271(3)(a) exempting from penalty a taxpayer whose income exceeds the exemption limit by less than Rs. 1,500, should be omitted. (Para II-5.5)

101. The provision in Section 271(3)(b) should be redrafted to make the intention clear and provide for the levy of a token penalty not exceeding Rs. 25 where a person, to whom a notice calling for a return has been issued and who fails to comply with it, proves that he had no income liable to tax. (Para II-5.6)

102. In the context of the recommendation that the eligibility for the exemption under Section 11 and 12 should be conditional upon the furnishing of the return before the close of the assessment year, the maximum penalty leviable for default in furnishing return of income by a trust which is entitled to exemption under Section 11 and 12 should be limited to Rs. 500. This limit should, however, apply only to cases where, after applying the provisions of Sections 11, 12 and 13, the trust does not have taxable income. (Para II-5.7)

103. The law should clearly provide for levy of penalty for default in furnishing return of income more or less as a matter of course except where the taxpayer proves that he was prevented by sufficient cause from furnishing the return. (Para II-5.8)

104. For default in complying with notices issued by the assessing authority calling for production of account books, documents and other material, the penalty should be a lump sum not exceeding Rs. 1,000 for each such default. While drafting the provision, it should be made clear that the onus of showing sufficient cause for failure to comply with the notices will be no the taxpayer. The penalties for such defaults should be levied without waiting for the completion of the relevant assessment proceedings. (Para II-5.9)

105. The provisions in the Management Act relating to penalty for concealment of income, wealth, etc., should uniformly apply to all the four direct taxes. There should be no minimum penalty and the assessing officer's discretion in this regard should be unfettered. The maximum penalty should be twice the amount of tax sought to be avoided. (Para II-5.10)

106. The power to levy penalty for various defaults under Section 271 should not be available to the Appellate Tribunal. The penalty for defaults in furnishing tax returns or in complying with the notices issued by the assessing authorities, should be leviable only by the assessing authority and not by any other authority. The power to levy

penalty for concealment should, however, be available uniformly to the first appellate authority and also to the Commissioner, in addition to the assessing authority, in respect of all the four direct taxes. (Para II-5.11)

107. If the recommendation in the Interim Report (Para 8.18) that the separate tax on a registered firm should be discontinued altogether is accepted and implemented but the Government, then the existing provisions for calculating penalty for default of a registered firm in furnishing the return of income should continue unchanged. If, however, the separate tax on registered firms continued to be charged, the penalty for defaulty in furnishing the return of income should also be calculated with reference to the tax payable by the registered firm itself and not on the notional tax which would be chargeable if it had been assessed as an unregistered firm. No change in the existing method of calculation of penalty of concealment of income in the case of a registered firm is called for. (Para II-5.12)

108. In the context of the recommendation that the procedure for the registration of firms should be extended to association of persons and bodies of individuals as well and that a registered association of persons or body of individuals should not be assessed to tax on its income as a single unit by that the shares of the members in the income of the association or body should be subjected to tax in their hands, the penalty leviable in the case of a registered association of persons or registered body of individuals for defaults in furnishing returns of income and also concealment of income should be calculated with reference to the tax that would have been payable if the association or body had been subjected to tax on its income as a separate unit. (Para II-5.13)

109. Section 271(4) which provides for the levy of penalty on a registered firm which distributes its profits otherwise than in accordance with the shares of the partners is virtually a dead letter and should be deleted. (Para II-5.14)

110. With a view to making the penalty for failure to keep, maintain or retain books of accounts, documents, etc., as required under Section 44AA serve the purpose underlying its levy, the penalty should be a lump sum not exceeding Rs. 5,000. (Para II-5.15)

111. In regard to defaults in payment of advance-tax, instead of having a separate provision for levy of interest and for levy of penalty for the same type of default, it would be sufficient if the interest to be charged for non-payment of advance tax or on short payments of ad-

vance tax is fixed at 18 per cent per annum of the tax payable on the basis of the return or, as the case may be, of the shortfall from such tax. Once this is done, it will be unnecessary to have separate penal provisions for this purpose and Section 273 may be omitted. (Para II-5.18)

112. There should be a certain degree of uniformity in the provisions for the levy of penalties for the defaults enumerated in Sections 270, 272, 272A and 272B and the provisions for the levy of fines in Sections 131(2) and 285(2), which are of a technical nature. These provisions should be modified as under:

(1) Penalty for failure to respond to summons under Section 131 should be brought on par with the penalty leviable under Section 272A(1) for refusal to answer questions and sign statements, and the necessary provision in this behalf should be made in the latter Section.
(2) Penalty for not complying with the provisions for obtaining a Permanent Account Number or quoting it under Section 139A, should also be covered under the provisions of Section 272A(1), subject to the exclusion of failure to quote the Permanent Account Number on routine correspondence for which no penalty should be levied.
(3) The penalties provided under Sections 270, 272 and 285A(2) should be integrated with the penalty for various defaults enumerated in Section 272A(2) and the amount of penalty should be fixed at a maximum of Rs. 20 for every day during which the failure or contravention continues.
(4) The penalties for the corresponding defaults under the Wealth-tax Act, Gift-tax Act and Surtax Act should be brought in line with these penalties. (Para II-5.20)

113. All procedural aspects in regard to levy of penalties should be uniform for the purpose of all the direct taxes. The Inspecting Assistant Commissioner's approval should be required to be obtained for levy for penalty for concealment, where the penalty exceeds Rs. 5,000. All orders levying penalties should be in writing. The law should also specifically provide that, where any authority other than the assessing officer levies a penalty, a copy of the order shall be sent to the assessing officer who shall thereupon issue a notice of demand and proceed to recover the amount. (Para II-5.22)

114. The time limits for completion of penalty proceedings should apply uniformly for all the four direct taxes and, further, that the extension of these time limits in specified circumstances should be so fixed as to expire on the 31st March of the financial year next following that in which event justifying the extension happens. (Para II-5.23)

115. Section 273A which gives powers to the Commissioners to reduce or waive certain penalties on interest in certain cases should provide as under :

(1) These should be uniformly applicable for all the four taxes.
(2) The provisions in this behalf should be placed in the Chapter dealing with the Commissioner's powers of revision in the Management Act, rather than in the Chapter relating to penalties.
(3) The existing requirement of obtaining the Board's approval before the Commissioner reduces or waives, under Section 273A(1) any penalty or interest exceeding the specified limit should be done away with.
(4) The provisions in Section 273A(3) should be amended to make it clear that it applies only to the exercise of the power under sub-section (1).
(5) The power of the Commissioner to waive or reduce penalty on the ground of hardship under sub-section (4) should be extended to cover interest including interest for delay in payment of tax, and its scope should be enlarged so as to empower the Commissioner to reduce or waive any penalty or interest even in cases not involving hardship but where, for any other reason, he considers such a course to be desirable or expedient.
(6) Powers similar to those under sub-section (4) should be given to the Board also so that, in case where the assessee does not get the necessary relief at the Commissioner's level, he should be in a position to approach the Board. (Para II-5.24)

Appeals References and Revisions (Chapter 6)

116. The first appellate authority's power to set aside an assessment or remand it to the assessing authority for further enquiry should remain but it should be limited to the following situations:

(a) Where the assessment was made *ex parte* and the appellate authority comes to the conclusion that it should not have been so made;
(b) Where the appellate authority admits any fresh ground of appeal not originally specified;
(c) Where the appellate authority admits any fresh evidence produced by the appellant at the stage of appeal; and
(d) Where any of the grounds of appeal relates to a matter which has not been considered by the assessing authority. (Para II-6.3)

117. The first appellate authority should be specifically empowered to admit, in its discretion, any ground even if it had not been raised before the assessing authority and considered by the latter subject to the safeguard that, where any such ground is admitted, the assessing authority should be allowed an opportunity to examine the matter on merits and make a report to the appellate authority setting forth the results of such examination. Similar power should also be given to the Appellate Tribunal to admit any ground not raised before any lower authority, subject to a similar safeguard. (Para II-6.4)

118. Appeal should be provided against the order of an Assistant Director of Inspection, levying a fine under Section 131(2), to the Commissioner (Appeals) having jurisdiction over the Income-tax Circle in which the assessee or the other person on whom the fine is imposed is assessable to tax. (Para II-6.5)

119. Section 252 of the Income-tax Act should be deleted and a separate statute enacted to deal with the constitution and composition of the Appellate Tribunal. (Para II-6.6)

120. Section 253 may be reworded to provide that appeal will lie to the Appellate Tribunal against all final orders of the Commissioner (Appeals) or the Commissioner and the reference to orders under Section 154 passed by the Inspecting Assistant Commissioner should be omitted. (Para II-6.7)

121. The Tribunal should not have the power to enhance an assessment or penalty under any of the direct tax laws. (Para II-6.8)

122. While abolishing the institution of Valuation Officers performing statutory functions, the earlier system of arbitration of the value by two Values at the stage of appeal to the Appellate Tribunal should not be revived. (Para II-6.9)

123. The Government should take steps for the early establishment of a Central Tax Court with all-India jurisdiction to deal exclusively with litigation under the direct tax laws in the first instance, with provision for extending its functions to cover all other Central tax laws, if considered necessary, in the future. Such a court should be constituted under a separate statute. In the meanwhile, the desirability of constituting special tax benches in the High Courts to deal with the large number of tax references by continuous sitting throughout the year may be considered. (Para II-6.16)

124. The Central Tax Court should initially have benches located at Ahmedabad, Bombay, Calcutta, Delhi, Kanpur, Madras and Nagpur. Each bench should have two judges. Judges of the Tax Court should be appointed from among High Court Judges or persons who are qualified to be appointed as High Court Judges and should be on par with High Court Judges in the matter of conditions of service, scales of pay and other privileges. (Para II-6.17)

125. The Central Tax Court should have the right to go into questions of the validity of the provisions of the tax laws or of the rules framed thereunder. (Para II-6.18)

126. The jurisdiction of the Central Tax Court should be appellate and not advisory. The appeals should be heard by a bench of two judges. Where, however, the judges do not agree, the appeal should be heard by a full bench of three judges. The judgment of a division bench should be binding on other division benches unless it is contrary to a decision of the Supreme Court or of a full bench of the Tax Court. (Para II-6.20)

127. In addition to legal practitioners, Chartered Accountants and also such other persons as may be permitted by the Court to appeal before it may also represent the appellant or the respondent in tax matters before the Central Tax Court. (Para II-6.21)

128. The time limit under Section 263 should be two years from the end of the financial year in which the order sought to be revised is served on the taxpayer. (Para II-6.23)

129. The Commissioner should be given the power under Section 263 to revise the order of any authority subordinate to him. (Para II-6.24)

130. The powers of revision under Section 263 should extend to reassessments made in pursuance of proceedings initiated without the previous approval of the Commissioner or the Board. (Para II-6.25)

131. The provision in Section 263(3) may be amended to secure that an order of revision under the circumstances mentioned therein may be passed at any time up to the end of the financial year next following that in which the order of the Appellate Tribunal, High Court or Supreme Court was received by the Commissioner. (Para II-6.26)

132. For the purpose of revision of orders by the Commissioner under Section 263, in a case where the assessee demands rehearing on account of a change of incumbent of the office of the Commissioner, the limitation should expire on the last day of the financial year next following that in which the demand of the assessee is received by the Commissioner. Similarly, in a case where the proceedings before the Commissioner the stayed by an order or injunction of any court, the limitation should expire on the last day of the financial year next following that in which the order of stay or injunction is vacated by the Court. (Para II-6.27)

133. The time limits under Section 264(2) and Section 264(3) should be increased from one year to two years. This period should be reckoned from the end of the financial year in which the order in question was communicated to the assessee. (Para II-6.28)

134. A specific provision should be made in the law requiring the assessing authority to pass in order in writing giving effect to the order in appeal, revision, etc., and also enabling the taxpayer to represent his case through a miscellaneous petition filed within 60 days of his receiving such order to the appellate authority in case he is aggrieved by the manner in which that authority's order has been given effect to by the assessing authority. The appellate authority may also be required to dispose of such an application in the same manner as if it were an appeal presented before it. The law may also specify a time limit of six months from the end of the month in which the order in appeal or revision is received by the assessing authority for giving effect to it by passing an order under this provision. (Para II-6.29)

135. An order giving effect to an order in appeal or revision should be made appealable on any new point arising out of it, in the same manner as other final orders of the assessing authority. (Para II-6.30)

Settlement of Cases (Chapter 7)

136. The provisions in the Management Act relating to settlement of cases should apply to all the four taxes. (Para II-7.1)

137. All restrictions on the powers of the Settlement Commission to entertain cases in its discretion should be removed. The Commission should be authorised to admit an application, even when the matter is pending before the High Court or the Supreme Court provided the taxpayer withdraws the reference or appeal. (Para II-7.2)

Payment and Refund of Taxes (Chapter 8)

138. The provisions in the Management Act relating to payment and refund of taxes should apply uniformly to all the direct taxes. (Para II-8.1)

139. The term "assessee in default" will be made applicable under the Management Act, not only to demands arising as a result of an assessment, imposition of penalty, etc., but also to defaults in respect of advance tax and tax deductible at source, so that the coercive process of recovery can be set in motion in all cases. (Para II-8.3)

140. Interest for delay in payment of tax, which should include advance tax payable under a notice of demand, should be reckoned from the first day of the month next following the month in which the amount was payable under such notice. In respect of tax deductible or deducted at source, the interest should be reckoned from the first day of the month following that in which it was deductible. In all cases, the interest should be charged up to the last day of the month in which the amount is paid. (Para II-8.4)

141. Interest should be calculated and recovered only after the tax demand has become final and it has been fully paid or recovered. It is also desirable that the taxpayer is furnished with a formal order showing how the interest is worked out and a demand notice issued for the amount of interest. The law should also make it clear that interest should be charged only on outstanding tax and not on penalty, interest or any other sum. (Para II-8.5)

142. The provision in the Management Act should make it clear that an assessee in default will be liable to pay penalty for defaulty in payment of regular tax as also for default in making deduction of tax at source or non-payment of the tax deducted to the credit of the Central Government, and for default in payment of advance tax demanded by a notice issued by the assessing authority. The relevant provision in the Management Act in the matter of levy of penalty should make it clear that the onus of establishing the existence of

good and sufficient reasons will be on the assessee. (Para II-8.6)

143. There should be a provision for proportionate reduction of the penalty in cases where the tax with reference to which the penalty was imposed is partly reduced as a result of appeal, revision, etc. (Para II-8.7)

144. The provision for grant of interest on delayed refunds should, in all cases, take effect only if the refund is not granted within three months from the end of the month in which the assessment is completed. In any event, there should be no question of the Government paying interest on refunds due to the assessee for any period prior to first October of the assessment year. (Para II-8.8)

145. In all cases where interest becomes payable to the assessee on a delayed refund, the same should be reckoned up to the last day of the month preceding the month in which the refund voucher or cheque is issued to the assessee. As the date up to which the interest runs would thereby become ascertainable, the appropriate amount of interest should also be added to the refund of tax, etc., in the same refund voucher or cheque. The format of the refund voucher or cheque should provide for showing the amount of interest separately from the amount of tax or other sum which is being refunded. (Para II-8.9)

146. The refund order should be, broadly, in the form of a cheque, whereas the certificates, etc., may be incorporated in the counter-foil to be retained with the Department. (Para II-8.10)

147. The provisions of Section 245 may be extended to cover amounts payable under other direct tax laws also and the assessee may also be given the right to ask for adjustment of refunds against demands payable and, in that event, the date of receipt of the request from the assessee should be taken to be the date of adjustment for the purpose of calculating interest payable or receivable. Where any refund is adjusted by the Income-tax Officer against demand, the date of passing the order of adjustment should be taken to be the date of payment of tax and grant of the refund. (Para II-8.11)

148. Government may consider the introduction of a system of tax accounts in public sector banks, on a compulsory basis in the case of companies and other big taxpayers, and on a voluntary basis in the case of other taxpayers. (Para II-8.12)

Recovery of Taxes (Chapter 9)

149. The institution of Tax Recovery Officers should be done

away with. The provisions in the Management Act corresponding to Section 222 should authorise the assessing officer himself to issue a show cause notice to the defaulter and, thereafter, proceed to recover the taxes by applying the various methods set forth in that Section and in the Second Schedule. The rules for recovery of taxes in the Second Schedule should be included as Sections in this Chapter of the Management Act with appropriate drafting changes to enable the assessing officers to exercise these powers instead of the Tax Recovery Officers. (Para II-9.4)

150. Provisions of Rules 86 and 87 of the Second Schedule should continue, with appropriate modifications and the appeal against the order of the assessing officer in recovery matters should like to the Commissioner to whom he is subordinate, and not to the Commissioner (Appeals). The order of the Commissioner in such appeal should be final. (Para II-9.6)

151. The notice of commencement of recovery proceedings should be permitted to be issued at any time before the expiry of three years from the end of the financial year in which the demand was made or in which the person concerned is deemed to be an assessee in default. (Para II-9.7)

152. The provision for extension of time in cases where recovery proceedings are stayed by any court should be made applicable also the stay of such proceedings by the Appellate Tribunal. (Para II-9.8)

153. Provisions of Sections 281 and 281B should be incorporated in this Chapter of the Management Act with appropriate changes. (Para II-9.9)

Liability in Special Cases (Chapter 10)

154. While incorporating provisions of Section 160 which defines "representative assessee" for the purposes of the Income-tax Act, in the Management Act, it should be ensured that these provisions apply uniformly to wealth tax, gift-tax and surtax as well. In order to ensure certainty and completeness, this provision may be enlarged to cover a trustee appointed under an oral trust also. (Para II-10.2)

155. The provisions in the Management Act corresponding to Section 168 should be so drafted as to ensure that, even where there are two or more executors, the assessment will be made in the status of an 'individual' both for income-tax and wealth-tax. (Para II-10.3)

156. The provisions in the Management Act corresponding to

Section 171 should be made applicable to a Hindu undivided family assessable as such for any year, whether or not the family had actually been so assessed at any time in the past, and it may be provided that the status of Hindu undivided family will continue as such, except where and insofar as a finding of partition is recorded by the assessing authority. (Para II-10.4)

157. A specific provision should be made requiring the assessing authority to give an opportunity of being heard to any director of a private company before the latter is fastened with the tax liability of the company which could not be recovered from it and also requiring such authority to pass a formal order holding such director to be liable for such tax (where justified) and specifying the amount for which he is so liable. Such an order should be made appealable. A time limit of two years from the end of the financial year in which the tax due from the company is found to be not recoverable from it should be laid down for passing an order holding the director to be liable for such tax. (Para II-10.6)

Registration of Firms, Association of Persons and Bodies of Individuals (Chapter 11)

158. The procedure for registration of partnership firms on the lines recommended in the Interim Report should be made applicable, *mutatis mutandis,* to registration of associations of persons and bodies of individuals also. (Para II-11.4)

Offences and Prosecution (Chapter 12)

159. The existing limit of Rs. 3,000, under Section 276CC, should be raised to Rs. 5,000 uniformly for the purpose of all the direct taxes. (Para II-12.2)

160. In the context of integration of the procedural provisions of the four direct taxes, the provision of Section 276D of the Income-tax Act and Section 35C of the Wealth-tax Act should be made uniformly applicable to all the four taxes. (Para II-12.3)

161. The provisions of Section 35E of the Wealth-tax Act should be incorporated in the Management Act. (Para II-12.4)

162. No prosecution should be launched for any default in respect of which the penalty levied or leviable has been waived or reduced. (Para II-12.5)

163. The provisions of Section 280 of the Income-tax Act should be made applicable to unauthorised disclosure of information relating to all direct taxes. (Para II-12.6)

164. The provisions of Sections 291, 292 and 292A of the Income-tax Act should be incorporated in the Chapter on offences and prosecutions in the Management Act. (Para II-12.7)

165. The provisions of Rule 89 of the Second Schedule to the Income-tax Act should form part of the Chapter dealing with offences and prosecutions and the punishment for such an offence should be the same as provided under Section 275A. (Para II-12.8)

Miscellaneous Provisions (Chapter 13)

166. The relevant rules in the Civil Procedure Code governing service of notices should be incorporated in the Management Act itself. (Para II-13.2)

167. The provisions relating to registered valuers in the Income-tax Act, Wealth-tax and Gift-tax Act should be incorporated in a single Section. (Para II-13.4)

168. A person who has a minimum of 10 years' service as an income-tax authority not below the rank of a Direct Taxes Officer should be declared eligible to represent an assessee before any tax authority or the Appellate Tribunal after leaving the service. (Para II-13.6)

169. Section 288(3) should be amended to secure that a person who has retired or resigned from service as a direct taxes authority, not below the rank of Direct Taxes Officer, shall not be entitled to practise for two years, at any station, where he had served at any time during the two years preceding the date of his leaving the service, without placing any such restriction against his practising any other station. Further, even this restriction should not apply for appearance before the Appellate Tribunal. (Para II-13.7)

170. Section 289 of the Income-tax Act, requiring grant of a receipt for money paid or received under the Act should be incorporated in the Management Act and made uniformly applicable to all direct taxes. (Para II-13.8)

Approvals under the Tax Laws (Chapter 14)

171. The applications for approval of agreements, contracts,

schemes, etc., for various purposes under the direct tax laws should invariably be submitted to the Board even where the approval is to be granted by the administrative ministry concerned. The procedures for making such applications, the forms to be used and the guidelines which would regulate such approvals, should be laid down in the Rules. (Para II-14.2)

172. Provision should be made in the law whereby approval will be deemed to have been given if an application is not finally disposed of within a period of 120 days from the date of receipt of the application by the Board. (Para II-14.3)

173. Uniform terminology of "approval" should be used in relation to provident funds, superannuation funds and gratuity funds. (Para II-14.4)

174. The provisions relating to approval of funds should be streamlined as follows:

(1) there should be certain general rules applicable to all the three funds, followed by special rules applicable to each type of fund; the general rules should cover such matters as procedure for making the application; requirements regarding maintenance of accounts; investment of fund money; grant of approval; date from which approval is to take effect; appeal against refusal or withdrawal of approval; and amendments to the rules of an approved fund;

(2) the applications for approval should in all cases, the required to be addressed to the Commissioner having jurisdiction over the Salary Circle and routed through the specified assessing officer of such circle;

(3) any fund which has been granted approval should be required to maintain proper accounts containing essential particulars specified in this behalf and get these audited every year; the auditors should be required to certify that the fund in question continues to satisfy the conditions of approval; copies of the accounts, along with the auditor's certificate, should be required to be furnished to the designated Income-tax Officer by a specified date every year together with such other particulars, as may be prescribed; it should also be laid down that the accounts should be maintained in India and all fund moneys should be invested in India;

(4) there should be uniform provisions governing the investment

of fund moneys in the case of all the three categories of funds, fund moneys should be permitted to be invested in short-term deposits with the public sector banks for kept in savings accounts, the investment pattern of fund moneys should be brought in par with that under the Employees' Provident Fund Scheme.

175. A common fund should be allowed to be set up for the benefit of employees belonging to a group of companies which are connected with one another, subject to whatever safeguards are considered necessary to prevent misuse. This would secure economy in administrative costs and also facilitate movement of employees from one concern to another within the same group. Side by side with these provisions, in order to meet a situation where a company in the group, having a common fund wishes to separate from the group for any reason there should be a provision for splitting up the common fund subject to suitable safeguards. (Para II-14.7)

176. There should be uniform provisions for transfer of the balance or accrued benefits from one approved fund to another approved fund of the same type, in respect of all the three categories of funds whenever an employee changes his employment. Further, an employer company may be permitted to make contribution to the account of an employee in a gratuity fund maintained by it after taking into consideration the past service of the employee under the former employer. Where, however, the new employer does not maintain a superannuation fund or where the employee does not take up another employment, the former employer should be required to purchase from the Life Insurance Corporation out of the balance in the superannuation fund account of the employee a non-surrenderable deferred annuity policy in favour of the employee under which payments should be made to the employee on his attaining the normal age of superannuation or on his prior incapacitation or to his widow children, dependents or nominees if he dies before attaining such age. (Para II 14.8)

177. The provisions in Rules 6, 8 and 9 of Part A, Rules 5 and 6 of Part B and Rule 7 of Part C of the Fourth Schedule to the Income-tax Act and Rule 72 of the Income-tax Rules are substantive in nature and should not be incorporated in the Management Act. (Para II-14.9)

178. In place of the existing Rules 76, 92 and 105 of the Income-

tax Rules, treating the consideration received for the assignment or creation of a charge upon his beneficial interest in a recognised provident fund, approved superannuation fund or an approved gratuity fund, as the employee's income, provision should be made in the Chapter relating to penalties for the imposition of a suitable monetary penalty on the employee in such a case. Such monetary penalty may be expressed as a percentage of the consideration, if any, received for such assignment or charge, subject to an alternative minimum amount which should be applicable where no consideration is received by the employee. (Para II-14.10)

179. The provisions in the Management Act and the rules thereunder governing provident funds should be brought in line with those in the Employees' Provident Fund Scheme. (Para II-14.11)

180. The provisions relating to availing of benefits should be made uniform for all the three types of funds and necessary amendments should be made to the rules relating to approval of superannuation funds to bring these in par with rules 67A and 101A of the Income-tax Rules. (Para II-14.12)

181. In the interest of uniformity and to avoid invidious distinction, the provisions in the Rule 90 may be brought in line with those is Section 10(10A). (Para II-14.13)

182. The term 'annuity', for the purpose of the provisions relating to superannuation funds, may be defined to mean an annuity payable for a period of not less than 10 years and may even extend to the life time of an employee. (Para II-14.14)

183. Option should be given to an employee participating in an approved superannuation fund either to have the payment of annuities secured by taking out annuity policies with the Life Insurance Corporation or to receive the annuities directly from the trustees. (Para II-14.15)

184. The provisions applicable to approval of gratuity funds for the purpose of taxation, should be brought in line with those under the Payment of Gratuity Act. (Para II-14.16)

Conclusion (Chapter 15)

185. The various suggestions for improving the administration of the tax laws, particularly in the area of levy, collection and recovery of the direct taxes should lead to a better climate of understanding between the taxpayers and the tax-gatherers. The rigours of a taxing

statute can be largely mitigated and made acceptable to the public by an enlightened and fair administration.

PART III

Introductory

1. Consolidation of the Estate Duty Act with any other direct tax enactment is not favoured. (Para III-0.5)

2. The Estate Duty Act should continue as it serves a socialistic objective. (Para III-0.6)

Definitions (Chapter 1)

3. The term "principal value of the estate" may be used to indicate the base for charge of duty and it may be defined to mean the aggregate of the market values of all property, settled or not settled, including agricultural lands, which passes or is deemed to pass on the death of a person, as reduced by the debts and incumbrances and after allowance of the admissible deductions. Any similar expression used elsewhere in the Act to denote the market value of a single item of the deceased's property as in Sections 20A, 34, 36, 39(3), etc., will have to be suitably modified for the sake of clarity. (Para III-1.2)

4. The term "gross duty payable" may be defined to mean the amount of duty calculated on the "principal value of the estate" in accordance with the rates specified in the Second Schedule to the Estate Duty Act, 1953; and the term "average rate of duty" may be defined to mean the rate arrived at by dividing the "gross duty payable" by the "principal value of the estate". (Para III-1.3)

5. It is necessary to constitute the Controller of Estate Duty, Deputy Controller of Estate Duty and Assistant Controller of Estate Duty as distinct authorities under the Estate Duty Act with powers and functions similar to their counterparts under the other direct tax laws. (Para III-1.4)

Basis of Charge of Estate Duty (Chapter 2)

6. The law should make it clear that, property held *benami* would pass under Section 5 of the Estate Duty Act, 1953 on the dealt of the real (beneficial) owner and that, on the death of the

benamidar, Section 6 would not be applicable on the mere ground that the *benamidar* was legally competent to dispose of the property. (Para III-2.2)

7. Complete integration of lifetime gifts with the estate passing on dealt would neither be practicable nor rational under our system of taxation. The statutory period under Section 9 of the Estate Duty Act may, however, be extended from two years to five years. Corresponding amendments may be made in Sections 10, 11 12, 22, 23, 33(1)(b) and 46. (Paras III-2.5, III-2.9, III-2.11, III-2.12, III-3.6, III-4.5 and III-6.11)

8. A clarificatory provision may be made in the law to the effect that payment of any premium by the deceased for effecting or keeping in force a policy taken out under the Married Women's Property Act, 1874 is not to be regarded as a gift for the purposes of Section 9 of the Estate Duty Act. (Para III-2.6)

9. The law may be suitably amended to provided that where cash gifts received by the done from the deceased, who was a partner in a firm, are deposited in the business of that partnership, such gifted property would not be available to duty under Section 10 of the Estate Duty Act regardless of the position whether the donee is a partner in the firm of not. (Para III-2.7)

10. The definition of the term "property" under Section 2(15) of the Estate Duty Act may be expressly made applicable to the provisions of Section 10. (Para III-2.8)

11. An Explanation may be added at the end of Section 10 to the effect that possession and enjoyment of the gifted property by the donor or any benefit reserved to him therein will not result in the charge of duty to the proportionate extent of the consideration in money or money's worth paid by the donor to the donee for such possession and enjoyment or benefit. (Para III-2.10)

12. With a view to preventing leakage of revenue through the divide of "grafting" and to keep up the efficacy of the provisions of Sections 5, 7 and 11, and suitable amendment may be made on the lines of Section 36 of the U.K. Finance Act, 1969. (Para III-2.11)

13. Section 12 may be amended to limit the charge under that Sections to a part of the settled property in proportion to the value of the interest reserved. (Para III-2.12)

14. A provision may be made in the law to the effect that moneys receivable under personal accident policies, if otherwise passing on the dealt, are not be aggregated with the other property of

the deceased. (Para III-2.13)

Exceptions from Charge (Chapter 3)

15. The concept of domicile of the deceased may continue in preference to that of either his citizenship or residence for purposes of Section 21 of the Estate Duty Act. (Para III-3.4)

16. Rule 7(g) of the Estate Duty Rules may be amended to make it clear that the interest of a beneficiary in an unadministered estate is moveable property even if the estate includes immovable property. (Para III-3.5)

17. Section 29 of the Estate Duty Act providing for relief from duty in cases where estate duty has been paid in respect of any settled property on the death of the spouse may be amended to secure that the relief will be available even where no duty was in fact paid on the first death due to the estate being below the dutiable limit or the property being exempt under any specific provision of the law. (Para III-3.8)

18. The word "dependents" in Section 29A may be replaced by the expression "relatives of the deceased dependent upon him for the necessities of life." (Para III-3.9)

19. The market value of the dutiable part of the annuity or pension for the purposes of Section 29A may be determined by the application of Jollicoe's formula with a rate of interest equal to that allowed by nationalised banks on long-term deposits of more than five years. (Para III-3.9)

20. An annuity payable to the widow or other relatives of the deceased dependent upon him for the necessaries of life, under a contract approved under Section 80E of the Income-tax Act, 1961, should be eligible for exemption under Section 29A of the Estate Duty Act to the extent of Rs. 15,000 per annum. (Para III-3.11)

21. The power to grant quick succession relief under Section 31 should be delegated to the assessing authority. (Para III-3.12)

22. The quick success in relief under Section 31 should be allowed if the second deceased has at his death adequate resources to cover what he inherited on the first dealt without the need for tracing actual dealings with the property through sale and reinvestment between the two deaths. (Para III-3.13)

23. The proviso to Section 31 may be amended to make it clear that, where the proviso applies, the reduction in the estate duty pay-

able on the second death will be worked out with reference to the amount of duty calculated on the value of the property as on the first death at the "average rate of duty" on the principal value of the estate computed on the second death. (Para III-3.14)

Other Exemptions and Rebates (Chapter 4)

24. In order to simplify calculations of duty, the exemptions under clauses (a), (b), (f), (g), (h), and (k) of Section 33(1) may be provided by way of straight deductions instead of rebates at the average rate. Relief under Section 35(3) in respect of agricultural land in the case of small estates may be given by way of a deduction of an amount equal to 10 per cent of the value of the agricultural land included in the principal value. (Para III-4.2)

25. The amount eligible for exemption under Section 33(1)(a) with reference to gifts for charitable purposes maybe increased from Rs. 2,500 to Rs. 5,000. The amount eligible for exemption under Section 33(1)(b) with reference to other gifts may be increased from Rs. 1,500 to Rs. 3,000. (Para III-4.5)

26. A consolidated exemption may be provided in respect of all kinds of tools and household goods, to the extent of Rs. 10,000, under Section 33(1)(c). (Para III-4.6)

27. The present limit and the restriction under Sections 33(1)(f) and 33(1)(g) should continue as these are equitable. (Para III-4.7)

28. The limit over the exemption in respect of moneys payable under policies of insurances, under Section 33(1)(h), should be raised to Rs. 10,000. Further, moneys payable from any provident fund referred to in Section 80C(2) of the Income-tax Act should also be covered by the exemption under Section 33(1)(h) within the same consolidated monetary limit of Rs. 10,000. (Para III-4.8)

29. The exemption under Section 33(1)(i) in respect of drawings, paintings, etc., should be extended to cover such collections made by the deceased himself if the conditions prescribed in that behalf are satisfied. (Para III-4.9)

30. The expression "retained in the family" of the deceased occurring in the clauses (i) and (j) of Section 33(1) may be substituted by the expression "retained by the legal heirs or legatees or donees". (Para III-4.10)

31. Rules 11, 12 and 13 of the Estate Duty Rules, 1953, relating to conditions for grant of exemption under Sections 33(1) and

33(1)(j), which create substantive liability to duty and cast statutory obligations on certain persons, may be made a part of the substantive law. (Para III-4.11)

32. The scope of the exemptions under Sections 33(1)(m) and 33(1)(mm) should be widened so as to cover the estate of any civil servant and any other person whose employment in the national cause is equally hazardous; and these exemptions should be available not merely where the deceased was killed in action against an enemy but also where the claim of exemption is supported by a certificate from the prescribed authority that the deceased had died either from a wound inflicted accident occurring or disease contracted at a time when the deceased was (a) on active service against an enemy or (b) on other service of a warlike nature or which involved the same risks as service of a warlike nature or where the deceased had died from a disease contracted at some previous time, the death due to or hastened by the aggravation of the disease due to the said employment. (Para III-4.12)

33. In valuing the property of the deceased which was exclusively used by him for his own residence for the purposes of exemption under Section 33(1)(n), the same principles as recommended in Chapter 14 of the Interim Report and Chapter 18 of Part I of this Report should be adopted. Further, the expression "one house" occurring in Section 33(1)(n) should be clarified to cover servants' or a gardener's quarters and garage. (Para III-4.14)

34. The period of five years specified in Section 33(1)(O), relating to exemption of the property gifted by the deceased to his spouse, son, daughter, brother or sister, should be increased to seven years. (Para III-4.15)

Value Chargeable (Chapter 5)

35. The method of valuation of property under all direct tax laws including estate duty should, as far as possible, be the same as suggested in Part I of this Report except where some special or distinguishing features of the estate duty law require a different methods to be adopted. (Para III-5.1)

36. The substance of Section 37 should be incorporated in Section 36 itself and at the same time, the exclusion of cases falling under Rule 15 of the Estate Duty (Controlled Companies) Rules from the scope of the general provision in Section 36 should be spelt out

clearly so as to avoid any controversy or ambiguity. Further, the special provisions at present contained in Section 37 should be extended for the purpose of valuation of shares in a private company under the Wealth-tax Act at the Gift-tax Act as well. In consonance with the recommendation made in Part I of this Report, rules will have to be framed by the Board for the valuation of unquoted shares on the basis of guidelines laid down by the Institute of Chartered Accountants for uniform application to all the direct taxes including estate duty. (Para III-5.6)

37. The provision in Rule 14(3) of the Estate Duty Rules may be excluded from application in respect of quoted shares, stocks and debentures, and trading assets, viz., stock-in-trade, consumable stores, spare parts, raw materials and semi-finished goods. In respect of trading assets, it may be expressly provided that the value as for the corresponding income-tax assessment of the deceased will be adopted. Further, the expression "within a short time after the death" in Rule 14(3) may be replaced by "within six months after the death". (Para III-5.8)

38. For the purpose of valuing interest in coparcenary property of a Hindu joint family ceasing on the death of the deceased, the principal value of the joint family property should first be computed without grant of any deduction under Section 33 and, thereafter, the deceased's interest in each of the exempted assets of the family should be projected into the assessment for being taken into consideration for exemption subject to the overall ceiling, if any, under Section 33. (Para III-5.10)

39. Rules 14(5) and 14(6) of the Estate Duty Rules should be deleted and the method of valuation of lands, whether agricultural or containing minerals, or otherwise, should, for estate duty purposes, be the same as for valuation under other direct tax laws. (Para III-5.11)

40. Power may be given to the Controller for granting relief in the duty payable in a case of a genuine hardship resulting from the sale (to a person not being a relative) of quoted investments within 12 months of the date of death of the deceased at a substantially lower value than that adopted in the assessment provided there is no purchase or repurchase thereof within two years of the date of death by any relative of the deceased. The relief may be granted only after making appropriate adjustments for factors such as issue of bonus shares right shares, payment of further calls, reorganisation of the

capital of the company, etc. The relief may be determined with reference to the difference between the duty on the assessed value of the estate and that on the value of the estate recomputed by taking the price realised on sale of the quoted investments (as adjusted). (Para III-5.13)

Deductions and Reliefs (Chapter 6)

41. The limit over the deduction for funeral expenses may be raised from Rs. 1,000 to Rs. 2,500. (Para III-6.2)

42. A clarificatory *Explanation* may be inserted in Section 44 to secure that any liability in respect of gift-tax outstanding against the deceased at the time of his death is not disallowed as falling within the scope of clause (a) or clause (b) of that Section. (Para III-6.3)

43. Debts or incumbrances which are in excess of the free estate may be allowed against property passing under other titles, e.g., property gifted by the deceased which is included in the estate, if such debts are actually discharged by the persons to whom such other property has passed, within a specified period of, say, two years following the date of death of the deceased. Such a voluntary discharge of the debts of the deceased by the donees of such gifts should also be exempted from any liability to gift-tax in the hands of the donees. (Para III-6.5)

44. Debts or incumbrances which are secured on property eligible for exemption from duty, e.g., foreign immovable property or residential house in India up to Rs. 1,00,000, should be considered for deduction from the remaining properties which are dutiable provided such debts are enforceable against such dutiable properties; if there is a deficiency the same should be allowed against property passing under other titles. (Para III-6.5)

45. The substance of the provisions in Section 16(2) may be incorporated in Section 46 itself in simple language so as to make it self-contained. (Para III-6.7)

46. Section 16(2)(c) may be amended to secure that only in the case of a settlement made by the deceased, the annual or periodical payments would be covered in the definition of "subject-matter" under that Section and that in other cases, the income of the property derived from the deceased is not to be regarded as property derived from the deceased. (Para III-6.8)

47. Section 46 may be amended to secure that its provisions do

not apply with reference to transactions which took place earlier than 15 years prior to the date of death of the deceased. (Para III-6.9)

48. Section 46 should be made expressly inapplicable where the property derived from the deceased is otherwise included in the estate under the provisions of Sections 9, 10 or 12. (Para III-6.10)

49. The actual expense of realising or administering foreign property should be allowed up to the limit of 5 per cent of its value, under Section 48. (Para III-6.12)

50. Section 50 may be amended to make it clear that the amount of court-fees paid means the amount paid in pursuance of a determination by the court of court-fees payable on the application for probate, letters of administration or succession certificate and that neither the assessing authority nor any other authority under the Estate Duty Act will be entitled to question such determination. (Para III-6.13)

51. Section 50A may be amended to limit the deduction on account of gift-tax paid to the proportionate amount of estate duty payable on the same property. (Para III-6.14)

52. The power to relax the time limit under Section 50B should be given to the Controller, instead of being centralised with the Board. (Para III-6.15)

53. Section 50B may be amended to cover transfer by way of compulsory acquisition of any of the properties included in the estate or delivery of any such property by the accountable person to the Government for adjustment of the price against the estate duty even beyond the period of two years stipulated thereunder. (Para III-6.15)

54. For purposes of the relief under Section 50B, the quantum of tax paid on capital gains may be spelt out to be the amount arrived at by applying the average rate of income-tax applicable to the total income of the relevant year, to the capital gains forming part of such total income, after the deduction, if any, under Section 80T of the Income-tax Act, and the "amount paid towards estate duty" may be clarified to mean the estate duty actually paid taken together with any court-fees paid out of the process of the transfer of the property. (Para III-6.16)

55. The relief under Section 50B may be computed with reference to the net proceeds of the transfer of the property, i.e., the proceeds after the deduction of the expenditure incurred wholly and exclusively in connection with the transfer, instead of the gross proceeds. (Para III-6.17)

Assessment, Penalties and Prosecutions (Chapter 7)

56. The account of the property passing on the death, required to be filed by the accountable person, should be termed as an estate duty return. Further, the verification of an estate duty return should be in the same form and should be made in the same manner as in the case of any other direct tax return and the requirement of a sworn statement before a magistrate or an oath commissioner should be removed. (Para III-17.1)

57. The provisions of Section 53(1)(b) may be amended so as to confer immunity from accountability on persons responsible for making payments out of provident funds referred to in Section 80C of the Income-tax Act, or gratuity funds approved under the Income-tax Act, in those cases where the aggregate amount payable out of such funds to the legal heirs, or the nominees of the deceased subscriber does not exceed Rs. 25,000. (Para III-7.2)

58. There should be a specific provision for treating an estate duty return field any time before the assessment is completed as a valid return and for charge of interest on the duty from the date of expiry of 6 months after the date of death of the deceased up to the date of filing of such return, irrespective of whether or not the accountable person had obtained extension of time from the Controller for filing the return. (Para III-7.3)

59. The time limit for initiation of assessment proceedings under the Estate Duty Act should be 8 years from the end of the financial year in which the death occurred and 16 years, in cases where the principal value of the estate is likely to be Rs. 5 lakhs or more, subject to the requirement that in the latter type of cases, approval of the Board is obtained before the issue of the notice. The time limit for commencement of proceedings for reassessments should be 4 years from the end of the financial year in which the death occurred in cases, falling under Section 59(b) and 8 years in cases falling under Section 59(a), subject to the approval of the Controller in the latter type of cases. There should also be a provisions for initiating such proceedings up to 16 years in cases where the value of the estate escaping assessment is likely to be Rs. 5 lakhs or more, subject to the approval of the Board. (Para III-7.4)

60. The time limit for completion of an estate duty assessment/reassessment should be 4 years from the end of the financial year in which the proceedings for such assessment/reassessment were in-

itiated, or 4 years from the end of the financial year in which the return or a supplementary return envisaged under Section 53(4) or under Section 56 is filed, whichever is later. Further, a specific provision should be made authorising a reassessment on the basis of a supplementary return envisaged under Section 53(4) or under Section 56, which is filed after the completion of the assessment, without the need to initiate formal reassessment proceedings. The introduction of the time limit as stated above should be suitably staggered in respect of pending proceedings. The time limit may be released in cases where:

(a) the accountable person demands the reopening of the whole or any part of the proceedings consequent on a change in the incumbent of the office of the assessing authority; or
(b) the proceedings are stayed by an order or injunction of any court; or
(c) the assessment/reassessment has to be made in consequence of, or for giving effect to, any finding or direction of any appellate or revisionary authority; or
(d) an application made before the Settlement Commission (in pursuance of the recommendation elsewhere in this Part for the provision of a machinery for settlement of disputes in estate duty matters) is rejected by the Commission or is not allowed to be proceeded with by it.

In such situations, the relaxation in the time limit should be broadly on the lines of the provisions in Section 153(3) of the Income-tax Act as suggested to be modified under the recommendations in Part II. (Para III-7.6)

61. Sub-Section (2) of Section 57 relating to provisional assessment should be amended to make the demand raised on such assessment liable to be recovered from any of the accountable persons and not merely from the accountable person on the basis of whose return the provisional assessment is made, after giving an opportunity to the other accountable persons of being heard. Section 70 should be amended to extend the provision for levy of interest on the demand raised on a provisional assessment under Section 57, which is not paid in time. (Para III-7.7)

62. The provisions of Section 70 and Rule 42 may be modified so that levy of interest is attracted in all cases where there is a delay

in filing the estate duty account or in the payment of the duty, whether on regular assessment or provisional assessment, even if there is a no application from the accountable person for extension of time, or the terms subject to which extension is granted are not fulfilled. (Para III-7.8)

63. The maximum rate of interest under Section 70 and Rule 42 should not exceed 6 per cent. (Para III-7.9)

64. As recommended in Part II in relation to Section 273A of the Income-tax Act, power may be conferred on the Controller to reduce or waive the interest chargeable under the Act. Further, the proviso to Rule 42(d) which makes in Controller's discretion to reduce the rate of interest subject to the general instructions of the Board should be deleted and the rate of interest to be actually charged in a given case, either for delay in filing the account or in the payment of duty, may be wholly left to the discretion of the assessing authority. (Para III-7.10)

65. The rate of interest payable by Government under Rule 19(3) on deposits in respect of estate duty made under Section 33(1)(g) may be increased to 6 per cent. This interest should continue to be calculated from the date of deposit to the date of death, as at present. In case the deposit is found to be in excess of the estate duty liability finally determined, further interest may be granted on such excess at the same rate from the date of death to the date when the excess is refunded. (Para III-7.11)

66. Interest may be granted at the rate of 6 per cent on any amount which is found to be refundable to the accountable person consequent upon any order in assessment, appeal, revision or rectification but which is not refunded within the period of 3 months from the end of the month in which the order is passed. (Para III-7.12)

67. Provisions relating to penalties under the Estate Duty Act may be modified on the following lines:

(i) Penalties for defaults relating to filing of returns or complying with notices should be leviable only by the authority before whom such default occurs and not by any other higher appellate or administrative authority. The penalty for concealment may, however, be allowed to be levied by the assessing authority as also by the first appellate authority and the revisionary authority. The Appellate Tribunal, which is the final authority on facts, should not have the power to levy penalties for any of the defaults; and

(ii) A provision similar to that Section 273A of the Income-tax Act should be introduced in the Estate Duty Act bestowing powers on the Controller to reduce or waive the penalty in appropriate cases. (Para III-7.13)

68. For completion of penalty proceedings under the Estate Duty Act, there should be a time limit of two years from the end of the financial year in which the assessment proceedings during which penal action is initiated are completed. Provision may also be made for extension of this time limit on the lines of the provision in Section 275(a) of the Income-tax Act and the *Explanation* thereto, as suggested to be modified in Part II of this Report. (Para III-7.14)

69. A provision may be introduced for prosecution for the making of a false statement in any verification or for delivering an account or statement which is false or which the accountable person either known or believes to be false or does not believe to be true, on lines of the provision in Section 277 of the Income-tax Act. (Para III-7.15)

Appeal Rectification and Revision (Chapter 8)

70. Provisions of the Estate Duty Act relating to appeals and rectifications need to be restructured to bring them in line with the corresponding provisions under the other direct tax laws. (Para III-8.1)

71. Instead of enumerating the various orders of the assessing authority against which an appeal lies to the first appellate authority, there should be a general provision to the effect that every final order (which is not in the nature of an administrative order or an interlocutory order) of the assessing authority should be appealable to the first appellate authority. The first appellate authority under the Estate Duty Act should be of the rank of Controller. (Para III-8.2)

72. The language of Section 62(4)(a) relating to admission of fresh grounds of appeal before the first appellate authority should be brought in harmony with that of Section 250(5) of the Income-tax Act as modified in the manner recommended in Chapter 6 of Part II of this Report. Further, provisions regulating the admission of fresh evidence at the stage of first appeal may be introduced on the lines of

Rule 46 of the Income-tax Rules. (Para III-8.3)

73. The proviso to Section 62(1) may be deleted so that an appeal against penalty levied for non-payment of estate duty would be competent even if the duty is not paid before the appeal is filed. (Para III-8.4)

74. The powers of enhancement given to the Appellate Tribunal under Section 63 may be withdrawn. (Para III-8.5)

75. The procedure for reference of any question of disputed value to arbitration, contained in sub-sections (6), (7), and (8) of Section 63, should be deleted. Further, the system of Valuation Officers obtaining under other direct tax laws, functioning in an advisory capacity as recommended in Part II of this Report, as also the system of registered valuers obtaining under other direct tax laws, should be extended to estate duty as well. (Para III-8.6)

76. A provision for the filing of a memorandum of cross objections may be incorporated in the Estate Duty Act as under other direct tax laws. (Para III-8.7)

77. In regard to further appeals/references against orders of the Appellate Tribunal, the provisions in the other direct tax laws as modified in the manner recommended in Part II of this Report should be made applicable for the purpose of estate duty too. (Para III-8.8)

78. The provisions of Section 61 relating to rectification of mistakes apparent from the record should be brought in line with those in the other direct tax laws as modified in the manner recommended in Part II of this Report. (Para III-8.9)

79. The provisions of Section 61 may be enlarged in line with the provisions in Section 155 of the Income-tax Act so as to provide extended time limits for various purposes under the Estate Duty Act such as, recomputation of the principal value to give effect to any revision in the income-tax or wealth-tax liability already allowed under Section 44; deduction of the duty paid in a non-reciprocating country under Section 49; deduction for court-fees under Section 50; granting of relief due under Section 50A or Section 50B with reference to the gift-tax or tax on capital gains, etc. (Para III-8.10)

80. Provisions corresponding to those in Sections 263 and 264 of the Income-tax Act may be introduced in the Estate Duty Act conferring power on the Controller to revise orders of any subordinate authority. Orders of the Controller revising an order prejudicial to the revenue should be appealable to the Appellate Tribunal, as under

the other direct tax laws. (Para III-18.11)

81. Section 71 of the Estate Duty Act, which authorities the Board to remit outstanding duty and interest, may be modified so that the power under that Section is exercisable by the Board any time after the expiry of three years from the date of finalisation of an assessment or reassessment proceeding under the Estate Duty Act. (Para III-8.12)

Recovery of Duty (Chapter 9)

82. The present procedure for collection and recovery of estate duty demands has not proved effective in tackling the problem of mounting arrears. (Para III-9.1)

83. The procedures for recovery of income-tax and other direct taxes, modified in the manner recommended in Part II of this Report, should be made applicable for the purposes of estate duty also. As this would entail the Department taking over the recovery matters already referred to the State Government authorities and pending with them, suitable transitional provisions will have to be made for such takeover. (Para III-9.2)

84. Section 52 of the Estate Duty Act, which provides for payment of duty by transfer of a property comprised in the estate to the Government at a price to be agreed upon, may be amended to secure that, when a property comprised in the estate is offered by the accountable person in payment of the estate duty, it should be obligatory on the Government to accept the offer; where there is a dispute about the price in such a case, the Government should be obliged to pay the value which has been finally adopted for the purpose of assessment. (Para III-9.3)

Settlement of Estate Duty Cases (Chapter 10)

85. A machinery for settlement of cases may be introduced in the Estate Duty Act on the lines of the provisions in Chapter XIXA of the Income-tax Act, keeping in view the recommendations in Chapter 10 of the Interim Report. (Para III-10.3)

Rates of Estate Duty (Chapter 11)

86. The maximum rate of estate duty should be fixed at 80 per

cent and the rates of duty in the slab of principal value exceeding Rs. 20,00,000 altered as under:

Slab of principal value	Present rate of duty	Rate of duty recommended
Over Rs. 20 lakhs but not exceeding Rs. 25 lakhs	85%	60%
Over Rs. 25 lakhs but not exceeding Rs. 30 lakhs	85%	70%
Over Rs. 30 lakhs	85%	80%

(Para III-11.3)

87. With a view to ensuring proper correlation between the gift-tax rates and the estate duty rates, the rate of gift-tax in the slab of taxable gifts over Rs. 20 lakhs up to Rs. 25 lakhs should be 60 per cent; that in the slab over Rs. 25 lakhs up to Rs. 30 lakhs should be 70 per cent; and the existing maximum rate of 75 per cent should operate on taxable gifts exceeding Rs. 30 lakhs. (Para III-11.4)

88. Section 20A of the Estate Duty Act imposing liability to estate duty in respect of shares and debentures in a foreign company held by a deceased not domiciled in India, in certain cases, and Part II of the Second Schedule specifying the rate of duty for the purpose of Section 20A be deleted. (Para III-11.6)

22

DIRECT TAX LAWS COMMITTEE, 1977 – INTERIM REPORT[1]

Chairman Shri N.A. Palkhivala, Senior Advocate, Bombay replaced by Shri CC Chokshi
Member Shri Harnam Shankar; Shri C.C. Ganpathi
M. Secy. Shri T.S.R. Narasimham

Appointment

In his Budget speech in the Lok Sabha in June 1977, the Hon'ble Shri H.M. Patel, Minister of Finance, Government of India, informed the House as under:

> "As Hon'ble Members are aware, the direct taxes statutes have become increasingly complicated and incomprehensible over the years. It is, therefore, necessary to take immediate action for simplification and rationalisation of these laws with a view to making them readily intelligible to the taxpayers, reducing litigation, and thus, subserving the interest of the national economy. It is also necessary to examine ways, and means of improving the administration of these laws and expediting assessment, appellate and other proceedings under these laws. It has, therefore, been decided to appoint a Committee of eminent experts to make recommendations for the simplification and rationalisation of the direct tax laws. It is my intention to ask the Committee to submit its report before the end of the year". [Para 82 of the Budget Speech, Part B]

In accordance with the above assurance to the Lok Sabha, the Government of India in the Ministry of Finance, Department of

---

1. Government of India, Ministry of Finance, December, 1977.

Revenue and Banking (Revenue Wing) passed a Resolution No. A-11019/70/77-Ad. VII, dated the 25th June, 1977 appointing a Committee of Experts to examine and suggest legal and administrative measures for simplification and rationalisation of the direct tax laws and such further alterations as are desirable in the interest of the national economy.

Terms of Reference

The Committee will:

(a) Recommend measures to simplify and rationalise, the laws relating to income-tax, surtax, wealth-tax, gift-tax and estate duty, and to alter those laws with a view to making them readily comprehensible to taxpayers, reducing litigation and thus subserving the interest of the national economy;

(b) Suggest ways and means of improving the administration of those laws and expediting assessment, appellate and other proceedings under those laws;

(c) Examine the advisability of consolidating the four laws relating to income-tax, surtax, wealth-tax and gift-tax into one Act;

(d) Prepare draft of the Bills for being presented before Parliament.

Contents

Introduction; Charitable Trusts; Depreciation; Amalgamation of Industrial Units under Section 72A; Taxation of Casual Incomes; Additional Income-tax on Undistributed Profits; Assessment Procedure; Registration of Firms; Advance Tax; Settlement of Cases; Appeals and Revision; Acquisition of Immovable Properties; Authorities Competent to Interpret the Tax Laws; Valuation of House Properties; Summary of Observations and Recommendations; Annexures I to IV.

Recommendations

Charitable Trusts (Chapter 2)

1. The provisions relating to the assessment of charitable and

religious trusts are one of the most complicated groups of sections in the Income-tax Act. (Para 2.1)

2. The provisions contained in the Income-tax Act should have only one underlying objective, viz., to regulate the extent to which and the circumstances in which tax concessions should be granted to charitable trusts. (Para 2.4)

3. A uniform central law governing registration of trusts, regulating their fund-raising activities, maintenance of accounts, application of income, investment of trust funds, involvement of trusts in corporate affairs consequent on holding of shares in companies and providing for machinery to deal with the abuse of trust property, etc., should be enacted as soon as possible. (Para 2.4)

4. The words "not involving the carrying on of any activity for profit" occurring in Section 2(15) should be deleted. (Para 2.7)

5. The amendment to Section 1(15) should have retrospective effect from 1st April, 1962. (Para 2.8)

6. The provisions of Section 13(1)(bb) should also be made applicable to the trusts with the fourth category objects, i.e., trusts for the advancement of objects of general public utility other than relief of the poor, education and medical relief, with effect from the 1st April, 1977, as in the case of trusts with the other three categories of objects. (Para 2.9)

7. Section 11(4) should be deleted with effect from the 1st April, 1977 as it would be inconsistent with the scheme of tax exemption outlined above. (Para 2.10)

8. The provisions of Section 13(1)(bb) should be further enlarged to permit business activity, mainly carried on by the beneficiaries even when the business itself is not carried on in the course of carrying out a primary purpose of the trust. (Para 2.11)

9. The law should provide for two different and totally independent computations, one for determining the assessable income, and the other for determining the amount that is to be applied for charitable purposes by the trust. The assessable income under the Income-tax Act should be computed strictly in accordance with the Act following the various provisions, taking into account even notional income and granting deductions specifically permitted under the Income-tax Act. On the other hand, the amount that is to be considered for the purpose of application to charitable objects should be the actual gross receipts of the trust less the expenses actually incurred in earning the income or in maintaining the trust property. In

this computation, notional incomes or incomes not received, and notional allowance and deductions for amounts not actually expended, will both be left out of account. If the actual income so computed is equal to or less than the statutory income, i.e., income computed under the provisions of the Act, the trust should be required to apply either 75 per cent of the statutory income or the whole of the actual income, whichever is less. However, where the income so worked out on actual basis exceeds the statutory income, it should suffice if the trust applies either 75 per cent of the actual income or the whole of its statutory income, whichever is less. We also suggest that the relevant provisions should be suitably illustrated in the Act itself to make the concept clear. (Para 2.12)

10. The existing provision for relating the amounts applied in the immediately following year to the earlier year, at the option of the trust should be retained, subject to the modification that the Income-tax Officer may be empowered to extend the time for exercise of the option in deserving cases independently of the time available for filing the return of income. (Para 2.13)

11. While the capital gains arising to a charitable trust could be given the same treatment as in the case of any other taxpayer, insofar as the application of funds for charitable purposes is concerned, only the net sale proceeds received by the trust during a given year should be considered for application (which, under the existing law, includes re-investment) in that year. Further, re-investment may be permitted until the expiry of the next following accounting year of the trust. (Para 2.14)

12. Charitable trusts should be allowed to accumulate their income even for a general purpose falling within the overall objects of the trust. Consequently, the provision in Section 11(3A), which empowers the Income-tax Officer to allow change of the purpose originally indicated for the accumulation, at the request of the trust, will be rendered superfluous, and may, therefore, be omitted. (Para 2.15)

13. The provisions relating to accumulation should continue to operate in relation to the income required to be applied for charitable purposes as recommended in para 2.12. (Para 2.16)

14. Section 11(2) should be amended to empower the Commissioner to condone delays in giving the notice as also in making the investment or deposit under that section. The Section may also specify: (a) The time within which the notice is to be given, which may (as

present, stipulated in Rule 17 of the Income-tax Rules) be "the time allowed under sub-section (1) or sub-section (2) of section 139, whether fixed originally or on extension, for furnishing the return of income" and (b) the time within which the amount accumulated or set apart is to be invested or deposited in the manner laid down in the section, which may be one year from the end of the relevant previous year (instead of six months at present stipulated in form 10). (Para 2.17)

15. There should be no objection to a trust making a donation from out of its corpus to the corpus of another trust. However, where a trust makes donations out of its income to another trust, while in the case of the donor trust these will continue to be treated as application of income, in the hands of the recipient trust, these should always be considered as normal income and any stipulation that the contributions are to the corpus of the recipient trust should be disregarded for the purposes of the tax exemption. (Para 2.18)

16. The provisions of Section 12A should be amended to provide for an application for registration being entertained at any time before the completion of the first assessment of the trust. Where a trust has failed to register itself within the time limit, it should still be open to it to register itself prospectively at least for future years. (Para 2.19)

17. The provision in Section 12A(b) may be amended to clarify that, where the accounts of the trust have been audited under the provisions in this behalf in any State law, such audit could be regarded as sufficient compliance with the requirements of that provision. (Para 2.19)

18. Insofar as the situations enunciated in Section 13(2) are concerned, the provisions of that section should be treated as exhaustive and the law should make it clear that, unless the features spelt out in Section 13(2) are present in any of those situations, the transaction will not be treated as use or application of the trust income of property for the benefit of the excluded persons, for the purposes of section 13(1)(c) so as to nullify the exemption in Sections 11 and 12. (Para 2.20)

19. The provisions of Section 13(2)(a) should be suitably amended so as to make the intention clear that, in a case where a loan is advanced to a person referred to in Section 13(3), it should be covered by adequate security and also ensure adequate rate of interest. (Para 2.21)

20. The provision in Section 13(2)(h) should be amended to clarify that it excludes from its purview the assets originally settled on trust or donated to the corpus of the trust including in either case accretion to such assets, by way of bonus shares. (Para 2.22)

21. As the restrictions in Section 13(2)(h) would be excluded from operation in respect of investments forming the original corpus of the trust and donations to the corpus irrespective of the date of creation of the trust, the operation of Section 13(2)(h) should be so excluded whether or not there is any mandatory direction in this regard in the trust deed. (Para 2.23)

22. The term "substantial contribution" should be defined to mean the aggregate contribution up to the end of the relevant previous year in a sum equivalent to 10 per cent of the value of the trust assets as at the end of the previous year in which the contribution was made, or Rs. 5,000, whichever is higher. (Para 2.24)

23. The definition of "relative" in Section 13 should be restored to the position existing prior to 1st April, 1973. (Para 2.25)

24. The provisions of Section 13(1)(d) together with those of Sections 13(5) and 13(6) should be deleted and, in their place, a general provision should be substituted giving the trustees freedom in the matter of investment subject to the restrictions under Section 13(1)(c). Section 153B of the Companions Act may also be simultaneously amended suitably to vest voting right in respect of all shares held by charitable trusts in the public trustee. (Para 2.26)

25. While the state need not encourage the growth of communal and non-charitable institutions, there should be no objection whatsoever, for these institutions existing with whatever resources they are able to muster without being put to an additional disadvantage *vis-a-vis* other taxpayer under the Act. The law should, therefore, be amended suitably to stipulated that the deeming provisions of Section 2(24)(iia) would not apply to a trust or institution referred to in Section 13(1)(a) or (b). (Para 2.27)

Depreciation (Chapter 3)

26. Depreciation under the Income-tax Act is not merely a provision for charging against taxable profits the capital expenditure incurred by an undertaking on depreciable assets over the useful life of the assets, but it is also aimed at working as a tax incentive measures affecting the cash flow of business enterprises and genera-

tion of internal resources for replacement of assets which have outlived their utility. (Para 3.3)

27. One of the recommendations of the Bhoothalingam Committee was to allow a taxpayer to write up his assets on a flat 20 per cent basis and allow depreciation up to 120 per cent of the cost of assets. Such artificial distortion of the concept of depreciation to serve the objective of providing funds for replacement of assets at the end of their useful life is not favoured. (Paras 3.4 to 3.7)

28. The present provisions relating to depreciation and the elaborate Schedule of rates under the Income-tax Rules are highly complex and complicated. (Para 3.8)

29. The existing practice of allowing depreciation on the reducing balance method, which provides for accelerated depreciation by larger write-offs in the earlier years for assets in general, should continue. The exception in the case of ocean-going ships, where the straight-line method of depreciation has been adopted should also be retained. (Para 3.9)

30. The taxpayer should have the option in respect of the actual quantum of depreciation be claimed against the profits from year to year subject, however, to a maximum rate specified in the law which will be applied to the written down value, except in the case of ocean-going ships where the existing pattern should continue. In this regard, the maximum rates of depreciation should be:

Building including roads, culverts, bridges, etc.	10%
Furniture and fixtures	20%
Plant and machinery	40%

(Para 3.10)

31. The option given to the taxpayer should be limited to his choosing one single rate for all assets falling within a class, namely, building, furniture and fixtures and plant and machinery, and he should not be allowed to adopt different rates for different items falling within the same class. (Para 3.11)

32. A total latitude to the taxpayers, in the matter of choosing depreciation rates is not desirable as that might disturb the budgetary position of the Government. (Para 3.12)

33. The tax incentive which flows from the degree of latitude allowed in the matter of choice of depreciation rates should not be permitted to be frittered away by the taxpayer but should be retained

within the business for further development. To ensure this, depreciation under Section 32 should be allowed in the manner indicated above only where the quantum of depreciation claimed for income-tax purposes is actually debited to the profit and loss account of the relevant previous year. (Para 3.13)

34. Full write-off (i.e., depreciation at 100%) should be allowed in the case of all assets where the actual cost of any asset does not exceed Rs. 10,000. In the case of those taxpayers who avail of the option to vary their claim for depreciation to suit the performance of their business from year to year, such depreciation should also be debited to the profit and loss account of the taxpayer of the relevant previous year in which the taxpayer chooses to claim such depreciation, while in other cases it will be allowed in the year in which the assets are brought into use for the purposes of the business. (Para 3.15)

35. In cases where no books of account are maintained, depreciation should be allowed at the uniform rate of 10 per cent on buildings and 20 per cent on plant and machinery and furniture and fixtures, on the reducing balance method. (Para 3.16)

36. The basic concept of depreciation as a charge in determining the true and fair profits under the Companies Act should not be disturbed. The quantum of such depreciation should be left to the opinion of the directors under the provisions of the Companies Act. In cases where companies choose to make a higher claim in Income-tax law, the additional amount should also be debited in the profit and loss account "below the line" (that is to say in the appropriation section of the profit and loss account) and such amount should be credited to a depreciation reserve. The Income-tax Act should provide that such reserve should not be utilised for purposes of declaration of dividends. (Para 3.21)

37. If a company desires a nil allowance in income-tax, it should not charge the profit and loss account of that year but should disclose such arrears of depreciation by way of a note on the accounts, as permitted by the Companies Act. (Para 3.22)

38. The Government may, therefore, consider consequential amendments to the provisions of the Companies Act so as not to result in any inconsistency with the scheme for allowance of depreciation under the Income-tax Act as recommended above. The distinction between the charge of adequate amount of depreciation and the additional amount which may be claimed at the taxpayers' option (as a measure of incentive and simplification under the Income tax law)

should be clearly maintained for all purposes. It would then not result in any in consistency with other questions such as payment of dividend, bonus, managerial remuneration and provisions relating to capital issues, etc. (Para 3.23)

39. In dealing with business concerns as going concerns not operating with a view to liquidation, calculation of depreciation separately for each item of asset is unnecessary. At every stage of addition of new assets, the cost of the new assets should be aggregated with the written down value of the existing block and depreciation allowed on such consolidated block. (Para 3.24)

40. With a view to obviating meticulous calculations, the entire sale proceeds (or scrap sales, insurance or salvage monies realised) of assets which are sold, discarded, demolished, or destroyed should be reduced from the written down value of the asset block and that, if at any stage, the realisations exceed the written down value of the block, the excess should be taxed as profit. As the entire block of assets whether they be (a) furniture and fixtures, or (b) buildings, or (c) plant and machinery, will continue to be depreciated until ultimately brought down to zero, there should be no deduction by way of a terminal allowance under Section 32(1)(iii) at any intermediate stage. The grant of terminal allowance should only arise with reference to the shortfall when the entire block of assets is sold on the closure of the business or the closure of a distinct and separate part thereof. (Para 3.25)

41. The provisions for extra-shift allowance in respect of machinery and plant used in factories (general of seasonal) and approved hotels should be discontinued. (Para 3.26)

42. The existing provisions for carry forward of unabsorbed depreciation should continue. The benefit of carry forward and set off of unabsorbed depreciation should be allowed whether or not the asset in question continues to be used for the purposes of the business in the succeeding accounting years. (Para 3.27)

43. On the analogy of the provisions of Section 54D, a provision should be made to secure that, where depreciable assets, of a business are taken over by the Government or any statutory authority, no profit will be taxed under Section 41(2) if the taxpayer re-invests the sale proceeds or compensation moneys in the acquisition of other depreciable assets for any business within a period of three years from the date of acquisition. (Para 3.28)

44. The law should be clarified to provide that no depreciation

under Section 32 shall be allowable in respect of capital expenditure for scientific research qualifying for deduction under Section 35. (Para 3.29)

45. The following items of expenditure, in particular, should also be eligible for amortisation against profits of a business over a ten-year period for tax purposes:

(1) Pre-operative expenses on administration and accounts departments and such other expenditure which does not directly relate to creation or acquisition of assets.
(2) Expenses on shifting of a factory.
(3) Payment for acquisition of intangible assets for which there is no other provision for amortisation.
(4) Expenses on construction of railway sidings and roads on land not belonging to the taxpayer.

As some of these items are not necessarily "preliminary" in character, but would be incurred in a running business, it would be necessary to enlarge the scope of Section 35D to cover these items as well. (Para 3.30)

46. Any instance of business expenditure which results in disallowance as revenue expenditure and non-allowance of depreciation, should be promptly notified under Section 35(2)(d) as and when the attention of the Government is drawn thereto. (Para 3.31)

47. The limitation on the totality of preliminary expenditure now appearing under sub-section (3) of Section 35D should be removed. (Para 3.32)

48. The following simple formula should be prescribed for amortisation of expenditure on production of feature films in place of the complicated procedure laid down in Rule 9A of the Income-tax Rules:

(a) If the film is released 90 days prior to the close of the accounting year in which the production is completed, the entire cost of production should be allowed as a deduction in the relevant previous year;
(b) If the film is released at any time within the period of the aforesaid 90 day prior to the expiry of the accounting year, 60 per cent of the cost of production should be allowed in that accounting year and the remaining 40 per cent in the im-

mediately succeeding accounting year. (3.33)

49. As the rupee is now de-linked from the sterling and the foreign exchange value of the rupee fluctuates from time to time as computed with reference to a "based of currencies, the provisions of Section 43A have become quite cumbersome and difficult to apply. The law should be amended to secure that the actual cost of assets acquired on deferred payment terms, etc., from abroad is taken as originally computed with reference to the exchange rates prevailing on the date of acquisition of the same. Thereafter, any gain or loss occasioned to the taxpayer at the point of actual remittance of instalment of purchase price or loan, as the case may be, should be treated as a revenue gain or loss of the business and the actual cost of the assets should not be disturbed. As regards cases where the actual cost has already been adjusted under the existing provisions of Section 43A, the gain or loss would be calculated with reference to such adjusted actual cost. In other words, as from the time the aforesaid suggestion is in force, no further adjustment should be made under Section 43A. (Para 3.35)

50. In the case of assets acquired under hire-purchase agreements, the purchaser should be entitled to claim the depreciation in his assessment provided that, as between the purchaser and the vendor, it is agreed that the purchaser alone shall be entitled to claim depreciation in respect of the same asset. The administrative instructions under which this is presently being secured should preferably be incorporated in the law itself. (Para 3.36)

Amalgamation of Industrial Units under Section 72A (Chapter 4)

51. Section 72A permits the carry forward and set off of the accumulated business losses and the unabsorbed depreciation of the amalgamating company (which is sick industrial unit not financially viable) against the income of the amalgamated company in the following years. The provisions as they stand are likely to give rise to certain practical difficulties in actual implementation and unless these difficulties are removed, the amalgamations aimed at may not take place to the extent desired by the Government. (Paras 4.2 to 4.4)

52. Under this section as it stands, it appears that the amalgamation has to be effected first and thereafter the "specified authority" has to be moved for the purpose of making a recommen-

dation to the Central Government. In the guidelines recently issued by the Government, it is indicated that an application for approval of the scheme of amalgamation may be made to the "specified authority" even before such amalgamation has actually taken place and that the "specified authority" may indicate to the amalgamated and amalgamating companies that, in the event of the amalgamation being finally effected on the basis of the scheme presented to and approved by the "specified authority", it would make a formal recommendation to the Government for making a declaration under Section 72A(1). While this assurance is indeed welcome, in the fitness of things, the substance of the assurance should be incorporated in the law by a specific provision to permit an application to the Central Government by the concerned company with a scheme of amalgamation for consideration as to whether the terms of the proposed amalgamation as set forth in the scheme are such as to meet the requirements of the section. Once the application is approved, then the companies concerned can go ahead with the scheme and obtain the Court's approval to the same and implement it accordingly. Natural justice requires that the Central Government should give an opportunity to the companies concerned to explain the scheme and, if there are any objectionable features, the companies should be allowed to modify the scheme suitably so that it meets with approval. (Para 4.5)

53. The declaration to be issued under Section 72A should clearly specify the previous year of the amalgamated company in which the accumulated loss and unabsorbed depreciation of the amalgamating company shall be deemed to be the loss and depreciation of the amalgamated company so as to eliminate controversies arising from the time lag in the completion of formalities as to the date on which the amalgamation may be considered as effective. (Para 4.6)

54. When a scheme is submitted to the Central Government under the above-mentioned procedure, the Central Government should examine it only with reference to the conditions spelt out in the section itself and any other conditions which may already have been notified pursuant thereto. In other words, further notifications which may be issued by the Central Government should only apply prospectively to schemes of amalgamation which may be submitted for approval after the date of issue of the notification. (Para 4.7)

55. There is, at present, unnecessary duplication of proceedings, one before the "specified authority" and the other before the Central

Government; the former to make the recommendation and the latter to issue the declaration. These should be coalesced. The section should provide for a declaration being issued by the Central Government (or in the alternative, by the "specified authority") on an application by the amalgamated company as a single proceeding. (Para 4.8)

56. The section should be amended to provided for the laying down of conditions by the approving authority (Central Government or the "specified authority") upon which the scheme of amalgamation is approved under sub-section (1). These conditions may relate, among things to,—

(a) Employment of workers,
(b) Use of productive capacity,
(c) Finance to be raised.

The actual allowance would then be subject to the fulfilment of these conditions by the amalgamated company and the satisfaction of the assessing authorities at the time of assessment in the matter of such fulfilment. No further approval of the Central Government (or "specified authority") should be necessary. Thus, if the conditions as laid down by the approving authority in according approval under sub-section (1) are compiled with, the set off and carry forward of accumulated losses and unabsorbed depreciation should follow as a matter or course. If, however, the assessing authority finds a breach of the conditions, such set off and carry forward would lapse as from the year of infringement of the conditions. As this would be a decision by the assessing authorities, it would automatically be subject to the normal appellate proceedings under the Act. (Para 4.9)

Taxation of Casual Incomes (Chapter 5)

57. The present scheme of taxation of casual income is unduly complex and provides a fertile field for mistakes in assessments and causes needless confusion in the mines of the taxpayers. In its well-meant attempt to bring into the net all items of income which are of casual and non-recurring nature and to make them bear the full brunt of tax with a concessional treatment only to lottery winnings in the case of non-corporate taxpayers, the Government seems to have failed to achieve the intended objective. (Paras 5.3 and 5.4)

58. Collections from the sources mentioned in sub-clause (ix) of clause (24) of Section 2 are a little over Rs. 1 crore only. Jackpot payments all over the country alone are estimated to run into several crores of rupees. To devise some procedures for getting some tax at least from such winnings, Section 194B should be enlarged to encompass in its fold all the items appearing in sub-clause (ix) of clause (24) of Section 2 where the payer is an organised body. (Para 5.5)

59. To ensure that taxpayers, as far as possible, obtain their winnings from various recognised sources such as race clubs and other social clubs, Section 80TT should be amended to include, in addition to lottery winnings, all the other items which are mentioned in sub-clause (ix) of clause (24) of Section 2. All these items should be treated in the same way as lotteries by deducting 50 per cent of the amount in computing the total income, with the difference that, in respect of these additional items, the initial deduction should be limited to what is allowable under Section 10(3), viz., Rs. 1,000. In the case of companies having any such income, the position under the present law may continue, with the modification that the provisions for deduction of tax at source under Section 194B, modified as suggested above, should apply also to payments of casual income made to companies. (Para 5.6)

Additional Income-Tax on Undistributed Profits

60. The scheme for levy of additional tax under Section 104 has to be considered in the light of the totality of the tax incidence on companies. At present, closely-held companies are already subjected to higher rates of tax than widely-held companies. (Para 6.4)

61. The question of declaration of dividends and adequacy of dividends has to be considered objectively, judged by business considerations. Reasonable requirements of the future have also to be considered, apart from the financial position of the company, etc. In the face of such widespread considerations of business exigency, it is very difficult to sustain assessments of additional tax under Section 104 in a large majority of cases. (Para 6.5)

62. Considerable emphasis is currently being placed on the need for restraint in dividend distributions with a view to encouraging plough back of resources for development. (Para 6.6)

63. The provisions relating to "deemed" dividends, under Section 2(22), are an effective check on the use of companies' resources

for private purposes. Apart from this, there is already a provision for levy of wealth-tax on shares, levy of capital gains tax on transfer of shares and levy of gift tax or estate duty on transmission of shares *inter vivos* or on death. (Para 6.7)

64. The trend of company legislation in recent years has been to ensure at least a minimum plough back of profits and further of restrict the withdrawals from reserves for payment of dividend under Section 205(2A) and Section 205A of the Companies Act, 1956. (Para 6.10)

65. The latest provision exempting closely-held industrial companies from the ambit of Section 104 is a step in the right direction. There is likewise justification for excluding the other categories of companies as well, inasmuch as trading companies and service companies do contribute to economic growth and employment and supplement the role of industrial companies in this regard. The provisions of Sections 104 to 109 should be applicable only in the case of closely-held investment companies, while other closely-held companies should be excluded from their purview. (Para 6.11)

66. Investment companies should continue to be subjected to the restrictions under these sections as these companies enjoy a concessional tax treatment in relation to their main source of income, namely, dividend income. Again, investment companies are capable of, and are, being used as a medium for holding investments and for acquiring further investments as a means of gaining share-holding control. Non-compulsion in the matter of distribution of dividends in such cases is likely to contribute to concentration of economic power, which needs to be checked. (Para 6.12)

Assessment Procedure (Chapter 7)

67. Mounting arrears of work has plagued the Income-tax Department for many years. The various procedures experimented with by the Department have not helped to solve this problem. (Paras 7.2 to 7.4)

68. The problem faced by the Department is one of extreme strain on its man-power and other physical resources. The system of planning man-power requirements to match the work-load overlooks the fact that whereas work multiplies without notice, man-power cannot be multiplied instantaneously to keep pace with workload. Planning to fit work-load to man-power seems to be the only answer to

the problems confronting the Department. (Paras 7.5 to 7.8)

69. The Department must so gear itself that, by deploying its entire work-force, it would be in a position to check whether the returns are complete and payments adequate, within a period of 3 months from the receipt of the returns. To facilitate this, the particulars to be submitted with the return should be clearly indicated in a manner easily intelligible to the taxpayer. At the same time the particulars should be such that a rapid scrutiny would reveal compliance by the taxpayer and instances of non-compliance would be readily discernible. In particular, the return should contain:

(i) Statements showing computation of income under each head separately, disclosing all allowances and deductions claimed;
(ii) Statement showing computation of the tax payable, along with claims for credit for tax deducted at source, advance tax paid and self-assessment tax paid, supported by the relevant certificates and receipted challans;
(iii) Attested copies of trading and profit and loss account or income and expenditure account, balance-sheet, partners'/proprietors' capital accounts, etc.; and
(iv) Compulsory deposit receipts. (Para 7.9)

70. The taxpayer should be cautioned in regard to the following matters:

(a) If the return is not complete in all respects, it is liable to be treated as an invalid return, with the consequences that the taxpayer will be regarded as being in default for the purposes of interest, penalty and prosecution, as if there is a failure on his part to file the return.
(b) Although the assessment may, in the first instance, be completed under Section 143(1), the taxpayer will become liable to penalty and prosecution in case the computation of income and deductions is found to be inaccurate and/or any escaped income is brought to assessment. (Para 7.10)

71. With a view to encouraging the filing of complete returns, there should be a specific legal provision according to which incomplete returns will be treated as invalid ones, attracting consequential interest for delayed submission, to be calculated till the date of filing

a correct and valid return. Wherever, it is observed that the return is incomplete in any respect, a standard form of notice should be sent to the taxpayer directing him to supply all the relevant missing particulars so as to enable the return to be treated as duly filed. The return itself need not be sent back to the taxpayer except in cases where some error of commission or omission therein requires to be rectified by him. (Para 7.11)

72. Notices under Section 139(2) need not be issued to taxpayers already on the registers of the Department. Such notices need be issued only to new taxpayers discovered in the course of searches or survey operations, or persons who have failed to file returns within the time limit. (Para 7.12)

73. The law may be amended whereby an assessment is deemed to be completed on the sending of an acknowledgement attached to the return itself as a tear-off slip. (Para 7.13)

74. Returns where any unusual features like partition of H.U.F., cession of business, dissolution of a firm, etc., are noticed during rapid scrutiny should be referred to the Commissioner for directions for inclusion in the scrutiny group. Taking into account the man-power available the Central Board of Direct Taxes should issue an annual programme laying down the criteria for selection of cases for scrutiny. The cases selected for scrutiny should cover the following types of cases:

(i) All company cases.
(ii) Sensitive cases, e.g., tax evasion cases.
(iii) A certain proportion of other cases picked up by random sampling, depending on the man-power available. (Para 7.14)

75. Belated returns should be left to the discretion of the Commissioner to decide on merits whether the circumstances justify the case being taken up for scrutiny. (Para 7.17)

76. In any scheme of voluntary compliance it should be for the taxpayer to buy time and the cost is to be metered right from the date on which the return is due up to the date of filing the return. While the rate of determining the cost may be retained at 12 per cent per annum, it should be applied to the gross tax on the total income as determined on regular assessment, that is to say, the tax without deduction of advance tax and taxes deducted at source. The taxpayer should be required to calculate this additional sum for each com-

pleted month of default on the basis of his return and pay it before filing the return, failing which the Income-tax Officer also should be empowered to calculate the amount at the time of the regular assessment. (Para 7.18)

77. The provision in Section 140(3) for levy of penalty for non-payment of self-assessment tax should be deleted. (Para 7.19)

78. In the event of delay beyond a period of 90 days from the due date, the penal provision should come into play. In such cases, if the default persists, the Income-tax Officer should also complete the proceedings on a best judgement assessment basis even before the end of the assessment year concerned. (Para 7.20)

79. The provision for levy of a cost for delayed filing of returns would not be a sufficient deterrent in cases where no tax is payable at all as, for example, returns showing a loss, returns of trusts, etc. In such cases, the law should provide for an outside time limit to coincide with the end of the assessment year and secure that any such return received after the end of the assessment year will not be treated as a valid return. Claims for refund of tax deducted at source will, however, continue to be entertained up to 2 years from the end of the assessment year, as under the present law. (Para 7.21)

80. There need be no apprehension that, by accepting returns, substantial revenue will be lost, as the bulk of the taxes is collected before the assessment by way of tax deducted at source, advance tax and self-assessment tax. (Para 7.22)

81. Income-tax Officers have not been able to pay adequate attention to search and seizure cases, which are all sensitive cases, where considerable revenue is likely to be involved. The Department has all the talent needed to effectively administer the tax laws. The problem is one of overwhelming workload. No Income-tax Officer has been able to give undivided attention to cases of fraud, evasion, etc. Completion of assessments on the basis of the returns on the lines suggested above will free the Income-tax Officer to carry out scrutiny in depth in such cases. (Paras 7.23 to 7.24)

82. Concentration of complicated and tax-evasion cases in Central Circles has not resulted in any significant success in handling such cases. Central Circle should be abolished. Instead, each Commissioner should have an investigation unit within his own charge for handling cases requiring intensive investigation. Officers posted to these circles must have adequate experience in investigation work and should be allowed special pay. It would even be desirable to

entrust investigation cases to two Income-tax Officers exercising jurisdiction concurrently under the close supervision of an Inspecting Assistant Commissioner. Reasonable disposal targets should be fixed for such investigation work allowing adequate time for scrutiny in depth. Each Commissioner may also have his own intelligence unit which would work in close liaison with the Central Intelligence Units organised on an all-India basis. (Para 7.25)

83. Section 146(2) should be amended to provide that, if the Income-tax Officer fails to dispose of the application within the specified period of 90 days, the assessment shall be deemed to have been cancelled and proceedings reopened. (Para 7.26)

84. Under the scheme suggested above an Income-tax Officer will have only 200 scrutiny assessment to handle in a year, and would be in a position to pay adequate attention to them. This would ensure a sufficiently intensive scrutiny and quality of assessment leading to reduction of appeals and better taxpayer compliance. Better administration of the laws in relation assessment procedures will also have a beneficial effect on the problem of arrears of taxes. The measures outlined by us will also reduce the public contact in a large majority of cases. This would necessarily have a beneficial effect in reducing he opportunities for corruption. The completion of the major portion of assessments virtually by acceptance of the returns would also reduce the areas of litigation between the taxpayers and the Department. The energies of the taxpayers would also be conserved and directed towards productive channels with consequential beneficial effects on the national income and the tax revenue of the Government. (Paras 7.28 to 7.33)

85. The beneficial results of the scheme can be enhanced by the personal involvement of the higher authorities like the Commissioner of Income-tax and the Inspecting Assistant Commissioner, and a dynamic approach towards its implementation. They should also inspire confidence in the Officers at lower levels and assure them that there will be no general suspicion of, or reflection on an officer, where loss of revenue may have been occasioned through the *bona fide* operation of the scheme. (Para 7.34)

Registration of Firms (Chapter 8)

86. Registration of partnership firms for purposes of taxation is one of the most controversial areas in the administration of the

Income-tax Act. This has generated an enormous amount of litigation but there are very few cases in which refusal of the registration on the ground of non-genuineness has been sustained by Courts, Simplification of these procedures is an urgent necessity. (Para 8.1)

87. The work relating to registration of firms should be centralised with the Commissioners of Income-tax, instead of leaving it with the various Income-tax Officers as at present. For this purpose, every firm should be required to make an application to the Commissioner before the end of the accounting year. (Para 8.4)

88. Full particulars of representative capacity of partners, if any, should be declared in the application for registration of the firm with the Commissioner. (Para 8.5)

89. As at present, the application should be signed by all the partners and should be accompanied by the original instrument of partnership along with a certified copy thereof or, in the alternative, two certified copies of the Deed. In the latter case, the original should be produced before the Commissioner, if and when called for. Particulars of the permanent account numbers of the partners and the Income-tax Circle/Ward where each of the partner is assessed should also be disclosed. (Para 8.6)

90. The Commissioner will record the receipt of the application in a register and intimate such registration to the firm and the Income-tax Officer within 30 days of the lodgement of the application. Where an application is complete and lodged with the Commissioner, registration of the firm should be automatic. (Para 8.7)

91. In subsequent years, so long as the constitution of the firm continues without change, all that is necessary will be a declaration to that effect to be furnished as a part of the return of income which should contain a provision for such declaration. (Para 8.8)

92. In cases where there is a change in the constitution of the firm, the firm will have to file a fresh application to the Commissioner and a fresh entry of registration would be made by the Commissioner. Likewise, when a firm is dissolved, intimation should be given to the Commissioner to enable him to make appropriate entries in the register. (Para 8.9)

93. A firm, which is registered with the Commissioner in accordance with the above procedure, will be assessed in the status of a registered firm. The income of the firm would be apportioned amongst the partners in accordance with their profit-sharing proportions and taxed directly in the hands of the partners. In a case where

a partner is in a representative capacity, the income in question would be taxed in the hands of the beneficial owner. (Para 8.10)

94. In the case of an unregistered firm, tax should be levied at a single stage on the firm itself and the scheme of further including the share of a partner in the firm in his personal assessment (even for rate purposes) should be discontinued. (Para 8.13)

95. To encourage firms to seek registration, unregistered firms should be required to pay tax at a flat rate of 65 per cent (which is the rate presently enacted under Section 164 in the case of discretionary trusts). No separate power need be vested in the Income-tax Officer to assess the unregistered firm as a registered firm as presently provided in Section 183(b). (Para 8.14)

96. In the case of the smaller firms, i.e., firms having incomes below Rs. 25,000 the Commissioner shall condone delays and technical lapses and afford full opportunity to such firms to comply with the registration formalities. In other cases, the Commissioner may condone the lapse if he is satisfied that the delay was due to just and reasonable cause. The powers of the Commissioner in this regard should be comprehensive and cover all forms of non-compliance including non-existence of a deed of partnership within the accounting year. (Para 8.15)

97. The procedure for assessing a firm as unregistered should be such that the Income-tax Officer cannot, on his own, accord the status of unregistered firm and he can only do so on the basis of a direction from the Commissioner. As an additional safeguard, the order of the Commissioner should be appealable to the Appellate Tribunal and the firm should not be entitled to agitate the question of status as an unregistered firm before the Appellate Assistant Commissioner. (Para 8.16)

98. Where registration accorded to a firm is subsequently cancelled in relating to any assessment year, consequential provision would be necessary to ensure that the partners' assessments are appropriately rectified as if there were mistakes apparent from record in respect of the shares of income from the firm assessed in their hands. (Para 8.17)

99. Double taxation of the some income may be justified where the taxable entities are legally and factually district from one another. This is not the case with firms and their partners. The present system is also regressive in the sense that the impact of double taxation is more acute in the case of a partner having a smaller share and in-

come than in the case of a partner with a larger share and income. The separate tax on a registered firm cannot be justified on any consideration of justice or fairness or sound principle of taxation and its only justification may be that it yields some revenue. But this yield is largely illusory because if the tax were to be discontinued a good portion of it will come back to the exchequer by way of increased tax on the partners. The separate tax on registered firms should, therefore, be altogether discontinued. (Para 8.18)

100. The law should provide for an obligation on registered firms to file returns of income as in the absence of a direct tax liability, there may be no obligation to file a return. (Para 8.20)

Advance Tax (Chapter 9)

101. Advance payment of tax is another area where the principle of voluntary compliance can be usefully extended. The present procedures involve considerable outlay of clerical labour and time and there is scope for introducing labour saving procedures in this field without adversely affecting the revenue. (Para 9.1)

102. The system of issuing advances tax notices be discontinued and the law amended to provide that every taxpayer liable to pay advance tax should furnish an estimate of the advance tax payable by him on the basis of the last assessment completed in his case or the return by him for a later year, before the date of the first instalment and pay the same in 3 equal instalments. The Income-tax Officer may, however, continue to have the power to issue a notice for advance payment of tax to any taxpayer who does not comply voluntarily with this requirement by the due date of the first instalment. (Para 9.5)

103. Advance tax should be uniformly payable on 15th September, 15th December and 15th March by all liable taxpayers. (Para 9.6)

104. To obviate difficulties and to impart some flexibility to the system, the Board should issue a general direction, under the provisions of Section 119(2)(a), that delays in payment of any instalment of advance tax for any period not exceeding 10 days should be condoned and the payment treated as having been made on the due date of that instalment in cases where the Income-tax Officer is satisfied that the delay was attributable to reasonable cause of circumstances beyond the control of the taxpayer. (Para 9.7)

105. The provisions relating to deferment of advance tax on com-

mission not received or adjusted may be deleted. (Para 9.8)

106. The right of the taxpayer to furnish a lower estimate on the basis of his estimated current income should remain in the statute. (Para 9.9)

107. The provisions requiring taxpayers to revise upwards the advance tax payable when the tax payable on the basis of their estimated current income exceeds the advance tax payable on the basis of past income by more than 33.5 per cent of the latter amount should be deleted. (Para 9.10)

108. The minimum income limit for liability to pay advance tax in all cases other than companies and registered firms should be Rs. 5,000 above the minimum taxable limit. (Para 9.11)

109. The provisions relating to grant of interest on excess payment of advance tax should be retained. (Para 9.12)

110. The charge of interest on short payments of advance tax should terminate on the date a valid and proper return of income is filed and should be computed with reference to the tax payable on the basis of such return. Such interest should be chargeable only where the advance tax actually paid falls short of 75 per cent of the tax payable on the basis of the return of income. (Para 9.13)

111. While there should be no charge of interest with reference to instalments paid on the basis of the last completed assessment or the latest return, interest at the rate of one per cent per month should be charged on the shortfall in any instalment paid on the basis of the taxpayer's own estimate, computed with reference to one-third of the tax payable on the basis of the return, from the due date for payment of that instalment up to the date the return is filed. Interest should similarly be chargeable when any instalment of advance tax is not paid on the due date. (Para 9.14)

112. Estimates should be deemed to be invalid, if appropriate payment of advance tax on due dates is not made. (Para 9.15)

113. The provisions relating to self-assessment should be suitably amended to require taxpayers to work out and pay voluntarily the interest due on shortfalls in the payment of advance tax along with the self-assessment tax. (Para 9.16)

114. The taxpayer should be made liable to penalty when he has failed to make payment of advance tax which is due or when the advance tax actually paid on the basis of his estimate falls short of 75 per cent of the tax payable on the basis of the return of income. (Para 9.17)

115. As there will be no need to levy penalty under Section 221 or to recover advance tax by coercive process under the scheme suggested above except where a notice has been issued by the Income-tax Officer, the provisions of Section 218 be modified suitably. (Para 9.18)

116. To provide a safeguard to the revenue against under-estimates of advance tax followed by under-statement of income in the return, interest at the rate of one per cent per month should be charged on the difference between the tax eventually assessed and the tax payable on the basis of the return from the date of filing the return up to the date of completion of the assessment made after due scrutiny. To avoid frequent recalculation of interest every time the income is modified in appeal, etc., the Income-tax Officer may be authorised to revise the interest, where necessary, while giving effect to the last appellate, etc., order. (Para 9.19)

117. The conditions for reduction of waiver of interest payable by the taxpayer as contained in Rule 40 should continue to apply in all cases of levy of interest. (Para 9.20)

118. To save hardship when an amalgamation takes effect retrospectively on account of the time take for obtaining the Court's sanction to the scheme, the law may be clarified to deem the payment of advance tax by an amalgamating company in respect of the income of the period falling after the date of amalgamation included in the assessment of the amalgamated company, as payment of advance tax by the amalgamated company in respect of such income. (Para 9.21)

Settlement of Cases (Chapter 10)

119. The existing provisions in the Act relating to 'Settlement of Cases' need some modifications in order to make them more effective and meaningful as well as to facilitate the smooth functioning of the Settlement Commission. While the Settlement Commission should not become an escape route for tax evaders who are caught by the Department, the doors for taxpayers who realise and admit their past mistakes of omission and commission and want to adopt the path of rectitude should not be closed. (Para 10.1)

120. The definition of "Case" in Section 245A(a) should be suitably amended to include (1) cases where no proceedings relating to assessment or re-assessment are pending on the date of the application but the taxpayer wishes to settle his past evaded or avoided

taxes which have escaped the notice of the Department, and (2) cases where no proceedings were commenced by the Department, viz., cases of taxpayers who hitherto have escaped the notice of the Department. (Para 10.2)

121. The provisions of Section 245B(2) may suitably be modified to enable the Commission to function with even less than its full strength. (Para 10.3)

122. The objection by the Commissioner under the second proviso to Section 245D(1) should be subject to review by the Commission. (Para 10.4)

123. The Government should examine the desirability of vesting powers in the Settlement Commission to compound the tax liability in the cases which are settled by it. (Para 10.5)

124. The authority for writing off, wholly or in part, any part of the Government revenues can be exercised only by the Government as such or by any of its subordinate authorities to whom the power is delegated and such write off is open to Parliamentary scrutiny. The Settlement Commission is a quasi-judicial body and is to act within the provisions of the Income-tax Act. If it were given such powers of write off, it would thus lay itself open to Parliamentary scrutiny which would detract from its quasi-judicial status. It may not, therefore, be desirable to give the Settlement Commission the powers of write off or scaling down the tax liability of a taxpayer generally. (Para 10.6)

125. The Commission may be specifically given the power to make rules regarding its functioning. (Para 10.7)

126. The existing provisions of Section 245F may be suitably modified to expressly provide delegation of power by the Settlement Commission to its subordinate officers. (Para 10.8)

127. Section 245F be suitably modified to enable the Commission to return a case of the Department after it has been admitted, if there is non-co-operation by the applicant. The Commission should remit a case only after giving the applicant an opportunity of being heard. (Para 10.9)

128. The law should vest power in the Settlement Commission to grant immunity from penalty under other Central Act also but a proviso should be added that such immunity may be granted only after due consultation with the appropriate authorities under the concerned Acts. (Para 10.10)

129. The rigours of the provisions in Section 245M may be mitigated by providing that, with the concurrence of the Commis-

sioner of Income-tax, a case could be taken up by the Settlement Commission where an Income-tax Officer has filed an appeal before the Income-tax Appellate Tribunal under Section 253(2) of the Income-tax Act. (Para 10.11)

130. Suitable modification needs to be made in Section 155 of the Income-tax Act to facilitate rectification of assessments in partners' cases or in the case or in the case of members of an association of persons, where settlements have been effected in the case of the firm or association of persons, as the case may be. (Para 10.12)

131. The Chairman of the Settlement Commission should be of the status of the Secretary to the Government of India. The tenure of office of the Chairman and the members should be five years or till attaining the age of 65 years, whichever is earlier. (Para 10.13)

132. The provisions for settlement of cases under the Wealth-tax Act, incorporated in Chapter V-A of that Act should also be amended on the same lines as indicated above. (Para 10.14)

Appeals and Revision (Chapter 11)

133. In our country, tax litigation has been proliferating in an alarming measures in recent years. Not merely is there too much of litigation, but the delays in the administration of such litigation is equally disheartening. (Paras 11.1 and 11.2)

134. This problem can be tackled by ensuring that the area of litigation is minimised and, at the same time, by ensuring that whatever litigation is inevitable, the same will be disposed of as expeditiously as possible. (Para 11.3)

135. The measures should be aimed at:

(a) Avoiding litigation;
(b) Reducing litigation;
(c) Simplifying and rationalising the existing provisions and accelerating disposal of appeals, references and connected matters. (Para 11.7)

A. *Measures to Avoid Litigation*

136. There should be a specific provision in the Income-tax Act and other direct tax laws, enabling the Central Board of Direct Taxes to give advance rulings at the request of taxpayers on specific issues,

not being purely issues of fact, on payment of the prescribed fees. (Parás 11.9 to 11.10)

137. A taxpayer should be entitled to seek an advance ruling both with reference to facts already obtaining in his case for a past year or with reference to a proposed transaction which he intends to enter into. A reference in the former types of cases may be made at any time before the completion of the assessment for the relevant year or where the assessment has already been completed and the matter is pending in appeal provided he withdraws the appeal on that point. The Board may give a ruling on such a reference or even decline to give any such ruling. In the latter event, the fees should be refunded and the appeal, if withdrawn, shall be divided. The ruling given by the Board should be binding on the income-tax authorities. However, it should bc open to the taxpayer to take the matter by way of appeal to the Delhi High Court, with a further right of appeal to the Supreme Court by either party. Where the point referred to the Board relates to a proposed transaction while the Board's ruling will be binding on the Departmental authorities, the taxpayer will be free to put through the transaction in such form as he deems fit, but he will not have the right of appeal to the Delhi High Court against the Board's ruling. (Para 11.11)

138. A provision may be introduced in the law enabling the Board to approach the Supreme Court and seek its advice even at an earlier stage before any litigation has arisen. (Para 11.12)

139. To avoid public funds being frittered away in futile litigation, disputes between public sector undertakings or Government companies and the Income-tax Department should, instead of being taken in appeals, etc., be resolved by the Central Board of Direct Taxes by discussion with the Administrative Ministry of the Central Government or the local Government concerned with the undertaking or Company and, where necessary in consultation with the Ministry of Law. (Para 11.14)

B. *Measures to Reduce Litigation*

140. Where a taxpayer claims before the assessing authority or any of the appellate authorities, that, on any issue arising in his case, an appeal or a reference is pending before any higher authority, including a High Court or the Supreme Court, in his own case for an earlier year or in the case of any other taxpayer for any year, and

gives an undertaking that he would abide, in respect of his own case, by the decision of the higher authority or the High Court or the Supreme Court, as the case may be, as governs such pending appeal or reference, then, the law should provide that the taxpayer's case should be disposed of in conformity with such decision, as and when it becomes available, without his having to agitate the matter by way of further appeals or references. If the assessment is completed taking a view adverse to the taxpayer, the same should be suitably modified by the (appropriate authority) when the final decision becomes available, as if it were a mistake apparent from the record in the taxpayer's own case for the relevant year and such modification should be made within four years from the date of such final decision. (Para 11.15)

141. Further, where the Supreme Court decides a point of law in any case, it should be open to any taxpayer to claim before the appropriate authorities the benefit of that decision in his own case for any past year for which the assessment has attained finality even though he might not have kept the matter alive by way of appeal or reference Department also to revise any completed assessment in the case of any taxpayer in the light of Supreme Court's judgement in any other case, if this is necessary in the interest of revenue. In either case, such action by the taxpayer or the Department should be permissible within a period not exceeding one year from the pronouncement of the Supreme Court's judgement. (Para 11.16)

C. *Measures to Simplify and Rationalise the Existing Provision and Accelerated Disposal of Appeals, etc.*

(i) *Proceedings before Appellate Assistant Commissioner/ Commissioner (Appeals)*: 142. To avoid controversies and also simplify the provisions, instead of enumerating the various orders of the Income-tax Officer against which an appeal lies of the Appellate Assistant Commissioner or, as the case may be, the Commissioner (Appeals), in Section 246 of the Income-tax Act, there should be a general provision to the effect that every final order (i.e., an order which is not in the nature of an administrative order or an interlocutory order) of the Income-tax Officer will be appealable to the Appellate Assistant Commissioner or the Commissioner (Appeals), as the case may be. Insofar as the Commissioner (Appeals) is concerned, the law should specify a monetary limit so as to demarcate his jurisdiction from that of the Appellant Commissioner. In addition, his jurisdiction may also be demarcated in terms of a class of orders, more or less on the lines of the existing provisions in Section 246. (Para 11.17)

143. To avoid the controversy as to whether a taxpayer is entitled to urge before the appellate authorities a ground which he had not raised before the lower authorities, the condition that the taxpayer should be "Aggrieved" appearing in Section 246 should be omitted. (Para 11.18)

144. Specific, right of appeal to the Appellate Assistant Commissioner should be provided against the Income-tax Officer's failure to pass an order on the taxpayer's application for rectification of relief within a period of six months of such application. (Para 11.19)

145. With a view to obviating delays in disposal of appeals finally, the powers of the Appellate Assistant Commissioner/Commissioner (Appeals) to set aside or remand a case should be taken away and he should be required to decide the points raised in the appeal finally after himself conducting any further enquiry that he may consider necessary for the purpose. (Para 11.20)

(ii) *Proceedings before the Appellate Tribunal*: 146. The minimum service qualification for appointment of a member of the Central Legal Service as judicial member and for appointment of an Assistant Commissioner of Income-tax as Accountant Member should be raised to 5 years. (Para 11.22)

147. The Members of the Tribunal should have a tenure of office similar to judges of High Courts, i.e., until 62 years of age. The President of the Tribunal should have the rank corresponding to a Secretary to the Government of India and other Members should correspond to Additional Secretaries. As the office of the President involves administrative powers and responsibilities only persons who are already vice-President of the Appellate Tribunal should be eligible for appointment as President of the Tribunal. (Para 11.23)

148. Section 253 should be amended on the same lines as Section 246. (Para 11.24)

149. The rules should be amended so as to permit a memorandum of appeal being signed by the Power of Attorney-holder of the Appellant. (Para 11.25)

150. The Appellate Tribunal should be given specific powers to dismiss an appeal or reference application before it on the ground of non-appearance of the Appellant/Applicant and it should not be re-

quired to pass an order thereon on merits. However, there should be a provision for reopening the matter by the Appellate Tribunal at the instance of the Appellant/Applicant within a period of 30 days. The Appellate Tribunal should also have the power to permit the withdrawal of an appeal or reference application by the Appellant/Applicant. (Para 11.26)

151. The law may be amended to provide that such a single member bench may dispose of any appeal where the amount of variation in the income or less in dispute does not exceed Rs. 25,000. (Para 11.27)

152. Where the members of a bench differ in opinion, that matter should be re-heard by a bench of three or more members which may include the members who originally heard it. (Para 11.28)

153. As publication of important order would go a long way in achieving certain judicial harmony among all the Benches in the country and will also enable the taxpayers to secure easily the official views of the final fact finding authority under the Act, the Tribunal should permit a reliable agency to publish an authentic and full text of its orders which it regards to be of general importance. (Para 11.29)

(iii) *Proceedings before High Courts*: 154. The Government should consider the establishment of a Central Tax Court to deal with all matters arising under the Income-tax Act and other Central Tax Laws. (Para 11.30)

155. For liquidating the heavy pendency of reference in the various High Courts pending the establishment of a Central Tax Court, the Government may advise the High Courts to constitute, as soon as possible, special tax benches on an *ad hoc* basis to hear and dispose of the pending matters by continuous sittings throughout the year. To achieve uniformity in this matter, judges with experience in this branch of law should be appointed on tax benches of High Courts. (Para 11.30)

156. The law may be amended to enable the High Court to dispense with the formality of calling for statement of the case under Section 256(2) where it is satisfied that the papers filed before it are sufficient to enable consideration of the question, and thereupon proceed to treat the application itself as a statement of the case and decide the question. (Para 11.32)

157. Section 256(3) may be amended to permit a refund of the fee paid also in a case where the application is withdrawn by the ap-

plicant before the Tribunal considers it. (Para 11.33)

158. Section 258 may be amended to give power to the High Court and the Supreme Court to alter or reframe the question referred to it without remitting the matter back to the Appellate Tribunal. The Court should also have the power to amend the statement of the case suitably and, thereafter, decide the matter without sending of back to the Appellate Tribunal for making the amendment. The Court should, however, be given the power to direct the Appellate Tribunal to take additional evidence on any point, where it considers this necessary for the purpose of deciding the matter before it. (Para 11.34)

(iv) *Proceedings before the Supreme Court*: 159. Section 257 may be amended to provide that, if the appellant makes a specific request to the Tribunal in a case were there is a conflict in the decisions of the High Court, it should be incumbent upon the Tribunal to make a reference direct to the Supreme Court. We further recommend that the power to make a direct reference to the Supreme Court may also be given to the Tribunal in the following situations:

(a) Where the High Court has already decided the matter in other cases;
(b) Where the point at issue is of a recurring nature in the case before the Tribunal year after year;
(c) Where the point at issue is one of public importance. (Para 11.35).

160. The requirement of obtaining a certificate of fitness from the High Court before filing an appeal to the Supreme Court be dispensed with so as to enable either party to move the Supreme Court directly in a special leave petition, without obtaining the certificate of fitness from the High Court. Such a provision will be similar to that under Article 136(1) of the Constitution for grant of special leave. (Para 11.36)

(v) *Proceedings by way of Revision by Commissioner*: 161. The provisions in Section 264 relating to revision by the Commissioner should be amended to make it clear that the Commissioner will not be debarred from dealing with any matter under this section except where the same point has been agitated in an appeal to the Appellate Tribunal or the Commissioner (Appeals). (Para 11.37)

162. As a corollary to the above, the provision in Section 263,

empowering the Commissioner to revise the Income-tax Officer's orders which are prejudicial to the revenue, should also be amended so as to clarify that the Commissioner will not be debarred from revising any such order except where the particular point on which he proposes to revise the order has been made the subject-matter of appeal before the Appellate Assistant Commissioner, the Commissioner (Appeals) or the Appellate Tribunal. (Para 11.38)

(vi) *General*: 163. The taxpayer should be given the right to set off any refund due to him as a result of any order in appeal against any tax or other sum payable by him for any year by giving an intimation in writing to that effect to the Income-tax Officer. (Para 11.39)

Acquisition of Immovable Properties (Chapter 12)

164. The experience regarding the working of the provisions of Chapter XXA, which was inserted in the Income-tax Act on the basis of the interim report of the Wanchoo Committee for the last 5 years should be adequate for judging the utility and effectiveness of the provisions. The statistics relating to the progress of work in this area during the past few years in Bombay, where the evil of understatement of property values is considered to be widely prevalent, show that notices of acquisition have been issued in only about 20 per cent of the cases where intimations were received from the Registrar and acquisition orders have been actually issued only in a very small fraction of these cases. The acquisition order has been upheld in only one case. The conclusion is inescapable that the provisions have failed to achieve their intended purpose. (Para 12.3)

165. There is no evidence of the deterrent effect of these provisions. The statistics do not disclose any steep rise in the yield from capital gains tax. Increases in stamp revenue, if any, may merely be part of the general phenomenon of rising tax revenues or the result of increased rates of stamp duty. There is also no indication of any unusual rise in the value of immovable properties disclosed for wealth-tax purposes. (Para 12.5)

166. There has been a change in the complexion of the situation after the Wanchoo Committee submitted their interim and final Reports. The law relating to ceiling and regulation of urban land, which came into effect in the course of 1976, has considerably reduced the magnitude of the problem. With the recent enactment of Section 54E, any temptation for understatement of the sale con-

sideration in the deed with a view to evading or reducing the capital gains tax liability has largely disappeared. (Paras 12.6 and 12.7)

167. The effectiveness of the provisions in Chapter XXA for acquisition of property also depends entirely on the ability of the administration to sustain the estimated market value before the Courts. If the market value can be effectively established, the remedy under Section 52(2) would be more direct and less cumbersome even from the Department's point of view. (Para 12.8)

168. Chapter XXA of the Income-tax Act should be deleted. (Para 12.9)

Authorities Competent to Interpret the Tax Laws (Chapter 13)

169. With varied interpretation put forth by different authorities on the complicated provisions of the Income-tax Act, there is a marked tendency, in the Department, to re-open post haste and indiscriminately, completed assessments on the basis of any opinion advocated against the taxpayer. (Para 13.1)

170. A rigid interpretation, followed quickly by a wooden application of the legal provisions, simply because an adverse view against the taxpayer has been propounded by another authority, has to be strictly eschewed for reducing unnecessary litigation. (Para 13.3)

171. There should be a reasonable degree of finality in assessments. As observed by the Supreme Court in Parashuram Pottery Works Co. Ltd. *vs.* ITO (106 ITR-1) stale issues should not be reactivated beyond a particular stage and lapse of time must induce repose in and set at rest judicial and quasi-judicial controversies. (Para 13.3)

172. A new Section 293A may be inserted in the Income-tax Act, to provide that the only authorities competent and authorised to pronounce upon the interpretation of the provisions of the Act should be the income-tax authorities, the Income-tax Appellate Tribunal, the Settlement Commission, the High Court and the Supreme Court. (Para 13.5)

Valuation of House Properties (Chapter 14)

173. One of the vexatious problems confronting both the Income-tax Department and the taxpayer is the question of valuation of house properties for the purpose of determining the wealth-tax

payable in wealth-tax assessments. (Para 14.1)

174. Ordinarily, the engineers of the CPWD have been determining the value of house properties by what is commonly known as 'land and building method'. Where land is inseparably rented out along with the building, this method may not give the correct valuation. (Para 14.2)

175. Values of house properties should be determined by the method of capitalisation of the return actually received for which could reasonably be received from those properties. (Para 14.2)

176. The rates of capitalisation should be notified by the Board from year to year. (Para 14.3)

177. In all fairness and equity, owners of self-occupied properties too must be allowed the facility of determining post 1971-72 assessment properties at actual cost or at market rate based on the multiplier method, which ever is lower. (Para 14.5)

23

COMMITTEE TO STUDY THE FUNCTIONING OF PUBLIC SECTOR BANKS, 1977 – REPORT[1]

Chairman James S. Raj
Members Shri V.C. Patel; Shri T.D. Kansara; Shri B.K. Dutt
Secretary Kum. N.K. Ambegaokar

Appointment

The nationalisation of the 14 major scheduled commercial banks in July 1969 brought in its wake a rapid growth in branch expansion, particularly in the rural areas, accompanied by considerable rise in deposits and advances. It also had a material impact on the pattern of development of banking funds, particularly to the priority sectors. Commendable as was the progress of public sector banks, it was felt that there was further scope for banks in meeting the needs of economic development. It was also felt that the growth of banking should be directed more towards rectifying the regional imbalances, not only in respect of credit disbursal, but also of branch expansion. Despite efforts in these directions, however, there remained large-scale regional imbalances in banking facilities and operations, particularly for the weaker sections. It was with a view to examining the present position and future scope for a more balanced growth of banking as well as finding ways for getting banks more directly involved in the process of rural development that the Government of India set up, in July 1976, a Banking Commission.

It was in this background that the Reserve Bank of India set up a Committee to study all aspects of the functioning of the public sector banks and in the light of such findings to make recommendations June 1977.

---

1. Bombay, Reserve Bank of India, 1978, 145, Various Paging, 15 Tables (mimeographed)

10.4 For the present, the formula for branch licensing should be operated in the following manner:

(i) The existing banks should be categorised into 3 groups depending on the proportion of their rural branches to their total number of branches and the branch licensing formula for opening branches in rural unbanked, metropolitan/Port Towns and banked centres should be worked out on the following basis, subject to the limit on the size of the banks;

(a) Those having 40 per cent or more of their total number of offices in rural areas may be given a formula of 2: 1: 1;
(b) Those having 35 to 40 per cent of their branches in rural areas a formula of 3: 1: 1; and
(c) Those having below 35 per cent of their total number of branches in rural areas a formula of 4: 1: 1.

(ii) This formula should also be applied to the 5 zonal units to be carved out of the State Bank of India after its restructuring on the lines suggested earlier, and (Para 3.9)
(iii) In this process no bank should be forced to open branches in an area very remote from the area of its operation, unless it so desires. Voluntary exchange of such branches may be permitted among banks with a regional character for the sake of better control and management of branches. (Para 3.12)

10.5 In regard to the direction of branch expansion and its balanced growth in all areas, the Committee suggests:

(i) Depoliticalisation of the co-operative banking system and professionalisation of the management of the Apex Co-operative Banks, District Central Co-operative Banks and Primary Agricultural Credit Societies. It is possible that for some reasons, it may be found difficult to execute this proposal. In that case, we suggest the following course of action; (Paras 3.15 and 3.16)
(ii) At village level, co-operative institutions – PACs or FSS or LAMPS – may continue to operate provided they have reached a satisfactory level of functional efficiency; the commercial banks and/or RRBs may adopt such societies as is

possible after they are duly reorganised and their management professionalised; (Para 3.16)

(iii) RRBs may open branches in rural areas and wherever and whenever RRBs are well established, offices of commercial banks in the operating rural areas of RRBs may be taken over by RRBs, and their powers of lending may be widened to include not only small borrowers but also others. Their area of operation should be clearly demarcated to cover one district or more than one district, depending on the size of the district/districts; and (Para 3.16)

(iv) Commercial banks, particularly the public sector banks and other fairly big private banks may open branches upto the level of district headquarters or at most up to mandi or block level. (Para 3.16)

10.6 In regard to the question of evolving a pattern of branch expansion which will meet the needs of rural development and at the same time remove regional imbalances in banking, the Committee found that more intensive measures should be taken to cater to the banking needs of the Northern, North-Eastern and Central regions of the country which are sparsely covered by bank branches. For this purpose, the Committee recommends that:

> Three new public sector banks with strong financial and managerial position be established, one each in the North-Eastern, Central and Northern regions of the country to cover specifically (i) the North-Eastern States, viz., Arunachal Pradesh, Assam, Manipur, Meghalaya, Mizoram, Nagaland and Tripura, (ii) Eastern Uttar Pradesh and Bihar and (iii) the States of Madhya Pradesh and Orissa, respectively, with Head Offices located at suitable places in these regions, taking into account the need for rural development. These new banks will have their own branches for the present and the Committee do not recommend any transfer of branches from the existing branches to the new banks till they get going. (Para 3.22)

B. Lending to Priority Sectors

10.7 As regards agricultural sector, the Committee recommends that:

(i) State Governments which have not yet enacted the legislation recommended by the Talwar Committee, or which have not framed rules in that respect, should do so on a priority basis, covering within its scope, not only agricultural advances, but also other advances to priority sectors; (Para 4.9)

(ii) State Governments should expedite the implementation of land reforms and conferment of tenancy/cultivating rights on farmers, and issue certificates of possession of land; (Para 4.10)

(iii) The procedure for issuing a 'non-encumbrance certificate' to farmers should be simplified by the State Governments and suitable instructions issues to concerned officials to promptly respond to the requests for such certificates; (Para 4.10)

(iv) State Governments may waive the stamp duty in the execution of mortgages in respect of small loans to the weaker sections of borrowers such as small farmers, artisans, DIR loanees, etc., upto an amount of Rs. 10,000 each; and (Para 4.11)

(v) Early action may be taken to introduce crop insurance. (Para 4.12)

10.8 The Committee noted that the scheme of banks financing the PACs ceded to them was working satisfactorily. In view of the suitability of commercial banks using intermediaries for financing the rural sectors, the Committee recommends that:

(i) The scheme of bank financing the ceded PACs should be continued and extended to other areas also; (Para 4.13)

(ii) The State Governments should expedite the reorganisation of the PACs financed by commercial banks and appoint full-time paid secretaries in consultation with and approval of banks to which they are ceded; where PACs are not effective, the State Governments should organise the Farmers' Service Societies (FSS) which will be used as channels for lending by banks and RRBs; and (Para 4.13)

(iii) State Governments should evince more interest in setting up of RRBs in suitable areas. RRBs may land either directly to farmers or theory of PACs wherever the latter effective. (Para 4.14)

10.9 As regards the small-scale industries (SSI) sector, inadequate equity base in small entrepreneur's business is on of the serious impediments to banks' lending to this sector. The Committee, therefore, recommends that:

(i) The IDBI may give due consideration to a suggestion that it will provide refinance to banks which may grant soft loans (quasi-equity) without interest, repayable in 7 to 10 years; (Para 4.19)

(ii) Alternatively, Central Government may favourably consider the proposal made by State Bank of India to the Government sometime ago, that a "National Equity Fund" may be set up by the Government of India for providing equity support to the small-scale industrial units. This Fund may be administered by the IDBI. (Para 4.19)

10.10 In order to bring about better co-ordination among the different financial institutions, such as banks and SFCs, certain recommendations were made by the Working Group appointed by the IDBI. Early action may be taken on these recommendations. (Para 4.20)

10.11 As many of the small-scale units have become sick and are, therefore, to be nursed back to health, a suggestion has been made that a soft loan assistance fund should be set up by the Government of India to provide rehabilitation loans to these sick units without interest or at a nominal rate of interest. We suggest that this proposal may be given due consideration by the Government of India and Reserve Bank. (Para 4.21)

10.12 It was represented by the Associations of small industries that the small-scale units were asked to give collateral security such as house property, LIC policy, shares, third party guarantee, etc., in order to be able to avail of bank finance. Banks considered such additional security necessary because of difficulties experienced by them in getting the losses reimbursed by the Credit Guarantee Organisation. The Committee, therefore, recommends that:

(i) ordinarily, security other than the fixed and current assets of the SSI's should not be asked for by the banks; (Para 4.22)

(ii) the Reserve Bank may consider simplifying the claim procedures in consultation with the Government of India and deleting Clause 7(1) of the Credit Guarantee Scheme so as to enable the banks to make effective use of the Scheme and to remove the hardship to small-scale industrial units. (Para 4.22)

10.13 As regards the long delays experienced by small-scale units in getting payments from large-scale units as well as from Government departments/undertakings, for goods supplied to them, we recommend that:

(i) banks should ordinarily allow full drawings against such supply bills given to small-scale units and a suitable time limit should be specified for payment of such bills by the large units as well as the Government departments/undertakings; (Para 4.24)

(ii) a part of the credit limit given to the large-scale units may be specifically and compulsorily set apart as a sub-limit to be used only for making payments to small-scale units in respect of goods supplied by them; (Para 4.24)

or

(iii) existing credit limits granted to small-scale units against supply bills be continued even against overdue bills to a reasonable extent; (Para 4.24)

(iv) Reserve Bank of India may provide refinance to banks in respect of bills/notes drawn by the small-scale units on the large-scale units/Government departments/undertakings; (Para 4.24)

(v) Reserve Bank of India may also consider providing refinance facility to banks in respect of their lending to small-scale units, as was done in the past, and as in now being done in respect of bank lending to small farmers; and (Para 4.24)

(vi) alternatively, the Government of India may consider setting up a separate Refinance Corporation for Small-scale Industry for refinancing a specified portion of banks' lending to small-scale sector.(Para 4.24)

10.14 The Committee felt that if total charges levied by banks on small-scale units by way of interest, service charges, inspection charges, etc., were taken into account, the rate structure for this sector could be considered to be on the high side and, therefore, recommends:

(i) a maximum rate of interest which should be not more than one per cent above the Bank rate on advances to small-scale sector, including small-scale industrial units for amounts upto Rs. 2.5 lakhs and 3 per cent above the Bank rate for advances of more than Rs. 2.5 lakhs, but not exceeding Rs. 10 lakhs; (Para 4.25)

(ii) banks should not charge penal rate of interest on the *entire* outstanding amount of borrowing by small scale units, but only on the amount of overdue bills discounted by banks. (Para 4.25)

10.15 In regard to application of Tandon Committee's norms, we recommend that:

> such norms should not be applied by banks to advances availed of by small-scale units, even if such advances exceed Rs. 10 lakhs. (Para 4.26)

10.16 The Committee recommends that the portfolios of lending to priority sectors should be directly under the charge of senior executives who will give proper policy directions for any changes required to be made for carrying out this work with more dynamism and sincerity. This should be possible with the changes in the pattern of branches which has been suggested earlier. (Para 4.30)

10.17 In the case of small loans (say upto Rs. 1 lakh), in order to avoid frequent renewal in documents which is a time-consuming and, therefore, costly procedure, the period of validity of documents be extended from 3 to 6 years. (Para 4.32)

10.18 Banks should attempt to reach the target of lending to priority sectors fixed by the Government of India and also aim at a higher target, say 40 per cent to be reached in 3 years subsequent to March 1979. (Para 4.35)

C. Efficiency in Banks

10.19 In regard to the efficiency in banks, the Committee classified the problem into 3 broad groups, viz., those relating to (i) internal efficiency; (ii) external efficiency and (iii) managerial control. While making recommendations on these, the Committee has taken into account the assessment and recommendations made by the PEP Committee. Our recommendations are given below:

Internal Efficiency

10.20 In regard to internal efficiency we recommend that:

(i) Banks should evolve a suitable machinery to ensure that the procedures prescribed for operational efficiency are followed through periodical visits by the senior management and the procedures be modified whenever necessary, so that new management techniques are sufficiently and widely adopted in all branches. This should be in addition to the present monitoring systems prevalent in banks. Efforts should also be made to improve the working conditions and environment in branches where necessary. (Para 5.4)

(ii) Banks should make advance man-power planning for both recruitment and training to take care of the planned expansion in branches and in the concerned types of business. (Para 5.5)

External Efficiency

10.21 In regard to external efficiency, we recommend that:

(i) In order to improve the customer services, we endorse the recommendations made by the Talwar Committee in regard to the banking transactions, motivation of staff, servicing of loan proposals and follow-up action for supervising loan operations; (Para 5.7)

(ii) Banks must try to dispel the general prejudice on the part of workmen unions against the use of computers, so that partial and judicious use of computers for selected services could be resorted to; (Para 5.8)

(iii) The scheme for regional or national clearing system suggested by the Indian Banks' Association may be examined and necessary action taken thereon; (Para 5.9)

(iv) The suggestion made by the PEP Committee in regard to forming customer service committees at the branch level for better counter service by securing the involvement of the staff should be adopted; (Para 5.10)

(v) Since most of the work in banks is routine and repetitive in nature, banks should consider recruiting a higher percentage of personnel at the clerical level with educational qualification down to matriculation and give them appropriate job training; (Para 5.11)

(vi) Central Offices of banks should issue to branches detailed manuals of instructions in regard to the appraisal of different types of loan proposals, preferably in the form of check lists. The branch managers may also be given powers such that 75 to 80 per cent of the proposals can be disposed of by them without reference to higher authorities and necessary confidence should be created so that such powers are actually used; (Para 5.12)

(vii) In regard to consortium loan arrangements, the recommendation made by the Indian Banks' Association, viz., that an expert group of senior bank officers should assess the viability of the project and that their assessment should be accepted by the participating banks, should be implemented; (Para 5.13)

(viii) The question of enforcement of the Tandon Committee norms should be reviewed by the banks and Reserve Bank in consultation with representative organisations of borrowers, with a view to introducing an element of built-in flexibility in the scheme. The Reserve Bank should review the actual working of such norms every year at the time of the annual review of its credit police; and (Para 5.14)

(ix) The procedure for transfer of borrowal accounts from one bank to another should be further simplified so as to make such transfer ordinarily permissible. (Para 5.15)

Managerial Control

10.20 For dealing with the problem of delays in operations and dilution of control resulting from the wide-spread branch network and communication gap between Head Offices, Regional Offices and branches, we recommend that:

(a) an operational and controlling unit of a bank (be that a Regional/Divisional/Zonal/Area Office) should have a controlling charge of around 100 offices, depending on the magnitude of business and the area of operation. The criterion should be that the credit and other proposals sent from branches to the higher offices and the decisions taken thereon should not take more than 2 to 3 weeks from the date the borrowers furnish the full particulars; (Para 5.16)

(b) there should be a three-tier management structure in each bank, viz., (i) the Head Office, (ii) the Regional or Zonal or Divisional Office; and (iii) the branch office. In the context of the suggestions made by us in Chapter 3 on the compactness of the size of a bank and the demarcation of the area of operation of the commercial bank vis-a-vis primary co-operative credit society and/or the RRB, we consider that the organisation of a bank on a 3-tier basis would be desirable and practicable; (Para 5.16)

(c) the problems faced by middle management of officers may be dealt with by delegating to them adequate powers of sanctioning loans, seeing to it that they use there powers and assuring them full support from senior management in *bona fide* cases of doubts or mistakes; wider powers could be granted for exercise by 2/3 executive officers jointly; and (Para 5.16)

(d) at the top level, i.e., at the Head Office, an Executive Committee of senior officers be set up to take decisions on important matters and issue instructions to the Middle and Branch offices, and powers at all levels be increased, wherever they are currently low. (Para 5.16)

D. *Vigilance Arrangements*

10.23 In order to reduce the scope of malpractices and frauds in banks and for better vigilance arrangements in banks, we recommend that:

(i) two or three or more officials, as required by the exigency of the situation, should be involved in any particular decision on advances or on any other matter involving outlay of funds, or important executive decisions or two/three senior officers may take a joint decision; (Para 6.11)

(ii) the Central Bureau of Investigation Organisation should be strengthened, in dealing with banking offences, by induction of suitable experienced banking personnel into their ranks; and (Para 6.12)

(iii) alternatively, the Inspection Wind of the Department of Banking Operations and Development in the Reserve Bank which would be a better agency should be entrusted with the function of enquiring into the cases of frauds and corruption in banks. (Paras 6.12 and 6.13)

E. Management-Employee Relations

10.24 The solution for the malaise affecting the banking industry seems to lie largely in better management-staff relations and in this context, we recommend that:

(i) A high-level dialogue should be organised between the management and unions on the whole question of norms of work, to be subject to a biennial revision and the unions should be induced to under-take responsibility for getting work done in accordance with these agreed norms; (Para 7.13)

(ii) Unions should be induced to agree to the induction of efficiency bars every 4 to 5 years in a 20-year clerical grade which could help banks in punishing the inefficient workers and to accept the principle of accelerated promotion for efficient workers; (Para 7.13)

(iii) since banking is an important service in the national economy, it would be useful that in any law governing industrial relations, special provision is made for banks to ensure that there is no disruption of work by strike, work-to-rule, etc., and that disputes are settled by a special machinery; (Para 7.15)

(iv) there is a case for declaring banking as an 'essential' service; (Para 7.15)

(v) to avoid conflict of interests and loyalties, it should be laid down that (a) officers cannot continue as members of workmen staff unions, and (b) officers who have to discharge executive functions at Head/Central/Zonal/Regional/Divisional/District/Area offices of banks, should not be members of officers' associations; and (Para 7.15)

(vi) there should be uniformity of laws pertaining to industrial relations in banking and that, for that purpose, the appropriate Acts/provisions of the Central Government laws should apply, instead of those of the various State Governments. (Para 7.16)

F. Training Facilities for Bank Personnel

10.25 The Committee has noted that notwithstanding the existence of training institutions at the levels both of the banks and the industry, there is a wide gap between the demand and supply because of the limited capacity of the staff training colleges. On the qualitative side, there are many new tasks to which the staff training colleges have still to address themselves. The Committee, therefore, recommends that –

> a Standing Committee consisting of the Chairman of 4 or 5 banks (to be nominated by the Indian Banks' Association), the Director, NIBM, the Principals of the BTC and CAB, the Chief Secretary of the Indian Institute of Bankers and a representative of the Government be constituted under the Chairmanship of a Deputy Governor of the Reserve Bank of India. The Committee would have its secretariat in the Reserve Bank for assisting the Deputy Governor in making proper assessment of the requirements of the training of staff for banks, taking into account their future branch expansion programme, and in the overall formulation of the policy in regard to the training programmes. The Committee would also monitor the progress of training from time to time and provide for effective co-ordination of the working of the training institutions at the national level. (Para 8.18)

10.26 In view of the importance of the training arrangements for bank staff and the urgency to deal with this problem, the Committee strongly recommends that –

> a separate department to set up in the Reserve Bank to deal with the problem of training of bank staff. This department may and can be under the charge of the existing Deputy Governor holding charge of the DBOD, but having regard to the size of the problem in respect of staff training, there is a case for creation of a post of Deputy

Governor to be exclusively in charge of staff training throughout the banking system. He will be also in charge of the BTC, NIBM, CAB, IIB and other apex training institutions likely to be set up in future. (Para 8.19)

10.27 The Committee has considered whether the BTC and NIBM should continue as separate institutions or be merged as was recommended by the Working Group headed by Shri B.N. Adarkar and recommends, at this stage of the evaluation of the two institutions, that –

the Reserve Bank consider this question in detail for appropriate decision. (Para 8.20)

10.28 We feel that the faculty members of the various training colleges should be selected according to their aptitude and experience and recommend that –

the selection of personnel for the colleges should be done on a rational basis and these positions should be made attractive by giving suitable incentives and by making provision for them to return to the operational side if they so desire after a specified period of say, 3 years. (Para 8.21)

10.29 In view of the urgency to remedy the inadequacy of training facilities for bank staff in the Eastern and North Eastern regions, we recommend that –

(i) Priority may be given to the establishment of a training college combining the functions of BTC and CAB at Patna to serve the needs of the Eastern and North Eastern regions;
(ii) Similar types of institutions in the Northern, Central and Southern regions of the country be established in a phased manner, the location being decided by RBI in the light of the various factors involved. (Para 8.22)

10.30 We have given careful consideration to the question of continuance of the Indian Institute of Bankers as an examining body for bank personnel. It serves a useful purpose in enabling the clerical staff working in banks to qualify themselves for promotion to higher cadres. We feel that –

> the Indian Institute of Bankers should organise correspondence courses on the lines of May's correspondence courses in U.K., with necessary changes/additions there to meet our national requirements. (Para 8.23)

10.31 The Committee is convinced that the existing training facilities are not adequate quantitatively for meeting the requirements of large number of personnel still untrained and the future entrants to the banking profession. We, therefore, recommend that –

> the training facilities available in the banks be expanded and improved both in the infrastructure and faculty membership. The Reserve Bank may, therefore, give serious consideration to this problem and take quick action to bring about all-round enlargement and improvement in the training facilities. (Para 8.24)

G. General Problems

10.32 In regard to problems of a general nature, the Committee recommends that :

(i) on the question of the composition of Boards of Directors of the 14 nationalised banks, while it is not intended that heads of large industrial and trading houses on the Boards be brought back, trade and industry may have their representation through appointment of professionals who are familiar with the various sectors of the economy, including retired Chairmen of banks, provided they are put on boards other than that of the banks where they served; (Para 9.4)

(ii) the posts of Chairman and Managing Director should be separated and both be made full-time, in view of the enormous volume of work they have to handle now; (Para 9.5)

(iii) 2/3 wholetime executive/functional directors may be appointed on the Boards of banks; (Para 9.6)

(iv) Reserve Bank may be asked to recommend a panel of candidates for appointment of Chief Executive of a public sector bank and Government should choose one of them; as far as possible, the selection of the Chairman should be within the respective banks; (Para 9.7)

(v) the Chief Executives of banks should be appointed for terms of at least 3, preferably 5 years; (Para 9.8)

(vi) it would be desirable for the Boards of banks of comparable size to have uniform items of Agenda; Government of India may issue appropriate guidelines to banks in this regard; (Para 9.9)

(vii) credit limits for consideration of (loan) proposals by Boards be generally raised by delegation to a smaller and more compact body such as an Executive Committee of the Board. Similarly, there be further delegation of powers to deal with administrative matters from the Board to the Executive Committee. This Committee should meet once a week. The Board should meet more frequently than now for disposal of work. The Board and the Executive Committee may meet in alternate weeks; (Para 9.10)

(viii) banks may consider ways and means of charging fully for the services they render to customers but before doing so, they should take care to see that the cost which they might incur on such services, does not exceed the amount of such charges; (Para 9.11)

(ix) In order to strengthen the capital funds of banks, the following measures be taken:

(a) banks should be required to transfer 40 per cent of their disclosed profits to the published reserves, free of tax, as has also been recommended by the PEP Committee; (Para 9.13)

(b) since the banks are performing a major developmental function, a developmental grant should be made to them as is the case for State Bank of India since its inception; (Para 9.13)

(c) Reserve Bank should pay, on the entire quantum of the statutory cash reserves of the banks held with Reserve Bank, interest at the same rate as the coupon rate which the Government of India pay on their long-dated securities, subject to an annual review and revision if required: this would be without prejudice to the interest which is being paid at present on the impounded deposits;

and (Para 9.13)

(d) the tax levied by Government on income earned by banks on account of the interest charged on advances be abolished. (Para 9.13)

Conclusions

The Committee believes that the recommendations made by it have taken in to account the objectives with respect to economic development, particularly of the backward areas and social justice which were the objectives of the nationalisation as well as restoring financial health to the banks. Some of the recommendations made may take some time to be implemented, especially those which involve legislation. If all the measures recommended by the Committee are implemented, even with some delay, the Committee believes that the twin objectives of fulfilling the socio-economic objectives of nationalisation, and vigorous and growing banking system covering all the area of the country and all sections of the population will be achieved.

January 11, 1978
by B.K. Dutt (Member)

REPORT
COMMITTEE ON PUBLIC SECTOR BANKS

Introductory

1. No study of the working of the public sector banks can be useful without, at the same time, having a reference to the banking system as a whole, the environment in which the banks (including the private sector banks) operate and the basic objectives of the banking operations. The expression "to study all aspects of the functioning of the public sector banks" is, therefore, to be interpreted accordingly. A study of only the public sector banks themselves on the basis of their present status of functioning with a view of finding out what further improvements can be made, can only be a superficial exercise yielding hardly any useful results. The approach has to be to try and find out what is needed, by way of a banking system, for assisting expeditious growth of the economy where the common man is important and not to advise a patch work on the existing structure, organisation or system and then to expect the people to fit into it.

1.1 Traditionally, borrowing from the system abroad developed in a completely different socio-economic situation, banking in India has developed itself into a service for the minority group of elitists, leaving the overwhelmingly large portion of the population out of its scope. But since the social control of banks, the concept has been changing and with the nationalisation in 1969 a completely different orientation has been brought into play.

2. The basic objectives of the public sector banks now can briefly be stated as follows:

(a) Mobilisation of deposits by covering a large sector of the economically active population, who are not at present within the banking fold, and servicing the depositors in a manner as would assist spread of banking habit;
(b) Servicing the organised sectors of industry and commerce by providing credit and rendering collection, remittance and similar other services;

(c) Assisting the hitherto neglected sectors to become economically more active (particularly in the case of agriculturist, small scale industrial units, artisans, etc.), in developing their economy and in enabling them to generate incremental income and thus improve their standard of living;

(d) Assisting establishment of social overhead at micro-level essential for implementation of Plans (e.g., roads and bridges) where toll is realisable and social services (e.g., Hospitals, etc.) where fees may be charged, particularly in the semi-urban and rural areas; and

(e) Generating reasonable profit to be retained for strengthening the banking system and also for contributing a reasonable return to the owners of the banks.

Importance of Adequate Profit

2.1 It is being held that while profit has to be there, even a low profit would be enough if the social objectives (vide (c) and (d) above) are achieved satisfactorily. However, this particular point needs a more realistic appraisal. Admittedly "Maximisation" is not the objective. But what can be regarded as an adequate profit?

3. Viability of banks would depend on the adequacy of profits and profitability. Adequacy of profit has to be so determined that losses incurred in the new areas, (vide (c) and (d) in para 2), may be absorbed without shock, that losses arising out of industrial units and others turning sick may be borne, that the pressing requirements of continuous and adequate growth of the capital funds (capital and reserves) may be met. The network of the banks has to be strong and adequate. It would be a misconception to feel that Government ownership has eliminated the need for institutional strength of the banks and building up of the capital funds and internal reserves. Irrespective of ownership, a credit institution which is not self-sufficient, is bound to be an inadequate instrument in fulfilling its objectives, whether the traditional ones or those of social needs enjoined on them in recent time.

Achievements of Public Sector Banks – 1969-76

4. At this stage, it may be relevant to have a look at the comparative position of the public sector banks between 1969-76 in rela-

tion to the important items of their operations; this is reflected in the table in Appendix-I.

4.1 It will be seen from Appendix-I, that in relation to the position of the public sector banks in 1969, their progress with regard to deposits, advances, advances to priority sectors, opening of branches (with emphasis on rural areas) is really noteworthy. Indeed it can be said that expansion of this order is perhaps unmatched in the history of banking development in this country so far.

5. However, this growth has brought about in its wake certain trends which are all but heartening. The ratio of capital funds to deposits has sharply gone down while the ratio of net profit to deposits has, by and large, been maintained by mark up of the lending rates significantly. At the same time staff in-take has markedly gone up, the cumulative effect whereof well be a sharp rise in the ratio of staff cost to deposits.

6. The quality of banking services has deteriorated significantly. (It is necessary here to controvert the popular impression that the quality of customer service of the banks had deteriorated on account of nationalisation. The quality of services as it existed during the first two years after nationalisation was about the same as it was a few years before the nationalisation. It must be remembered, that since early sixties, the services of the banks started deteriorating and relatively it was no worse during 1970 and 1971. However, the sharp decline in the quality of services is noticeable from 1972 due mainly to the fast rate of growth and expansion).

6.1 At the same time, the normal safety measures have become a casualty. Inter-branch accounts remain unreconciled. This involves risk to the banks themselves and also cause suffering to customers because of avoidable delay in credit of collections/remittances. Balancing of personal ledgers and other accounts (e.g., clearing) remains in arrear for the long stretch of time involving tremendous risk both to the banks as well as to the customers. I would quote here the observation of State Bank of India, which mentions that the branch expansion programme was 'forced'.

> "In achieving this performance we have, however, been compelled to accord less than due priority to several important aspects of our working, like customer service, house keeping . . . ."

7. While the management is kept busy with the rush of expansion and development and are worried out of wits by disuse of the safety tools, workers go on deferring their work and manipulating for lesser and lesser work thus having spare time to undertake activities not related to banking operations. The management loses control as demand for higher and higher rewards for lower and lower per capita work goes on mounting. All this has contributed to a general deterioration in industrial relations and proliferation of various agitational patterns.

8. The overall impression is paradoxical. On the one hand there has been growth on which the public sector banks may be congratulated and on the other a situation has developed where peaceful teamwork is practically absent.

8.1 On top of this, there has developed a new feature in the environment arising from public gaze. Retrogatory headlines in newspapers on the face of any complaint against a bank, without assessing the merit of such complaint, and appointment of committees for post mortem examination of certain decisions taken in the past, at a time when the imperatives of the circumstances under which the decisions were taken are completely lost sight of.

9. This has contributed to fostering a fear phychosis amongst the bank managers leading to abdiction of decision-making authority at various levels, resulting in delay and indecision, further contributing to deterioration in the banks' services and also to the general atmosphere of near-chaos in the operation of the banks themselves.

9.1 Any study of the public sector banks which ignores this overall climate would be unrealisation and infructuous.

10. Going back to the progress made by the public sector banks, while, in terms of their relative position in the time period, there admittedly, has been significant and creditable growth, when this performance is related to the overall requirements of the nation, it would be seen that the performance has not touched even the fringe of the basic needs.

11. Take the case of finance for agriculture – Only about 3 million accounts have been covered under this head by all scheduled commercial banks in the country. Of these, about 2.6 million accounts have been covered by the Public Sector Banks. Considering that, on an average, every farmer would have at least two loan accounts because of seasonal requirements and considering that rural households in the country are about 70 million, bank finance to

agriculture would seem to have barely scratched the surface of the needs.

11.1 Similar is the position with regard to artisans, small scale industrial units, small business and professionals. Where man is important, any suggestion for 'orderly balanced growth' of bank credit to fulfil the "needs for rural development and removal of regional imbalances" needs to be made in relation to this horizon.

Specific Terms of Reference

12. At this stage an itemwise discussion of the Terms of Reference is relevant. For this purpose items 1 and 2 of the Terms of Reference may be clubbed together and similarly items 4 and 5 may be taken together. The points to be considered would be as follows, viz:

A. Items 1 & 2

"1. To assess the impact of branch expansion that has taken place since 1969 and to examine whether any change in the tempo and direction of such expansion is called for;
2. To enquire into the present pattern of branch expansion of public sector banks and to recommend the future course of action keeping in view the need for rural development and removal of regional imbalances."

Observations

12.1 To find the impact of branch expansion, at least four essential objectives of the recent branch expansion of the Public Sector Banks need to be looked into. These are as follows:

(a) *Area-wise distribution of branches:* According to the present branch licensing policy, about 2/3rds of the total new branches to be opened by a bank must be in the rural area and preferably at unbanked centres. Since 1969, until recently, it was required that 50 per cent of such new branches to be opened should be in the rural and unbanked areas. This loading in favour of rural and unbanked areas, with regard to branch expansion, has been in consonance with the declared objectives give to the public sector banks. The question that, therefore, needs to be looked into is whether the area-wise distribution of branches has been according to the objectives and, if so, how many of the unbanked rural and semi-urban areas have already been covered by the public sector banks through their branches and what proportion does it bear to the total of such centres as were in 1969? The performance is not unsatisfactory in this regard.

(b) The next question is whether such branches have been able to Generate banking habit and to mobilise deposits at their respective centres? In five years, if the average deposits per rural branch have grown to the vicinity of Rs. 10/12 lakhs, one would say that the impact in this regard has not been too bad. However, an assessment of number of accounts and the activities of the deposit accounts would give a further and better appreciation of the situation in this regard. A general observation indicates that a large segment of the potential depositors still remains untapped.

(c) (i) The next point is what has been the impact of priority sector advances made by the bank branches? This has been a basic objective given to the public sector banks. The assessment in this regard may take two bases, both of which need be appraised;

(ii) First, quantum-wise: The total number of priority sector advance accounts, classified category-wise (e.g., small scale industrial unit, transport, agriculture and other allied activities, etc.), is to be seen against the assessed total number of such units which need result oriented supervised credit. By this token, as already pointed out in the foregoing, achievement to the Public Sector Banks has not yet touched even the fringe of the total requirement. It, however, has to be understood and borne in mind that never were the Public Sector Banks expected to cover the entire ground; indeed they cannot reasonably to expected to do that. What is to be seen is whether they have been able to make a *marginal* impact which they were expected to do. Even here, perhaps, the impact has remained below marginal; and

(iii) Secondly, in these accounts (or in the majority of them), have the banks been able to provide result oriented credit in a supervised manner calculated to improve the operational technique and thus to bring about at least some elevation in the economic standard of the concerned loanees? This is to be a qualitative study. Many banks of their own have made sample study of their finances to different categories in the priority sectors, in order to assess their achievement in this particular sphere. Copies of such studies have also been fed into the Department of Banking, Government of India. One might say that, by and large, in overwhelming majority of cases such financing has not been adequately supervised and, therefore, has failed to produce the desired impact.

(d) Another item of enquiry is the impact of fast branch expansion (with weightage for rural branches), on the total profit and loss situation of the banks. In this regard it is to be borne that admittedly, a portion of the total profit of the banks should be diverted towards achieving certain social objectives. The question is what should be the proportion? However, it has at the same time to be borne in mind that on account the state of the national economy in the past few years, there has been a high mortality in the enterprises, particularly in the industrial field. This has faced the banks with the problem of carrying sick accounts, which means reduced earning from these units and need for adequate provision for them.

12.2 There is thus enough evidence to show that the impact of branch expansion with emphasis on rural areas, has not been enough in relation to the needs of the economy in general and the priority sectors in particular. It has been mixed in relation to the banking system itself. The latter aspect can be specified as follows, viz.:

(a) While deposits have grown sharply, – and this is a good thing– the banks have been left with a small margin of profit, even after substantial mark-up in lending rates, which is not enough to build the capital funds and to service the sick accounts adequately;
(b) The sizes of banks have suddenly increased in a manner that it has not been possible for the banks organisationally to match up with the requirement large recruitments, almost in masses,

have regularly been made, rendering it impossible to induct properly training and orientation to the new staff before posting them at the branches. There is, today, by and large, a preponderance of new and untrained (or inadequately trained) staff in relation to the experienced and trained ones. The load, therefore, falls unevenly on the latter group resulting in tilted functioning. Quick expansion in size requires frequent changes in the organisational set-up and this creates confusion;

(c) With sharp and continuous expansion of size, the lines of communication have elongated out of proportion. This has resulted in inadequacy of communication (because, despite everything, regular verbal and personal communication is not only effective but is also essential; this, however, has become impossible). Thus, the objective and purpose visualised and planned at the top level gets diluted as it filters through the different tiers of the organisation and most times gets distorted when it reached the operating points. Lack of rapport as between the different levels in the organisation produces a system of working which is more mechanical than innovative; and

(d) Deterioration in services as a result of the impact, as has been discussed earlier.

12.3 It flows from the above discussion,

(a) That there should be considerable slowing down of branch expansion of the public sector banks for a period of time, say, 3 years, when consolidation of branches already opened and or the organisational structures that have been evolved, can take place;

(b) That the public sector banks can hardly provide the required banking service to vast rural areas of the country and that there is need for some other mechanism of providing banking services to the priority and weaker sections of the society, both in the rural and urban areas, as complementary to the present public sector banking system. Only then can the banking system make an effective contribution towards orderly and balanced growth of different regions; and

(c) That is should urgently be considered whether banks should not be allowed to transfer to their internal reserves at a maximum rate of one-half of one per cent (1/2%) of their credit portfolio every year without any tax whatsoever.

B. Item No. 3 of the Terms of Reference is as follows:

> "To evaluate the performance of public sector banks in the matter of lending to the priority sectors and weaker sections of the society and to suggest ways for the orderly and balanced growth of such advances.

13. The evaluation is to be on three different counts, namely,

(a) Quantitative, in relation to the needs in the economy. It has been seen that the performance has not yet come up to the expected level except of a marginal impact;

(b) Yet from the aspect of relative change in the position from that upto 1969 and to that at the and of 1976, the growth of finance to these concerned sectors has been significant, as has never occurred before. (Appendix II provides details of the occupation-wise classification of outstanding credit extended by banks). If this is considered with the organisational limitation of the banks, as has already been discussed, and the limitations owing to delay in lack of assistance from quarters like the State Governments, it may be observed that the performance, as far as the banks themselves are concerned, has been commendable;

(c) Although the performance in relation to the needs of the economy has fallen short, there has been market and noticeable qualitative impact inas much as the activities of the public sector banks have at least made the small entrepreneurs in the concerned sectors conscious of the facilities available from the public sector banks, either in launching of a new project or in improving/expanding their existing activities. And a section of loanees in these categories have derived economic benefit. This qualitative impact is indeed a break through and can be expected to gather momentum and to have a demonstrative effect towards more and better utilisation of the banking services in this area, albeit in limited geographical areas; and

(d) It should also be remembered in this regard that a complete re-orientation of the bank staff who have already been conditioned for years together to a different approach to business, need time for absorption of the concept and effectively to apply it in their day to day working. At the same time a thorough re-orientation has to be given by the bank staff to the proposed borrowers/loanees in these sectors not only to make their proposals bankable but also to guide them in their day to day activities for conforming to the imperatives associated with improved techniques necessary for realising incremental income; this is a new approach as far as these borrowers are concerned. Seven years cannot be regarded as too long a time span for this purpose.

C. Terms of Reference No. 4 & 5

"4. To advise on improving the efficiency of banks with a view to rendering better and speedy service to the public.

5. To examine the operation of vigilance work in the banks and to make recommendations to bring about improvements."

Observations

14. The efficiency of banks as already pointed out, can be improved only if there is complete rapport as amongst the staff at different levels and when the organisational structure has some breathing time to consolidate and achieve adequate control. This can hardly be achieved in a state of flux. Thus, there is need for hastening slowly. The criteria stated here for achieving efficiency are basic and essential.

14.1 Bank service has not only to be speedy but has also to be personalised. By that token there is need for striking an optimum size for a bank. It has been found and proved that a new branch provides better service to its customers, whether by way of speed or by way of personalised service, than an old branch. The reason, it has been found, is that as the branch becomes older its business and activities increase with consequent increases in staff strength; there is then loss of personal contact with customers and in service. Eventually a point is reached when rapport of the branch management with different levels of staff gets diluted and then the control is lost. This has every time been found in the life of the branches over the years. The situation is exactly the same with regard to the total organisation of a bank.

14.2 There is hardly an agreed formula by which the optimum size of a bank can be ascertained. Whereas some hold that a bank should not have more than say 1000 branches, some hold that the number of branches should not exceed 500, yet others think that 5000 branches can easily be managed. Similar disparity exists in the matter of total number of staff for a bank which may be regarded as the optimum size.

14.3 If past experience is any guide and the coverage of a large geographical area is the objective and where test of efficiency is not only prompt but also personalised service, any claim of efficiently managing a branch network of even 500 with all the variety of demands pressing at different directions, is only wishful thinking.

15. At the same time, the vastness of the country and wide varieties of the economic status and situation at different regions, would not allow waiting for a long time for spreading banking services far and wide. This makes it essential that there should be banks each devoted to rather small territories, spread out in different parts of the country to provide banking services, primarily to the rural and semi-urban areas, where the gap is the widest. This then points to the validity of the scheme of District Banks as discussed hereafter.

16. Operational vigilance work in the banks is not quite effective. The situation is bound to be so, because of the size and spread of each bank. It is absurd to imagine development of a large staff of vigilance officers at the different operation points (particularly when there is acute dearth of trained staff even for day to day operations). There is much validity in the theory that the need for extra vigilance is substantially narrowed down if the organisation is well-knit, purposive and capable of establishing and maintaining rapport all along the line. Personal discussions, understanding and examples are more effective in such organisations than in a loosely-knit colossal one. The optimum size of a bank, therefore, again has its relevance.

Recommendations

17. The above discussion indicates that, what with the imperatives of rural development and the need for equally servicing the organised industrial and business sector in the metropolitan and urban areas at the same time, the present banking structure would seem to

be deficient and inadequate. The first pre-requisite for the banking service is personalised dealing with customers. This cannot be achieved through monolithic organisations.

18. Again, the basic requirements of banking service for these two major sectors of the economy, are completely different in nature and content and are wide apart from each other. The so called neglected sector requires complete understanding of not only its need for finance but also of its problems and potentialities. Plenty of zeal and attention, innovation and development is required of the bank staff in this area. This cannot be a routine function to be achieved through circulars and manuals of instructions. At the same time the organised industrial sector equally needs specialisation of a different type and constant attention.

18.1 Further, it has been seen that expansion and growth of bank business in a variety of areas (geographical as well as functional) has brought in its wake a number of problems effecting the efficiency of banking operations and evaporation of zeal and determination. Innovation and ability to service the common man in very small units of activity are what is required. Credit has to be made available to the weaker section of the society on a "tailor-made" basis and not on a "ready-made" basis.

19. Finally, in such a vast country with divergent geographical, social and economic situations in different areas, the required coverage, if it is to be achieved with the existing pattern of structure, would take such a long time that the process itself could frustrate the objectives.

20. The situation, at present, is such that a bank with its main centre of activities say in South Canara district opens up offices in the far corners of North-Eastern area or in the North-Western area. A Calcutta bank perhaps is the lead bank for a district in an underdeveloped area of Jammu & Kashmir, or for that matter in Rajasthan. Such criss-cross banking does good to none, and least to the people of the concerned areas. This system not only fails to achieve the national objectives but also results in wastage of time, energy and money and creates vigilance problems.

21. "Delegation" cannot achieve the objectives of providing "tailor-made" customer service in the rural areas in the broad canvas of the nation with varying and divergent local conditions and situations. In a big organisation delegation is limited to the extent of functioning within clearly laid down procedural directives and opera-

tion systems. Manoeuvrability is so limited as to be insignificant.

21.1 What then is needed is transfer of centre of authority into the district and rural areas.

21.2 The recommendations have, therefore, been divided into two basic heads, viz. (a) structural, and (b) operational, the latter being recommendations with regard to specific aspects of influence on the operation of banks.

Structural

22. The structure that is visualised is as follows:–

(a) There is to be a category of banks devoted to metropolitan, big urban centres and port-towns and operating nationally for industry, trade and business including transactions as amongst these centres. The existing structure of public sector banks can effectively render this service primarily devoted to the industrial and business requirements of the urban, metropolitan and port-town areas;

(b) There would be banks for the common man (generally referred to us 'neglected sector'): (i) one type for the rural sector, operating only within a particular district (where a district is rather large there may be two banks and where contiguous districts are small in size there may be one bank for two districts), and (ii) the other type at the urban areas for servicing smaller people like small industrialists, traders, artisans; etc.;

(c) At the grass-root level, i.e., at the village level, there would be primary co-operatives (say one for every 1000 rural households) linked to the nearest branch of the district bank, the district bank having branches mainly in the block headquarters and the growth centres at the village level, within the district, as well as in the urban and semi-urban areas. Such linking should be only for common planning and mutual business interest, without in any way disturbing or altering the structure of co-operation; and

(d) While for business with the rest of the country the district banks will have correspondent relations with assigned public sector banks, the former will not be allowed to operate outside the district so that their whole focus is confined to the district, (or the defined area of a town as the case may be), thus making it imperative on them intensively to mobilise deposits and use such resources within this area of operation for its economic development.

22.1 District banks, which would primarily be village-oriented should be former by merging all the existing branches of nationalised and non-nationalised banks and RRBs.

22.2 In larger towns, including metropolitan towns, there will be 'Small Sector Banks' to provide credit to the weaker sections of the community. These banks are to be encouraged to intensify their coverage of specified areas, rather than engage in wasteful competition by adding to the branch network all over the cities. Such banks shall not accept any demand deposits and shall not do other business than making loans to the weaker sector of the community. To ensure adequate mobilisation of resources and face the competition from larger banks they may be permitted, if need be, to pay a higher rate of interest on deposits, and provide marginally added facility.

22.3 Each district bank and small sector bank would organise function-wise Associations, Groups, etc., (duly registered under the existing laws) for availing credit from the banks in an orderly fashion. These Associations will sponsor and monitor credit operations of their members, thereby relieving the banks much of the initial work, follow-up and recovery problems. These groups under the guidance and support of the banking and co-operative systems, can take to a large measure the micro-level infrastructural needs. For the purpose of feeding the 'Association' at the grass level, arrangements should be made to reach banking services to each 'Association' on the spot, as often as necessary.

22.4 Services of Farmer's Service Societies and suitable non-credit societies could continue to be availed of by the banks as far as possible.

23. To enable them to keep their refinance needs and operating consists down, the liquidity norms as prevalent now should not apply to the 'District Banks' and the 'Small Sector Banks'. The implementation of the scheme and follow up of the performance of development of the 'district' and 'small sector banks' can be ensured through a supervision machinery, created out of DBOD, including its Inspection Division, the Agricultural Credit Department of the Reserve Bank of India. There could also be members of the Agricultural

Finance Corporation.

> (*Note*: the intention in making this suggestion is to keep down the costs by reducing the low yielding assets to the minimum. It will be recalled that one of the objectives of additional liquidity norms is to control the availability of credit to the affluent sector but in the case of 'district' or 'small sector banks' there would be only large number of borrowers for rather small amounts and mostly in the priority sector).

23.1 All the 'District Banks' and the 'Small Sector Banks' should be owned by the Central Government. The Chairman of the 'District Banks' and the 'Small Sector Banks' should not be appointed notionally, but should be recruited by advertisement, from within the banks and outside. Selection should primarily be based on personal qualities, e.g., leadership, capacity to innovate, etc. and seniority and experience in banking may be given only secondary weightage. The maximum age should not be more than 35/40. The terms of employment of the Chairman of the 'District Banks' and the 'Small Sector Banks' should be the same for the nationalised bank's Chairman with longer tenure. This is because their services will be less glamorous and more strenuous.

23.2 The staffing pattern of the newly suggested banks should be officer-oriented. The work should be so organised that an officer gets fully acquainted with the full range of the banking needs of a given client or a group of clients. In the process, he may have to do some work which is now handed over to the clerical staff.

23.3 The salary structure (for the clerical staff and the officers) should not be different from that of the existing bank of the same size. For, in the short run this will create various difficulties and in the long run the differences will disappear.

23.4 Recruitment of officers and other staff should be made by advertisement. The old staff at different bank branches who may have to be taken over by a District Bank, being mostly of an average of three or four years of service, should not be difficult of assimilation by the District Bank. Since the District Banks will expand faster, after the first preparatory pause, the scope for promotion will be good.

23.5 Even though bi-partite arrangement is same for all, work style and norms are different in different banks depending on what was initially there. So a new bank can set up its own style, establish new norms and staggering hours (this is most essential for rural areas). Gradual replacement of the old staff will then create a new atmosphere.

24. The State Bank of India should be given all possible support to develop international business through branches in a big way and in a speedy manner. In addition to the State Bank of India, there may be few other selected banks to undertake and perform International Business.

25. In view of the suggested reorganisation, the role of private banks would have to be confined only to the regions where they are operating. They have functioned successfully in their chosen fields and hence they should be allowed to operate but not beyond their respective chosen regions, as in that case they would merely add to the wasteful competition and diffuse the sharpness of their focus.

Operational - 'Management'

26. Coming to the operational aspects, the first and foremost is Management. It is probable that more than credit problem, 'Management' is the most important problem in the banking industry. Up to date, the basic management principles have hardly been applied in the banks and management is regarded as synonymous with 'management by crisis'.

27. Even at the risk of repetition it must be said that in an industry like banking, management is bound to be a nagging problem as the banks have grown at a quick pace, and beyond a manageable optimum. The basic distinction between a manufacturing industry and the banking industry is to be recognised. Banking deals with an intangible product called 'service' and the entire range of services marketed by the banks, multifarious in nature as these are, is by and large, the product of clerical activity. There is no work-output norm established and accepted in the industry. On top of that, banking is devoted to 'retail' marketing through a large number of branch offices, which may be called 'shop windows'. With such shop windows spread out extensively throughout the country, there is bound to be breakdown of communication and loss of touch with and control of the day to day activity. It, therefore, has to be reemphasised that for the sake of better management, which alone can ensure better serv-

ices, the sizes of the banks should be kept within controllable optimum and operations limited to compact and easily accessible geographical areas.

The Board of Directors

28. There is need for rethinking on the composition of the Board of Directors of the public sector banks. While the representatives of the Reserve Bank, the Government, as well as the workmen and officers have to be there, the other directors perhaps could carefully be picked from known sources, preferably from those who possess technical knowledge and experience with regard to some of the important industries (of different scales) as well as with regard to the economic activities in the rural areas. Such directors may make useful contribution to the Board deliberations and also help the Chairman and other senior executives in formulation policies with regard to different matters of importance.

28.1 Further, the Board should form committees to deal with important matters of operation, viz., the normal traditional credit activities, credit to priority sectors, matters of management (particularly management development), etc. It has to be mentioned that the existing public sector banks in the suggested structure will continue to render priority sector finance at the city and urban branches.

Industrial Relations

29. There is an urgent need for developing suitable atmosphere with regard to industrial relations. Multiplicity of unions is a problem and either by tripartite discussions or by legislation, a situation has to be developed where there can be only one union in one bank. Even recourse to legislative measures is suggested because banking is a very sensitive area and has a special importance in the matter of development and growth of the economic activities in the country. The matter, therefore, cannot be allowed to drift.

29.1 The establishment charges should have a ceiling ratio (in aggregate or separately) for the emoluments of the officers, clerks and the subordinate staff that it may bear to the working fund or deposits. The ratios are not intended adversely to affect the emoluments, but to eliminate, as far as possible, the non-monetary facilities, restrictive practices and host of allowances. Ceiling ratio shall exclude, new District and Small Sector Banks for 3/4 years.

29.2 The concept of 'ceiling ratio' is not a new one. Justice Sastry had, in his award, commended the idea, which, unfortunately, was not properly taken up. This is not anti-labour. The idea is to make the management and staff cost conscious facing them with the constraints of a ceiling ratio. The ratio would periodically be negotiated and agreed upon on bipartite basis. This will also lead to a better understanding of the banks' obligation towards the community at large. A beginning has been made in this direction.

Training

30. Most of the public sector banks have made arrangements for formal training of their staff. However, such formal training continues to be somewhat detached from the mainstream of operations and the members of the faculty hardly have adequate touch with the day to day real situation. Further, in the training of officers even today, the entire emphasis is on the legal side and technicalities of operation. The management aspects of the job of an officer is either absent or bears an insignificant proportion to the total training curriculum. At the same time, the training courses, by and large, seem to be rather long drawn. There need for more study on the subject. At least two-thirds of the total training period should be on-the-job, with formal training relating to the different phases of the on-the-job training, sandwitched for brief periods. In other words, after a period of, say one month, on actual job in certain type of operation, the trainees may be called to the formal training centre for a short term of, say about two weeks, to obtain theoretical and technical insight into matters handled by them while on the job and to give them guidance with regard to the problems that they may have faced on the job during the particular phase. The batch then goes back to training on the job in some other operation and so on. However, there still would remain the need and scope for deeper study in theory and technicalities, after the trainees have reached a certain level. This may be pre-determined.

Capital

31. It has been emphasised earlier in this note that capital fund

has an important role to play in banking operations. It has also been pointed out how awfully poor is the ratio which capital fund bear to the deposits. There is need for quick building up of capital fund of the public sector banks. Besides the requirements of their respective operations, this is also necessary for commanding credibility with the bankers and customers overseas. It is the experience of public sector banks that on account of this particular aspect, often they find it difficult to make arrangement with their correspondent banks abroad for large commitments. In some countries letters of guarantee of Indian banks are not accepted by the buyers when the amount involved exceeds a certain limit.

32. The self suggesting method is for the Government to subscribe to enough capital of the banks to make it 6 per cent of the current deposits and to be paid in, say 5 instalments. Another way could be to issue 6.5 per cent/7 per cent preference shares, redeemable over a period of 20 years from the profits of the respective banks, if the profits are allowed to take care of it, and guaranteed by the Government so that the Life Insurance Corporation can subscribe a part in it.

33. In order that banks are enabled to make better contribution to the published reserves than heretobefore, the profitability of banks needs to be improved; certain steps which may be taken by the Government immediately are:

(a) Abolition of tax on gross interest earning of banks. This will achieve to purposes; viz.; (i) reduction in the lending rates, and (ii) marginal increase in banks' profitability;

(b) Up to one half of one per cent of the (excluding priority sector) credit portfolio of the respective banks should be allowed for building up of internal reserve free of any tax, on lines similar to the charge off allowed to the banks in America; and

(c) Interest charged on the sick accounts and kept in outstanding accounts, should not be taxed. Interest has to be debited to the accounts in order that this may not go by default at the time of settlement of claim either at the court or otherwise. But such interest cannot go to inflate the profit and has to be kept in outstanding account. In fact, this portion of the interest should be left out of the purview of tax until there is actual realisation. For this purpose a certificate from the bank should be acceptable, if necessary on due certification by the auditors of the bank.

34. Along with the published reserves the internal reserves also need to be strengthened. The system of commitment charge on loans sanctioned to medium and large business units should be revised and streamlined and the income from such commitment charge should be allowed to be put straight to the internal reserve and the amount so put in the internal reserve should be free of tax.

Profits

35. The cost of deposits has gone up tremendously during the last few years and the trend remains unabated. Here there is need for better rationalisation of the rates of interest both on temporary and short-term deposits (including savings accounts) as well as on advances. The recent directive issued by the Reserve Bank to the commercial banks in 1977 is a right step in this direction.

36. The staff cost needs to be controlled. On the one hand, the dearness allowance goes on mounting without commensurate increase in productivity or in general income; on the other, the output per employee goes on decreasing. In order to increase the productivity of the workers there is need for better rapport and understanding with the staff and their unions who have to make a conscious effort, by cooperating with the management, in improving the situation as a part of their duty.

36.1 At the same time there has to be a proper study, preferably by joint committees of representatives of the management and the representatives of the staff, to streamline the work procedures and to improve the per capita output. Admittedly this is not an easy task, more so because of the size of the banks. However, with better reorganisation and re-orientation, this should not be impossible to achieve.

37. The service charges, for remittances and collections as well as for maintenance of highly active accounts, need to be looked into the suitably revised so that the rates are formulated on cost basis. It may be mentioned here that a large part of the staff cost incurred by banks in the USA is covered by service charges. But in India the service charges constitute a very minor item of income in the profit and loss account of a bank.

38. Another leakage is the staff cost at the headquarters of the

banks. On account of the size of the banks the Head Offices grow and in the absence of any system and norm of work measurement, the growth follows the pattern of Parkinson's Law. An examination will indicate that a major operation of the Head Office and allied offices (which is non-earning), is indeed non-producing and, on most occasions, are deterrants to the efficiency and quality of services rendered at the operating levels. With a compact operational region, suitable organisation, and proper management much of this wasteful expenditure can be avoided.

Deposit Insurance

39. Since nationalisation of the banks, deposit insurance seems to have lost its impact and importance which however should not have been the case. There is a danger in continuing to propagate and strengthen the impression that the public sector banks being owned by the Central Government are quite safe. Such propaganda has, in response, created amongst the minds of the borrowers in the priority sector the same phychosis which is prevalent among the masses about the Government loans. By experience the people at large have found that Government loans need not be repaid and these are eventually cancelled out. They have also started thinking that the loans taken from the "Government-owned" banks similarly need not be repaid. This is a dangerous situation.

39.1 While, therefore, on the one hand the banks should be strengthened, on the other the emphasis on the Government ownership of the public sector banks has to be played down. Simultaneously, the safety of depositors on account of deposit insurance has to be projected and developed vigorously through various public communication media. This will assist better deposit mobilisation particularly in rural area and enable it to avoid the danger discussed above.

Advances

40. The credit to some corporate accounts by one bank continues to be high. It may be worthwhile to consider whether there should not be a ceiling given for individual bank, in line with the system in the USA, on the quantum that may be advanced to a single party, this being related to the bank's net worth by way of a fixed

ratio. Such a ratio, however, need not be as low as in the USA. Suiting our requirements the ratio may be fixed anywhere from 50 per cent upwards. This will necessitate consortium arrangements as amongst the banks. Consortium are already in vogue with regard to very large accounts. So the system may not be difficult of being developed for more extensive application.

Sick Accounts

41. Such Accounts have taken an alarming proportion in Banks' credit portfolio and judging by the trend now noticeable, there does not appear to be much prospect of an early reversal of the situation. Banks have to carry sick accounts and nurse them. While the stake is heavy, banks are unable to devote as much time and attention to these sick accounts as is necessary. In order that these accounts may be revived, they need to be nursed, guided and controlled by the banks effectively and on a pragmatic basis. In most cases sickness had developed years back, grew unnoticed and eventually when the accounts turned sick the problem was not amenable to any easy solution because the sickness in the meantime became deep-rooted and problems became multiheaded.

42. It is not only finance that is needed, (indeed in many cases if adequate steps are taken, need for fresh finance may be only marginal). The units also need supervision and guidance with regard to technical as well as managerial aspects; and few banks today are in a position to provide such service to the sick units, nor does there appear to be existing any suitable organisation for this purpose.

43. In the circumstances it is recommended that depending on the proportion of the sick accounts to the total credit portfolio, each bank should start a subsidiary for the purpose of reconstruction of the sick units. Such subsidiary of a bank should be headed by a person of the level of General Manager (age 35/40 years) and will have to a founded banker with keen faculty, knowledge of management and ability to take quick decisions. He should report directly to the Chairman and the Board, although he will have lateral and diagonal communication with his other compeers in the organisation. He must be supported by skilled and qualified technical executives belonging to the disciplines to which the preponderance of the sick units belong. There should also be a panel of experts whose services may be drawn upon as and then needed. In suitable cases it may be advisable for

this subsidiary also to organise and maintain its own industrial engineering cell to service the units. The subsidiary will provide a package service for the sick units in the manner that each unit may need.

43.1 The smaller banks or those whose proportion of such accounts is rather low, may engage the subsidiary of a sister bank for providing technical and managerial guidance and supervision to the units and for making recommendations to them.

43.2 Such an organisation in a bank will be able not only to provide timely, spontaneous and continuous service in adequate quality to the sick units – its objective being reconstructing the units and not to be a fault finding machinery. Such a subsidiary then will further be able to render assistance the normal credit department through periodical analysis of the bigger accounts and against not only in spotting any sickness that may be creeping in any account but also in providing remedial and prophylactic measures in good time to prevent sickness developing.

43.3 Such a subsidiary indeed would be an expensive organisation, with hardly much business return accruing to them. But since this is necessary and imperative, not only for the banking industry itself but also for the industrial scene as a whole, and therefore, to the national economy as such, it would be logical to provide adequate financial support to the banks from the Government exchequer in maintenance or such subsidiaries. This may be done indirectly by allowing the banks exemption from tax, such amount of profit as is proportionate to the cost of maintaining the subsidiary.

44. It may be noted that, the recommendations here is for asking the banks to form their own subsidiaries instead of recommending to the Government/Reserve Bank to set up a corporation on national basis. This has been done because one single corporation for this purpose will have to be a big organisation and being completely detached from the main stream of banking will tend to be a sophisticated organisation functioning from an ivory tower. This will not help the situation. Indeed it is likely further to complicate the problem. Every bank has its own personality, philosophy and knowledge of the local atmosphere and industrial culture. Individual banks thus will be better suited to serve the sick units through their respective subsidiaries than an independent national organisation.

24

REVIEW COMMITTEE ON THE CURRICULUM FOR THE TEN-YEAR SCHOOL, 1977 – REPORT[1]

Chairman Shri Ishwarbhai J. Patel

Members Prof. Ram Lal Parekh; Shri A.E.T. Barrow; Smt. Shanti Kabir; Prof. S.M. Chatterji; Shri A.R. Dawood; Dr. (Smt.) Chitra Naik; Dr. A.K. Narayanan Nambiar; Dr. S.N. Mehrotra; Shri U.T. Bhelande; Shri S.P. Singh Bhandari; Shri Manubhai Pancholi; Dr. G.L. Bakhshi; Smt. Lotika Ratnam; Dr. (Kumari) A. Nanda; Dr. R.C. Sharma; Shri S.N. Bhanot; Shri Rana Pratap; Shri R.K. Mohta; Shri R.R. Biala; Shri R.P. Singhal; Shri Babia Naidu; Shri A.L. Subrahmanyam; Shri G.S. Dhillon; Smt. R. Kumar; Prof. B. Sharan; Dr. Manmohan Singh Arora; Prof. B.S. Parekh; Prof. Anil Vidyalankar

M. Convener Dr. A.N. Bose

Appointment

The Recommendations of the Education Committee (1964-66) were considered by the Government of India and a resolution on the National Policy on Education was adopted after consulting both Houses of Parliament (1968).

Among other things the resolution "laid great emphasis on the fulfilment of the Directive Principles contained in Article 45 of the Constitution regarding the provision of universal and free education for all children in the age group 6-14. At the secondary stage, it highlighted the urgency to adopt the new pattern of the 10+2+3 for school and college classes with an intensive effort to diversify and vocationalise the +2 stage."

The Ministry of Education and social welfare appointed an expert

---

1. New Delhi, Ministry of Education and Social Welfare, 1977, 177 p.

group in 1973 to develop curriculum for the 10+2 pattern. The group drafted an Approach Paper in 1975, which was circulated for opinion of the State Governments and of teachers, planners and educational administrators.

A publication entitled "The Curriculum for the Ten-year school—A Framework" was published by the National Council of Educational Research and Training (NCERT) in 1975.

In 1975 NCERT prepared syllabuses, textbooks and other material in consultation with experienced teachers, subject-specialists and representatives of State Institutes of Education and Science Education, within the framework of the NCERT publication. This work was carried out in a phased manner: for the 1975-76 school session, materials for Classes IX and X were prepared in a few subjects; for 1976-77 materials for Classes I, III and VI were prepared.

The Central Board of secondary Education adopted some of the textbooks prepared by NCERT for class IX and X for the first set of candidates appearing for the secondary public examination held by the Board, at the end of standard X, in April 1977.

The syllabuses and textbooks prepared by NCERT, specially for class IX and X evoked criticism from the public: teachers, parents and children. The main criticisms were that the scheme of examination contained too many and too voluminous and, therefore, there was not time for self-study and physical activities.

Another major criticism was that work experience, which was intended to be an integral feature of the curriculum, at all stages, did not find a proper place in the teaching-learning process that followed the introduction of the new pattern, thus giving the impression that the curriculum and the syllabuses developed by NCERT would perpetuate the same old system of bookish education.

Dr. P.C. Chunder, Union Minister of Education and Social Welfare, in his capacity as President of NCERT felt that an objective assessment of the syllabuses and textbooks should be made and, therefore, he appointed a Review Committee on the curriculum for the Ten-Year School in June 1977.

Terms of Reference

(1) to review the stagewise and subjectwise objectives identified in the NCERT document "The curriculum for the 10-Year School.

(2) to scrutinise the NCERT syllabus and textbooks, in the light

of review as per (1) above.

(3) to scrutinise the scheme of studies, as given in the said document, and examine whether any suitable modifications in either the cheme of studies or the time table or both should not be madc and to propose suitable staffing pattern.

(4) to review the present scheme of studies and the time allocated for various subjects with a view to ensuring that:

(i) the institution/teacher has adequate time for experimentation, creative work, remedial instruction, etc.
(ii) to accommodate the needs of the bright child for advanced level courses; the specific interests and aptitude, or the lack of it, in children, in only certain subject areas, keeping in view the national goal of development and objectives of education.

Contents

Introduction; Objectives and Structure of School Education; Socially useful Productive Work; Implications, Appendices from I to VI.

Recommendations

General

We considered that the objectives of education, when viewed comprehensively, should enable and individual to acquire, knowledge, skills, habits, attitudes and values necessary for:

(i) a successful performance of his responsibilities as a citizen; and
(ii) a rewarding personal life by development of:

    (a) innate talent,
    (b) power of creative enterprise, and
    (c) the capacity to appreciate the splendour of life revealed from communion with nature and man with man.

Learning : Formal, Non-formal

We feel that education must be organised as a system to take the individual and society progressively towards higher reaches of human thought and behaviour.

We are of the view that the learning system should be organised through formal or non-formal arrangements—some institutional, some partly personal—and that the institutional arrangements should not be so rigid as to exclude those learners who wish to make use of them partially. It is our opinion that linked with such flexible arrangements within the learning system, the content of learning must also be flexible and arranged so as to suit the needs of individual learners or groups of learners. The curriculum too must be capable of catering to the requirements of a wide range of learners and learning circumstances. The curriculum we feel, has to be built round local situations, though there must be a core of basic contents for comparability of educational attainment and the acquisition of further skills and knowledge.

Attitude and Values

We consider that education during these 10 years should be capable of:

(a) promoting an understanding and appreciation of our cultural heritage while simultaneously stimulating desirable changes in our traditional culture pattern;
(b) moulding the learning after the image of the citizen as visualised in the Constitution;
(c) releasing learning from its bookishness and elitist character so as to relate it closely to socially productive manual work and the socio-economic situation of the country;
(d) encouraging rationalism and the scientific attitude;
(e) emphasising the qualities of simplicity, integrity, tolerance and cooperation in all aspect of life;
(f) being available to every individual irrespective of caste, creed, sex, age, place of birth, or economic circumstances and in such a way that working and learning can always be combined.

Specific Objectives of Primary and Secondary Education

We feel that the objectives of the structure and curriculum content for primary and secondary education should be reformulated as below:

Objectives of Primary Education (I-VII/VIII)

(1) acquisition of tools of formal learning, namely, literacy, numeracy and manual skills;
(2) acquisition of knowledge through observation, study and experimentation in the areas of social and natural sciences;
(3) development of physical strength and team spirit through sports and games;
(4) acquisition of skills for planning and executing socially useful productive work with a view to making education work-based;
(5) acquisition of skills of purposeful observation;
(6) acquisition of habits of cooperative behaviour within the family, school and community;
(7) development of aesthetic perception and creativity through participation in artistic activities and observation of nature;
(8) development of social responsibility by inculcating habits (individually as well as collectively) of appreciation of the culture and life styles of persons of other religions, regions and countries; and readiness to serve the weaker and the deprived;
(9) development of the desire to participate in productive and other processes of community life and to serve the community.

Objectives of Secondary Education (VIII/IX-X)

(1) acquisition of the skills and habits of self-learning;
(2) acquisition of a broad-based general education consisting of science, mathematics, social sciences, languages and socially useful productive labour;
(3) acquisition of habits of helpful living and participation in games, sports, and athletics for the maintenance of physical fitness;
(4) developing aesthetics appreciation and creativity through participation in artistic activities;
(5) exploring the world of work and understanding the realities of life in order to prepare for a confident entry into the world outside the school;
(6) participation in and promotion of social activities in the school

and the community in such a way as to imbibc dcmocratic values and to work towards the achievement of equality through service to the weak and the deprived.

Keeping in view the objectives of Primary and Secondary education enumerated above and also keeping in view the constitutional obligation under Article 45 and realising that the stage of school education which is some times termed 'middle', ending at VII/VIII, is a terminal stage of formal education for the great majority of the children in our country, we recommend that a general broad-based education be provided up to the end of the stage of compulsory education, so that children leaving school should have acquired a knowledge of our heritage and culture and are enabled to exercise their rights as citizen in a responsible manner.

Taking into consideration differences in aptitude and ability of children, we feel that while in classes VIII/IX and X there should be general broad based education, provision must be made for developing any special interests or talents in at least one area, outside the broad framework of general education.

Realising that a broad-based general education can make heavy demands on the capacity and energy of children at the secondary stage, we strongly recommend that the content of courses of individual subjects of learning must be designed, so as to keep the quantum of knowledge to the minimum essential for the understanding of the subject.

Structure, Curriculum Pattern and Time Allocations

We give below the structure, curriculum pattern and time allocation for the different sub-stages of school education which is illustrative and which we believe may apply in general throughout the country.

Structure, Curriculum Pattern and Time Allocation

Classes I-IV/V	Time Allocations
(1) One language	20%
(2) Mathematics	20%
(3) Environmental studies (Social Studies, Nature Study and Health Education)	20%

(4) Social useful Productive Work	20%
(5) Games and Creative Activities, such as, Music, Dancing and Painting	20%

Classes V/VI-VII/VIII	**Time Allocation** (per week)
(1) Languages	7 hours
(2) Mathematics	4 hours
(3) History, Civics and Geography	4 hours
(4) Science—An Integrated course	4 hours
(5) The Arts (Music, Dancing, Painting)	3 hours
(6) Socially Useful Productive Work and Community Service.	6 hours
(7) Games, Physical Education and Supervised Study	4 hours
	Total 32 hours

Classes VIII/IX-X	**Time Allocation** (per week)
(1) Languages	8 hours
(2) Mathematics: Alternative I: or Alternative II:	4 hours
(3) Science: (Theory and Practical) Alternative I or Alternative II:	5 hours
(4) History, Civics and Geography —as one course	3 hours
(5) One of the following: The Arts (Music, Dancing, Painting, etc.), Home Science, Agriculture, Commerce, Economics, Social Reconstruction, Classical Languages, etc.	2 hours
(6) Socially Useful Productive Work and Community Service	6 hours
(7) Games, Physical Education and Supervised Study	4 hours
	Total 32 hours

Important Note:

1. The scheme for classes VIII/IX-X is *illustrate only* and States/Education/Examination Boards may decided to make some subjects *Compulsory* and others *Elective.*

2. In the Public examination at the end of class X the number of subjects for external evaluation should not exceed seven.

(1) *Three-Languages Formula*

The recommendations in the Report of the Education Commission 1964-66 (pages 334-336) published by the National Council of Educational Research and Training, 1971, are reproduced:

"8.34

We, therefore recommend a modified or graduated three-language formula to include:

(1) The mother-tongue or the regional languages;
(2) The official language of the Union or the associate Official language of the Union as long as it exists : and
(3) A modern Indian foreign language not covered under (1) and (2) and other than that used as the medium of instructions."

"8.35

Implications of the Modified Formula

At the lower primary stage only one language should be studied compulsorily—the mother tongue of the regional language, at the option of the pupil. In the case of the vast majority of pupils, the language of study at this stage will be the regional language which will also be their mother-tongue. Some children belonging to the linguistic minorities may also opt for instruction in the regional language, because of its great advantages; but this cannot be forced on them, and they have the right under the Constitution to have facilities provided for their primary education through their mother-tongues. The State Governments should, therefore, provide primary schools teaching through the mother tongue for the children of linguistic minorities if they desire to have such an education, subject to the usual condition approved by the Education Ministers' Conference (1949) that the minimum number of such children should be 10 in a class or 40 in a school. It is desirable that such children should have a working knowledge of the regional language also. Facilities for its study should, therefore, be provided, on an optional basis, from class III onwards. We do not favour making the study of regional language compulsory at this stage for children of linguistic minorities, as has been done in some States at present. We are also not in favour of teaching English as a second language at this stage. This has been discussed further in a latter section."

"8.36

At the higher primary stage only two languages should be studied on a compulsory basis: (1) the mother-tongue or the regional language, and (2) the official or the associate official language of the Union. For almost all the pupils in the Hindi areas and for a majority of them in the non-Hindi areas, English will probably be the second language, but a large proportion of the pupils in non-Hindi areas may also opt for Hindi. In addition, facilities should be provided for the study of a third language on an optional basis, so that the children in Hindi areas whose mother-tongue is not Hindi and the children in Non-Hindi areas who have taken English as the second language may study the official language of the union, if they do desire."

"8.37

At the lower secondary stage (Classes VIII-X), a study of three languages should be obligatory; and a student should be under an obligation to study either the official language of the Union or the associate official language which he had not elected at the higher primary stage. By and large, the pupils in the Hindi areas will study Hindi, English and a modern Indian language, while the vast majority of pupils in non-Hindi areas will learn the regional language, Hindi and English. In the selection of the modern Indian language in Hindi speaking areas, the criterion should be the motivation of the pupils for studying that language.

For instance, in the border areas of a State, people are generally interested in studying the regional language across the border and this could well be the third language to be studied."

"8.38

It is true that English will be the most important library language to be studied at this stage. We however, think that it is also necessary to encourage the study of other important library languages like Russian, German, French, Spanish, Chinese or Japanese. Facilities for their study should be provided in a few selected schools in each state and it should be open to the students to study them, either in addition to, or in lieu of English or Hindi. Similarly provision should be made, in a few selected schools in the non-Hindi areas, for the study of modern Indian languages other than Hindi and the regional language. It should be open to the students to study these languages, as stated earlier with regard to library languages, either in addition to or in lieu of English or Hindi."

"8.39

In the higher secondary classes, which will serve largely as a preparatory stage for higher education, only two languages need be made compulsory and the students should have the option to select any two of the three languages studied earlier or a combination of any two languages take from the following groups: (1) modern Indian languages; (2) modern foreign languages; (3) classical languages — Indian and foreign. There is of course no bar to a student studying one or more additional languages on an optional basis."

(2) *Study of Classical Languages*

"8.48

We recognize the importance of the study of classical languages and of the special claim that Sanskrit has on the national system of education. But we do not agree with the proposal to include Sanskrit or other classical languages in the three-language formula.

In our opinion, this formula has to be restricted to the modern Indian languages only. We are in favour of the proposal of adopting a combined course of the mother-tongue and Sanskrit. But this is not a very popular proposal. Under these circumstances, classical languages can be provided in the school curriculum on an optional basis only. This may be done from Class VIII onwards."

Socially Useful Productive Work

Objectives

(i) prepare pupils to practise and perform manual work individually and collectively;
(ii) acquaint children with the world of work and services to the community and develop in them a sense of respect for manual workers;
(iii) develop a desire to be useful members of society and contribute their best to the common good;
(iv) indicate positive attitudes of team work and socially desirable values like self-reliance, dignity of labour, tolerance, cooperation, sympathy and helpfulness;
(v) help in understanding the principles involved in the various forms of work; and
(vi) lead children to participate increasingly in productive work as they go from one stage of education to another and, thereby, enable them to earn which they learn.

Programme

Problem Solving Approach

In order to ensure that the educational objectives of this programme are achieved it is necessary to follow the problem solving approach. Children should be made aware of the problems related to their needs; they should be led to arrive to solutions by discussing the material, tools and techniques necessary for performing such work and services. A built-in system of evaluation should be developed to enable them to improve their performance and to enable teachers to give a fair assessment of their work. As recommended later *Socially Useful Productive Work* must be given the status of a full-fledged subject in the final public examination taken at the end of Class X.

Teaching-learning process: Three phases

The teaching learning process in socially useful productive work will have three phases:

(i) study of the world of work through observation and enquiry;
(ii) experimentation with material, tools and techniques; and
(iii) work practice.

The first two are concerned with preparation for actual participation in production work and services and the third may lead to remuneration.

Work situations: Six areas

Thus, productive manual work situations relating to production of goods and services will have to be drawn from the areas of:

(i) health and hygiene;
(ii) food;
(iii) shelter;
(iv) clothing;
(v) culture and recreation; and
(vi) community work and social service

These work situations occur in the home, in the school and in the community. It has already been mentioned that such programmes will have two components:

(a) a common core programme
(b) work practice.

The purpose of the common core programme will be to bring about attitudinal changes and to develop readiness for work practice.

The purpose of work practice is to give a vocational bias to the programme. It will, therefore, be repetitive in nature and, it is hoped, remunerative in kind or cash.

Programmes by Classes

The programme of **Socially Useful Productive Work** may be summarised as follows:

(a) *Classes I and II*: Helping in work situations in the home, in the school in the community; manipulating simple material with simple tools for creative self expression.

(b) *Classes III-VII/VIII*: Common activities pertaining to the six areas mentioned, earlier:

(i) *Health and Hygiene*: Dusting of furniture; cleaning of class-rooms, school buildings, the school compound and its vicinity.
(ii) *Food*: Vegetable gardening or pot culture; cooking of meals.
(iii) *Shelter*: Construction with plastic, pliable and rigid material. Maintenance of articles of use.
(iv) *Clothing*: Spinning and simple handweaving or knitting; washing of clothes; stitching; mending.
(v) *Culture and Recreation*: Decorating the class-room, school and home; flower gardening; preparation for important national days (including hoisting and saluting the National Flag), festivals and school functions.
(vi) *Community Work and Social Service*: Cleaning the neighbourhood; preparation, maintenance and use of a compost pit; planting and care of shade trees; running of cooperative stones; the school panchayat; helping adults in productive work.

In *Classes V/VI to VII/VIII* activities as in the previous classes will be continued but they will be of an advanced type.

Work practice will be in the form of projects selected from the list give below:

Two projects at least be selected from the following illustrative activities in *each* class.

(1) *Health and Hygiene*: Making of tooth powder; soap; disinfectants; detergent powder; hair oil; brooms; waste-paper baskets; dustbins; compost manure; first-aid boxes; health posters; booklets on health and hygiene; keeping health records; keeping the neighbourhood clean; working at health centres.
(2) *Food*: Growing of selected vegetables and ornamental plants in plots or pots, where possible for sale.

Seed collecting; soil testing; experimentation with different kinds of social, different types of seeds, different kinds of manure; vegetative propagation by cutting; vegetative propagation by breeding; vegetative propagation by grafting;

vegetative reproductivity; layering; soil conservation.

Making of jam; jelly; ketchup sauce; pickles; fruit juices; confectionery or bakery items.

Working in canteens or stalls for a specified period.

Packing of food material.

(3) *Shelter*: Making articles of use with the help of any material, making stationery items; white washing; polishing doors, windows and furniture, caning chairs; repairs of furniture; casual labour work in the school.
(4) *Clothing*: Spinning; making. school bags; school uniforms; handkerchiefs; table clothes; pillow-cases, knitting; making mats.
(5) *Culture and Recreation*: Toy-making, artificial flowers; pottery painting, making games material; cards for festivals; fancy covers for books and book binding; fancy candle-making.
(6) *Community Work and Allied Social Service*: Helping adults in their work as projects, such as, keeping a specified area clean; helping in the care of the sick; first aid; helping at functions and during festivals; traffic control; helping in the literacy campaign.

(c) *Classes VIII/IX-X*

Greater emphasis should be placed on *work practice* in these classes.

Work practice will include *one* main craft or equivalent service and at least *one* subsidiary craft or equivalent service.

Main Crafts/Services

(i) *Health and Hygiene*: Growing medicinal plants; eradication of communicable diseases; paramedical service.
(ii) *Food*: Agro-industries; kitchen gardening; pot culture; crop and seed production; repair of farm implements; soil conservation and desert control; horticulture, animal husbandry and dairying; bee keeping; poultry farming; fish culture; bakery; confectionery; cooking.
(iii) *Shelter*: Poultry; masonry work; workshop practice (mechanical); workshop practice (electrical); workshop practice (electronics); cane and bamboo work; housecraft, blacks-

mithy; foundry work; carpet weaving.

(iv) *Clothing*: Production of cotton, wool, silk and other fibres; weaving; dress making; knitting; hosiery work; embroidery work; dress designing; leather work.

(v) *Culture and Recreation*: Making toys and puppets; making and repairing musical instruments; making games material; printing; book binding; making stationery; photograph.

Subsidiary Crafts/Services

(i) *Health and Hygiene*: Cleanliness of the neighbourhood, well and pond and the disposal of garbage; construction of toilet facilities and compost pits; making tooth picks; tooth powder; soap; detergents; disinfectants; first and boxes; construction of waste paper baskets; dustbins; garbage cans; brooms; brushes; cob-web cleaners; dusters; mops; etc., detection of adulteration.

(ii) *Food*: Distribution of fertilisers and insecticides; processing and preservation of food; hydroponics; mushroom; culture; *khandsari; gur* and candy making; catering; making jam, jelly, squashes, pickles, *bari* and *papad*; etc., packing food; marketing.

(iii) *Shelter*: Home, village and town planning. Lac culture.

Renovation and effecting minor repairs in buildings, fitting, furniture and household articles. Decorating the home; gardening; surface decoration; interior decoration; construction of decorative pieces; plaster of paris work; chalk and candle making; making limestone.

(iv) *Clothing*: Spinning of different fibres; dyeing and printing, repair of garments; laundry work.

(v) *Culture and Recreation*: Stage craft; making costumes; holding exhibitions.

Teachers

The provision of properly skilled teachers for the implementation of the programme of *Socially Useful Productive Work* is of the utmost importance. In order to give this area of work its proper place in the school programme it is recommended that:

(i) the professional status of teachers of *Socially Useful Productive Work* should be the same as that of other teachers;
(ii) there should be provision for the part time employment of skilled personnel for different activities;
(iii) there should be cells for *Socially Useful Productive Work* in the State Departments of Education and the State Institutes of Education to develop programmes of in-service training;
(iv) a scheme of course content of *Socially Useful Productive Work* for Teacher Training Colleges should be produced by NCERT in collaboration with such other institutes which have included manual labour in their regular programmes.

Implementation

Committees

Coordinated efforts should be made for the implementation of the programmes.

High level committees at the Central level and State level should be constituted by the respective Departments of Education so that the decisions made by them should invariably be accepted and implemented without delay. These Committees meet regularly to review the progress of work in these areas and remove difficulties in implementation and also create a climate of opinion in favour of this area of the curriculum.

25

RAILWAY ACCIDENT INVESTIGATION REPORT ON DERAILMENT OF 2 DSU PASSENGER TRAIN AT MODINAGAR STATION OF DELHI DIVISION OF NORTHERN RAILWAY ON 4th AUGUST, 1977[1]

One Man Commission Shri B.P. Sastry, Additional Commissioner of Railway Safety, Northern Circle

Officers Present Shri Inder Sahai; Shri L.C. Vaswani; Shri R.P. Singh; Shri S.P. Sharma

Appointment

The Commission was constituted under Ministry of Tourism and Civil Aviation (Commission of Railway Safety) in accordance with Rule 4 of the Statutory Investigation into Railway Accidents Rules 1973 vide Notification No. RS. 13-T(8)/71 dated April 19, 1973 on August 8, 1977.

Terms of Reference

To enquire into the Derailment of 2 DSU Passenger Train at Modinagar Station of Delhi Division of Northern Railway at about 12.42 hours on August 8, 1977.

Contents

Summary; Inspection and Inquiry; Relief Measures; The Train; Local Conditions; Summary of Evidence; Observations and Tests; Discussion; Conclusion; Remarks and Recommendations; Railway Board's Comments on Various Paras of Report; Annexures A to E.

---

1. Ministry of Civil Aviation (Commission of Railway Safety), Government of India, New Delhi, 1981, i + 26 p.

Conclusion

51. Having carefully considered the factual, material and circumstantial evidence at my disposal, I have come to the conclusion that the derailment of 2 DSU passenger train at points No. 30a in Modinagar station yard at about 12.42 hrs. on 4-8-77 was brought about by the facing points getting stuck up in mid-position with a gap of approximately 60 mm between the tongue and stock rails when the train entered, probably on clear signals, the reasons for such an unusual occurrence being poor maintenance of the interlocking installation at the station and in particular the mutilated condition of the reverse detector contacts of point machine at points No. 30a.

Responsibility

52.1 I hold the Railway officials in charge of the maintenance of the signalling installation at Modinagar responsible for its poor maintenance. The Railway Administration may assess the relative responsibility of individual officials taking into account the nature of their duties in regard to the maintenance of the installation. I do not hold any particular individual responsible for creating conditions for the train to enter point No. 30a in its mid-position.

Para 701 of the Indian Railways Signal Engineering Manual (Extract at Annexure A) has been violated.

Relief Arrangements

53.1 The accident having taken place at the station, which is in the centre of Modinagar town all concerned were immediately informed and local doctors promptly responded to the call and took care of the injured. By the time the Railway doctor with a medical van arrived from Ghaziabad at 14.05 hrs., all the injured who were required to be shifted to hospitals had been shifted. I consider that the arrangements made for their medical attention were satisfactory.

53.2 Restoration of through traffic was necessarily slow due to the extensive damages suffered by the locomotive and the first coach behind it. The driving wheels of the engine ploughed into the soft ground and the locomotive had to be lifted with heavy cranes. The coach which got compressed literally into V shape had to be cut in the centre before it could be cleared off the track. Taking these factors into account, I consider that the time taken to restore was reasonable.

Recommendations

54. The Driver of the Passenger train entered the loop line at a speed which is estimated to be between 30-35 kmph against 15 kmph at which he was authorised to run while entering the loop line. This is a dangerous tendency, which is unfortunately seen among Drivers very frequently and has to be curbed with firmness and determination.

55. Sophisticated Signalling and Interlocking installations are being introduced progressively on Indian Railways to meet the growing needs of traffic. A large number of these have been installed on the Northern Railway mostly around Delhi where the traffic is heavy. These sophisticated installations which permit swift operations in busy areas when handled properly, are also capable of resulting in accidents if adequate attention is not paid to their maintenance. The quality of maintenance or maintainers which such sophisticated installations should receive will obviously be different from the conventional interlocking systems in vogue. This aspect needs greater attention of the Administration.

56. It came to notice during my inquiry that rules prescribed for the procedure to be adopted for attending to failures of the signalling gears were not being followed at stations provided with panel interlocking and Route Relay interlocking installations and that short-cut methods were being adopted to attend to such failures creating unsafe conditions of train operation. The guiding principle for adoption of such short-cut methods appeared to be their anxiety not to cause detention to fact traffic. While this anxiety is understandable staff should be made to realise that safety should not be sacrificed in the process. This is all the more necessary in such sophisticated systems where a seemingly minor mistake may result in a serious accident.

57. From the extent of damages suffered by the coach next to the engine (YSY 3814-NR) and the case with which it got compressed into V shape at its centre even at a speed of 30-35 kmph in spite of its being a coach of Integral design, it appears that there was either a design deficiency or a flaw in the material used. Attention of the Integral Coach Factory Administration may be drawn to this aspect.

58. Crank handles are no doubt interlocked electrically in the panel but in the absence of proper recording arrangements their use in any particular situation cannot be established. Provision of automatic counting arrangements to register their release is suggested.

59. In the existing circuitry, detection of points is proved in the UCR circuit and in the signal circuit through UCR energised. In such an arrangement any false picking up of UCR (by a contact fault) can lead to the clearing of a signal irrespective of the position of the points. The following safeguards in the circuitry are suggested:

(a) Proving of position of points directly to the signal circuit also in addition to UCR.
(b) Provision of suitable cross protection for UCR to prevent its getting energised under fault conditions.
(c) Provision of suitable cross protection for WLR to prevent its picking up under fault conditions, when it is held in a route.

60. The desirability of having an official of the Signal Department among the safety consellors attached to Divisions with such sophisticated signalling systems may be examined and the safety organisation be strengthened where considered justified. Such an official would be of immense help to station staff and would also keep a watch on the short-cut methods currently adopted at such installations.

61. The failure recorded at Modinagar station on 29-5-1977, referred to in paras 17, 18 and 19 of the report, was serious and could have resulted in a serious accident had it not been detected in time. As such, it had really taken place, if it should have been reported to higher authorities even if no accident resulted from it, that it was not done and only a vague remark appeared in the signal failure register would indicate that station staff were not alive to their responsibilities when a serious failure developed in the installation. There should be a procedure that such failures do not get lost without being properly inquired into even if no accident has resulted from it.

62. In terms of Railway Board's letter No. 76-chg/II/14/1 dated 4-6-1977 marshalling of a wooden bodied coach as the outer most vehicle even if it be a SLR is prohibited. When inescapable, such a vehicle should be marshalled in side two anti-telescopic coaches. In the case of 2 DSU passenger both these directives were

violated in as much the rear SLR was marshalled as the outermost vehicle and the front SLR was marshalled as second from engine, although sufficient number of anti-telescopic coaches were available on the formation itself. Had the coaches been marshalled as per Board's directives, the coach 2nd from the engine which was wooden bodied on the train would have been replaced by an anti-telescopic coach and the damage in that event would have been lighter.

Railway Board's Comments on various Paras of Report

Para 54: Instructions in regard to checking of speeds by the Inspecting Officials already exist. These are being re-iterated to the Railways.

The Northern Railway is also being asked to take up with the Driver for entering the loop line at excessive speed.

Para 55: This has been accepted by the railway administration who have issued instructions that only qualified maintainers should be posted for the maintenance of sophisticated signalling installations and that such staff be given periodical refresher training also.

The remaining zonal railways are being advised to take similar action.

Para 56: Necessary instructions on the subject are being issued to all the Railways.

Para 57: The attention of the Integral Coach Factory has been drawn to see whether there was any design deficiency or flaw in the material used in the affected coach.

Para 58: As explained by the Railway, a satisfactory design, based on fail-safe principle, for automatic counter to work in conjunction with crank handles does not exist at present and would have to be developed. For the time being, instructions have been issued by the Railway to ensure that the Registers meant for the utilization of crank handles are maintained carefully.

It is seen that CRS has noted the action taken by the Railway.

Para 59: The circuitry used at Modinagar and other stations of Northern Railway are based on correct principles practised over the Indian Railways. In order to ensure a degree of uniformity in the circuit design, certain guiding principles and stipulations for the design of circuits, have been evolved for adoption by the Indian Railways and have been circulated by RDSO. The Railways will be asked to follow these guidelines while designing the circuits.

Action has been taken by the Northern Railway to avoid the possibilities of detector contact faults by mal-adjustments as suspected by the ACRS.

Para 60: The question of posting safety counsellors to the Signal Department to work under Chief Safety Supdts., of various Railways is under examination in the Board's office. While it is agreed that the posting of such Safety Counsellors would help to increase safety consciousness amongst the signalling staff and would also help the Chief Safety Supdts., in carrying out checks on the operations of the signalling installations as provided for, the quantum of staff to be posted is under consideration in the Board's office.

Para 61: Instructions on the subject are being issued to all the Railways.

Para 62: The railway is being asked to fix responsibility for failure to comply with the extent instructions regarding marshalling of coaches and take up with the defaulting staff.

Approved

17/6/99